African American Biographies

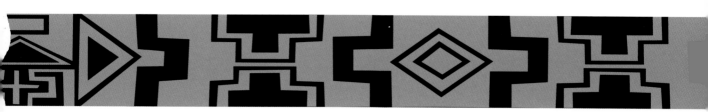

Volume 2

Bond, Horace Mann—Clarke, John Henrik

an imprint of

■SCHOLASTIC

www.scholastic.com/librarypublishing

First published 2006 by Grolier,
an imprint of Scholastic Library Publishing,
Old Sherman Turnpike
Danbury, Connecticut 06816

Set ISBN 978-0-7172-6090-4
Volume ISBN 978-0-7172-6092-8

Library of Congress Cataloging-in-Publication Data
African American biographies.
    p. cm.
    Includes index.
    Contents: v.1. Aaliyah–Blyden, Edward W.—v.2. Bond, Horace
Mann–Clarke, John Henrik—v.3. Cleaver, Eldridge–Edmonds, Kenneth
"Babyface"—v.4. Edwards, Herman–Greener, Richard —v.5. Greenfield,
Elizabeth–Jacobs, Harriet—v.6. Jakes, T. D.–Loury, Glenn C.—v.7. Love,
Nat–Oliver, Joe "King"—v.8. O'Neal, Shaquille–Satcher, David—v.9.
Savage, Augusta–Tyson, Cicely—v.10. Tyson, Mike–Zollar, Doris
    ISBN 978-0-7172-6090-4
    I. African Americans—Biography—Juvenile literature. I.
        Scholastic Library Publishing

E185.96.A439 2006
920'.009296073–dc22
[B]

                    2005050391

For information address the publisher:
Grolier, Scholastic Library Publishing,
Old Sherman Turnpike,
Danbury, Connecticut 06816

FOR THE BROWN REFERENCE GROUP PLC

Project Editors: Sally MacEachern, Aruna Vasudevan
Design: Q2A Solutions
Picture Researcher: Laila Torsun
Index: Kay Ollerenshaw
Design Manager: Lynne Ross
Production Director: Alastair Gourlay
Senior Managing Editor: Tim Cooke
Editorial Director: Lindsey Lowe

Academic consultants:

        Molefi Kete Asante, Professor,
            Department of African American
            Studies, Temple University
        Mario J. Azevedo, Chair and Frank Porter
            Graham Professor, Department of Africana
            Studies, University of North Carolina at
            Charlotte
        Scott M. Lacy, University of California Faculty
            Fellow, Department of Black Studies,
            University of California
        Mawusi Renee Simmons, Development
            Consultant and Museum Docent, University
            of Pennsylvania Museum Philadelphia,
            Pennsylvania

Printed and bound in Singapore

ABOUT THIS SET

This is one of a set of 10 books about the African Americans who have helped shape the past of the United States and who play a vital part in the nation's life today. Some were leaders of the abolitionist movement against slavery in the latter half of the 19th century; others excelled in their fields despite being born into slavery themselves. The abolition of slavery after the Civil War (1861–1865) did not mark the end of the prejudice that prevented most black Americans from fulfilling their potential, however. During the first half of the 20th century the African Americans who made their names in the arts, entertainment, sports, academia, or business remained exceptions who reached prominence as the result of a determined struggle to overcome discrimination and disadvantage.

The civil rights advances of the 1950s and 1960s removed legal and institutional barriers to African American achievement, but pioneers in many fields still faced greater difficulties than their white peers. By the start of the 21st century, however, black Americans had become prominent in all fields of endeavor, from space exploration to government.

This set contains biographies of more than a thousand of the many African Americans who have made a mark. Some are household names; others are largely—and unjustly—overlooked or forgotten. Their entries explain not only what they achieved, but also why it was important. Every entry has a box of key dates for quick reference. Longer entries also include boxes on the people who inspired great African Americans or people they themselves have influenced in turn. Most entries have a "See also" feature that refers you to related articles elsewhere in the set. If you want to find out more about an individual there are suggested books and Web sites. Addresses may change, however, and the accuracy of information on sites may vary.

Throughout the set are a number of guidepost articles. They provide an overview of particular aspects of African American experience, such as the civil rights movement or the Harlem Renaissance of the 1920s, and help place the individuals featured in the biographies in a wider context.

The biographies are arranged alphabetically, mostly by last name but also by stage name. Each volume contains an index that covers the whole set and will help you locate entries easily.

CONTENTS

Bond, Horace Mann 4
Bond, Julian 5
Bond, J. Max, Jr. 6
Bonds, Barry 7
Bonner, Marita 9
Bontemps, Arna 10
Boone, Herman 11
Boston, Ralph 12
Bouchet, Edward 13
Bowser, Mary Elizabeth 14
Boykin, Keith 15
Boykin, Otis 16
Bradley, Benjamin 17
Bradley, Thomas 18
Bragg, George Freeman, Jr. 19
Brandy 20
Branson, Herman 21
Brashear, Carl M. 22
Braugher, Andre 24
Braun, Carol 25
Brawley, Benjamin 26
Brent, John E. 27
Brice, Carol 28
Bricktop 29
Bridges, Sheila 30
Bridgewater, Pamela E. 31
Briggs, Cyril 32
Brisco-Hooks, Valerie 33
Brock, Lou 34
Brooke, Edward 35
Brooks, Avery 37
Brooks, Gwendolyn 38
Brooks, Tyrone 40
Brown, Bobby 41
Brown, Charlotte Hawkins 42
Brown, Clara 43
Brown, Clifford 44
Brown, Dorothy L. 45
Brown, H. Rap 46
Brown, Hallie Quinn 48

Brown, James 49
Brown, Jesse L. 51
Brown, Jim 52
Brown, Lawrence 54
Brown, Ron 55
Brown, Sterling A. 56
Brown, William Wells 57
Bruce, Blanche K. 58
Bryant, Kobe 59
Bubbles, John 60
Buchanan, Buck 61
Bullard, Eugene Jacques 62
Bullins, Ed 63
Bumbry, Grace 64
Bunche, Ralph 65
Burgess, John Melville 67
Burleigh, Harry T. 68
Burrell, Leroy 69
Burrell, Thomas J. 70
Burroughs, Margaret 71
Burroughs, Nannie Helen 72
Burton, Annie L. 73
Burton, LeVar 74
Busta Rhymes 75
Butler, Octavia E. 76
Calhoun, Lee 77
Caliver, Ambrose 78
Callier, Terry 79
Calloway, Cab 80
Campanella, Roy 81
Campbell, Milt 82
Cara, Irene 83
Carew, Rod 84
Carmichael, Stokely 85
Carnegie, M. Elizabeth 87
Carney, Harry 88
Carroll, Diahann 89
Carson, Benjamin S. 90
Carson, Julia 92
Carter, Benny 93

Carter, Betty 94
Carter, Cris 95
Carter, Eunice 96
Carter, Robert L. 97
Carter, Rubin 98
Carver, George Washington 99
Cary, Mary Ann Shadd 101
Cassell, Albert 103
Catlett, Elizabeth 104
Chamberlain, Wilt 105
Chapman, Tracy 107
Chappelle, Emmett W. 108
Charles, Ray 109
Cheadle, Don 111
Chenault, Kenneth 112
Cherry, Don 114
Chesnutt, Charles W. 115
Chester, Thomas 116
Childress, Alice 117
Chinn, May Edward 119
Chisholm, Shirley 120
Christian, Charlie 122
Chubby Checker 123
Cinqué, Joseph 124
Civil Rights 126
Clark, Kenneth B. 132
Clark, Septima P. 133
Clarke, John Henrik 134

Index 135
Credits 144

BOND, Horace Mann
Educator, Intellectual

A prominent and greatly respected educator and intellectual, Horace Mann Bond worked to improve African American education, advance civil rights, and promote cooperation among all races.

Bond was born in 1904, the son of two intellectuals, James Bond, a minister and the first director of the Kentucky Commission on Interracial Communication, and Jane Bond, a teacher and sociologist. He graduated from Lincoln University, Pennsylvania, in 1923 and by the age of 32 had published his first book, *Education of the Negro in the American Social Order*, and achieved an MA and a PhD in education. His PhD thesis won the University of Chicago's Susan Colver Rosenberg Prize for outstanding work in social sciences in June 1937 and was published in 1939 as the classic work *Negro Education in Alabama: A Study in Cotton and Steel*.

A dedicated educator

Committed to challenging the stereotype that African Americans possessed inferior intelligence, Bond wrote a series of articles attacking IQ test scores that were used to support racist educational policies, beginning with "Intelligence Tests and Propaganda" in 1924. Between 1928 and 1936 Bond held a number of teaching and research positions at Fisk University in Nashville, Tennessee. He was appointed president of Fort Valley State College, Georgia,

▼ *Horace Bond is pictured (right) in 1950 with Mary McLeod Bethune and W. E. B. DuBois, who had been awarded Lincoln University's Alpha Medallion.*

from 1939 to 1945 and went on to become the first African American president of his former school at Lincoln in 1945. During his presidency he successfully boosted the funding of the institution and established one of the first American centers for African studies. He also worked to outlaw the segregation of local community facilities. On his retirement from Lincoln University in 1957 Bond was appointed president honorarius for life. From 1957 he served as teacher and dean at Atlanta University in Georgia, eventually becoming director of Atlanta's Bureau for Educational and Social Research until his retirement in 1971.

Bond's legacy

Playing a vital role in the civil rights movement, Bond helped draft the brief for the landmark Supreme Court case *Brown v. Board of Education* (1954), which banned segregation in public education throughout the country. Bond died in Atlanta, Georgia, on December 21, 1972. His final work, *Education for Freedom: A History of Lincoln University, Pennsylvania*, was published after his death in 1976. Bond's legacy has continued through his son Julian, a leading civil rights activist and member of the Georgia House of Representatives.

KEY DATES	
1904	Born in Nashville, Tennessee, on November 8.
1939	Publishes his classic work *Negro Education in Alabama: A Study in Cotton and Steel.*
1945	Becomes president of Lincoln University.
1957	Appointed president honorarius for life on his retirement from Lincoln University.
1972	Dies in Atlanta, Georgia, on December 21.

See also: Bethune, Mary McLeod; Bond, Julian; DuBois, W. E. B.; Supreme Court

Further reading: Urban, Wayne J. *Black Scholar: Horace Mann Bond, 1904–1972.* Athens, GA: University of Georgia Press, 1992.
http://www.aaregistry.com/african_american_history/1822/%20Horace_M_Bond (Biography.)

BOND, Julian
Civil Rights Activist, Politician, Academic, Writer

Julian Bond has been active in the civil rights movement since his teens. He has served in the Georgia state legislature as both representative and senator for more than 20 years and is chairman of the National Association for the Advancement of Colored People (NAACP), a post he has held since 1998.

Born in 1940 in Nashville, Tennessee, Horace Julian Bond spent much of his childhood in Lincoln, Pennsylvania, after his father, Horace Mann Bond, became the first black president of Lincoln University, America's oldest black private college. After graduating from the George School in 1957, Bond entered Morehouse College, Atlanta.

Protest, politics, and beyond

In Atlanta Bond was a founder of a student organization that staged sit-ins to promote racial integration. In 1960 he was one of several hundred student founders of the Student Nonviolent Coordinating Committee (SNCC). After working as the SNCC communications director and in voter registration across the South, Bond dropped out of college in 1961 to join the *Atlanta Enquirer*. He later returned to Morehouse and graduated in 1971.

In 1964 Bond was elected to the Georgia House of Representatives but was prevented from taking his seat because of his opposition to the Vietnam War (1964–1973). He was reelected twice before the Supreme Court ruled his exclusion unconstitutional, and he was able to take up his seat. Bond was sworn in on January 9, 1967, and served as a representative until 1975 and then as senator until 1987. During this time he was sponsor or cosponsor of more than 60 bills that became law.

Early in his political career Bond was cochair of an alternative group of delegates to the 1968 Democratic National Convention. Bond's challengers unseated Georgia's regular Democrats, and Bond became the first black man to be considered as a vice-presidential nominee of a major party. He had to decline, however, because he was below the minimum age. In 1971 he helped establish the Southern Poverty Law Center (SPLC) and served as its president.

After an unsuccessful congressional race in 1986 Bond turned to academia, media, and writing. His poetry and articles have appeared in publications such as the *New York Times* and *Life Magazine*, and he was a commentator on the TV show *America's Black Forum* (1980–1997). He has been a professor at the University of Virginia since 1998, distinguished professor at American University, Washington, D.C., since 1991, and holds 21 honorary degrees.

KEY DATES	
1940	Born in Nashville, Tennessee, on January 14.
1960	Is a founder of the SNCC.
1964	Elected to Georgia House of Representatives but not sworn in until 1967.
1968	Is the first African American to be considered as a vice-presidential nominee of a major party.
1974	Elected to Georgia Senate.
1998	Becomes chairman of the NAACP.

See also: Bond, Horace Mann

Further reading: Jordan, Denise M. *Julian Bond: Civil Rights Activist and Chairman of NAACP.* Berkeley Heights, NJ: Enslow Publishers, 2001.
http://www.naacp.org/about/executive_bond.html (NAACP official site).

▲ *Julian Bond, chairman of the National Association for the Advancement of Colored People, addresses its 95th Annual Convention in December 2004.*

BOND, J. Max, Jr.
Architect

One of the United States's leading architects is J. Max Bond, Jr. In 2004 Bond's firm, Davis Brody Bond, was awarded the prestigious contract to work with architect Michael Arad and landscape architect Peter Walker on the design for the World Trade Center memorial project in New York, due to be completed in 2009.

Early life
Named after his father, the former dean of the School of Education at Tuskegee Institute, Alabama, James Max Bond, Jr., was born in Louisville, Kentucky, on July 17, 1935. While watching university buildings being constructed, Bond developed an interest in architecture.

Bond attended the segregated Booker T. Washington High School in Atlanta, Georgia. He graduated at the age of 13, but his parents thought that he was too young to go to college, and he was sent to the Cambridge School in Weston, Massachusetts. Aged 16, he went to study at Harvard College. While he was there, a lecturer advised Bond to give up his studies, claiming that he was wasting his time since there were no prominent black architects. Bond knew that this was not true: He was familiar with the work of Paul Williams, with whom he worked in 1956. Bond graduated Phi Beta Kappa from Harvard College with a BA in architecture in 1955 and gained his MA in 1958.

Making a name
After winning a Fulbright scholarship to study in Paris, France (1958–1959), Bond stopped off to visit his parents, who were then living in Tunisia. He became influenced by traditional Tunisian architecture, viewing it as high art.

In Paris, Bond was employed by Andre Wogenscky, Le Corbusier's former studio chief. Despite this fantastic experience, Bond found it difficult to get a job when he returned to the United States. In 1968 he went to work in Ghana, where he designed the Bolgatanga Library.

▲ *J. Max Bond believes that architecture should have an aesthetic relationship with culture.*

On his return to the United States Bond established and became executive director of the Architect's Renewal Committee of Harlem, one of the early community design centers that sprang up in the 1970s and 1980s. He was also a member of the New York City Planning Commission from 1980 to 1986. Bond's most memorable work includes the Martin Luther King, Jr., Center for Nonviolent Social Change in Atlanta (1981), the Birmingham Civil Rights Institute (1992), and major research laboratories at Harvard, Columbia, and Northwestern universities. He also worked in Zimbabwe, southern Africa, where he designed buildings for the National University of Science and Technology at Bulawayo.

Bond also taught at several universities, including Columbia University, where he was chairman of the graduate school of architecture and planning, and City University of New York, where he was also dean. He cofounded Bond Ryder, which merged with Davis Brody & Associates in 1990. In 1996 the firm became Davis Brody Bond.

See also: Williams, Paul

Further reading: http://www.wirednewyork.com/forum/showthread.php?t=4463&page=4 (Article on Bond).

KEY DATES	
1935	Born in Louisville, Kentucky, on July 17.
1958	Receives his MA in architecture at Harvard University.
2004	David Brody Bond company wins the contract to build the World Trade Center memorial project.

BONDS, Barry
Baseball Player

▲ *Barry Bonds in the Giants' dugout before a game against the New York Mets in 1997.*

Barry Bonds is generally recognized as one of the greatest baseball players in history. He spent most of his career with the San Francisco Giants, and by the end of the 2004 season had hit 703 major-league home runs, a figure exceeded only by Hank Aaron and Babe Ruth. He also held the record for the number of home runs hit in a season: 73. However, his huge achievements in the sport were mired in controversy when he was accused of accepting performance enhancing drugs from his personal trainer Greg Anderson.

Road to success

Barry Lamar Bonds was born on July 24, 1964, in Riverside, California. He came from illustrious baseball stock. His father was Bobby Bonds (*see box on p. 8*), who also played for the San Francisco Giants and set a number of records in a career that lasted from the late 1960s to the early 1980s. Barry showed considerable sports talent in high school, excelling not only in baseball but also in basketball and football.

Such was Bonds's skill in the batter's box that the San Francisco Giants drafted him on graduation. However, Bonds elected to continue his education at Arizona State University, where he played collegiate baseball as well as earning a degree in criminal justice. During his studies Bonds impressed onlookers with his talent on the field. However, the player also built up a reputation for arrogance and difficult behavior that would stay with him for his entire career.

Bonds graduated in 1986 and began his professional baseball career with the Pittsburgh Pirates, with whom he played until 1992. His debut season showed only glimpses of his potential; as a rookie he hit 16 home runs in 113 games at a relatively poor average of .223. His performances gradually grew better, but it was not until the 1990 season that Bonds hit the heights that would land him a place in baseball history. The improvement was partly the result of a change in attitude. In high school and college Bonds had often relied on his natural talent to get him through. However, he eventually realized that in order to fulfill his potential, he would also have to work hard. According to Bonds himself, the realization came to him suddenly in the fall of 1989 when he was sitting in a barber shop. A sports commentator on the radio was comparing two famous football players, one an all-time great, the other merely a "great talent." Bonds decided then and there that he wanted his achievements to match his ability.

In the following season Bonds scored 104 runs, stole 52 bases, hit 33 home runs, and led the league slugging averages with a figure of .565. He also won a Most

KEY DATES	
1964	Born in Riverside, California, on July 24.
1986	Graduates from Arizona State University and joins the Pittsburgh Pirates.
1990	Wins the Most Valuable Player (MVP) award for the first time.
1992	Joins the San Francisco Giants.
2001	Hits a record 73 home runs in the season.
2003	Defends himself against the charge of taking steroids.

INFLUENCES AND INSPIRATION

The player who cast the greatest shadow over Barry Bonds's career was his own father, Bobby Bonds (1946–2003). Like Barry, Bobby played for the San Francisco Giants. He joined the team in 1968 and made an immediate impact in the major leagues, hitting a grand slam in his first at-bat. In the following year Bobby went on to score 120 runs, becoming the joint highest scorer in the National League.

After considerable further success Bobby Bonds left the Giants in 1974. In the next seven seasons he played for seven different teams, finishing his playing days with the Chicago Cubs in 1981. Like his son, Bobby was not always popular with his teammates and was known for his abrasive nature.

Although Barry was not close to his father as a child, the latter had a considerable effect on his career. Barry inherited much of his father's talent, in particular his combination of speed and power. Many observers believe that the pressures of living up to his father's fame also shaped Barry's personality, making him overly defensive and confrontational.

Valuable Player (MVP) award, the first of seven that he would receive by the end of 2004. He was awarded his second in 1992, when he led the National League in both runs and slugging.

After the end of the 1992 season Bonds became a free agent. As the recipient of two MVP awards in the preceding three seasons, Bonds was aware that he could demand a high salary. Eventually he signed a six-year deal with the San Francisco Giants that was worth $43.75 million, making him the highest paid player in baseball.

In his first season with the Giants Bonds continued to display the form that he had shown at the end of his career with the Pirates. In 1993 he hit 46 home runs, ending the season with a slugging percentage of .677, the highest in the major leagues for 32 years. His efforts won him his third MVP award. However, individual success for Bonds did not translate into team glory for the Giants, and they narrowly failed to make the playoffs. This was a theme that was destined to run through Bonds's career. Despite reaching the playoffs three times during his seven seasons with the team, the Pirates had never gotten into a world series. The Giants would be similarly plagued; they reached the playoffs only once in the remainder of the decade, losing to the Florida Marlins.

Despite the lack of success for the Giants, Bonds continued to set new standards in his individual performances. His best season came in 2001, when he hit 73 home runs to break Mark McGwire's record for most home runs in a single season. He also posted the best slugging average of all time (.863), beating a record that was set by Babe Ruth in 1920. Bonds's achievements won him another MVP award, an honor that was repeated in 2002, 2003, and 2004. In April 2004 he overtook his godfather, Willie Mays, to reach third on the list of all-time

hitters of home runs. He hit his 700th home run later that year. During the course of his run Bonds appeared in his first world series in 2002; the Giants ultimately lost the series to the Anaheim Angels.

Controversy

From 2000 Bonds was trained by Greg Anderson, who was connected to the Bay Area Laboratory Cooperative (BALCO), a sports nutrition company that came under federal investigation for supplying illegal steroids to athletes. In December 2003 Bonds told a federal grand jury that Anderson had supplied him with a cream and a clear liquid to help combat fatigue and arthritis. He said that he believed that the medications were legal substances and that he only used them for a short period of time. In July 2005 Anderson and three top executives of BALCO pleaded guilty to distributing steroids and money laundering. The sports stars caught up in the scandal were spared a court appearance, but their reputations have suffered.

The suspicion that he may have taken steroids has made Bonds a controversial figure among fans. Some assume that he was guilty and argue that it undermines his achievements. Others protest his innocence and argue that even if his career had ended before the scandal, he would still have achieved enough to ensure that he would be remembered as one of the game's all-time greats.

See also: Aaron, Hank; Mays, Willie

Further reading: Travers, Stephen. *Barry Bonds: Baseball's Superman.* Champaign, IL: Sports Publishing, 2003.
http://www.barrybonds.com (Bonds's official site).
http://sports.espn.go.com/mlb/players/profile?statsId=3918 (ESPN page and links).

BONNER, Marita
Writer, Educator

Essayist, playwright, short-story writer, and teacher, Marita Odette Bonner was one of the leading female figures associated with the New Negro Movement or Harlem Renaissance, a group of creative African Americans working in the 1920s. She is perhaps best known for her unsentimental stories set in the imaginary multiracial Chicago community of Frye Street.

"Young—A Woman—and Colored"

Bonner was born in 1899 to middle-class parents and was one of four children. She was educated at Brookline High School near Boston, Massachusetts, where she showed a flair for academic studies, writing, and music, and contributed to the student magazine, the *Sagamor*. After high school she studied English and comparative literature at Radcliffe College in Cambridge, Massachusetts. After graduating in 1922, Bonner began her career as a high school teacher at Cambridge High School near Boston.

While teaching in Washington, D.C., she published her first literary works—mainly in *Crisis*, the magazine of the National Association for the Advancement of Colored People (NAACP), and *Opportunity*, the official journal of the Urban League. She also became friendly with some of the leading black writers of the time, including Countee Cullen, Langston Hughes, and Alain Locke, who regularly met at the Washington home of the black playwright and poet Georgia Douglas Johnson.

During the 1920s Bonner's work included mainly essays and plays, and was often experimental in style. Her first published work, written in 1925 soon after the deaths of both her parents, was the largely autobiographical essay "On Being Young—A Woman—and Colored," in which she described the double oppression faced by African American women in a white-dominated society. *Nothing New*, her first story set in Chicago, was published in 1926 and introduced readers to Frye Street, the fictional community where many of her subsequent stories were set. In her extraordinary and experimental play *The Purple Flower* (1928), which won the *Crisis* prize for Literary Art and Expression, she imagined a future in which conflict between black and white people was inevitable: In the play the Us's, who represent blacks, say to the White Devils, who represent whites, "You have taken blood. You must give blood... There can be no other way." Bonner intended her plays to be read rather than performed.

Frye Street

In 1930 Bonner married William Occomy, an accountant, and the couple moved to Chicago, where she continued to teach and write. Faced with the poverty and discrimination suffered by Chicago African Americans, her writing became more realistic and political. Most of her short stories were set on Frye Street—"that crooked little tumbled red brick place," which teems "with all the world"—and reflected the tense, multiracial environment of her adopted city. The stories often focus on the lives of working-class black women, who have to struggle to find jobs or to raise their children alone against the backdrop of an oppressive urban society.

After 1941 Bonner largely stopped writing, devoting herself instead to her teaching and to raising her three children. She died in 1971 after suffering injuries when a fire broke out in her Chicago apartment. In later decades her writing has been rediscovered, and a collected volume of her writing, *Frye Street and Environs: The Collected Works of Marita Bonner*, was edited by her daughter and published in 1987. Since then Bonner's contribution to the development of African American women's writing has become more widely recognized.

KEY DATES	
1899	Born in Boston, Massachusetts, on June 16.
1922	Graduates from Radcliffe College, Boston, and moves to Washington, D.C.
1925	Publishes the essay "On Being Young—A Woman—and Colored" in *Crisis* magazine.
1928	Publishes her play *The Purple Flower*.
1930	Marries William Occomy and moves to Chicago.
1971	Dies in Chicago on December 6.

See also: Cullen, Countee; Harlem Renaissance; Hughes, Langston; Johnson, Georgia Douglas; Locke, Alain

Further reading: Wall, Cheryl A. *Women of the Harlem Renaissance*. Bloomington, IN: Indiana University Press, 1995.
http://voices.cla.umn.edu/vg/Bios/entries/bonner_marita_odette.html (Biography).

BONTEMPS, Arna
Writer

Writer Arna Bontemps is probably best known for his involvement in the Harlem Renaissance, the black arts movement that took place in New York in the 1920s. Bontemps wrote over 20 books of poetry, history, biography, fiction, and anthology.

Arnaud Wendell Bontemps was born on October 13, 1902, in Alexandria, Louisiana. The Bontemps moved to Los Angeles when he was three. His bricklayer father and school teacher mother taught Bontemps that education was important. He attended both public and private schools: At boarding school his father told him to not to "act colored."

Bontemps's first poem, "Hope," was published in 1917 in *Crisis* magazine. He studied at Pacific Union College, Los Angeles, from which he graduated in 1923.

A writing career

From 1924 to 1931 Bontemps taught at the Harlem Academy, New York. He met several writers involved in the Harlem Renaissance, including Langston Hughes.

His poem "Golgotha Is a Mountain" won *Opportunity* magazine's Alexander Pushkin Award for poetry. In 1927

▼ *Arna Bontemps in 1939, when he published* **Drums at Dusk,** *a novel about the 18th-century black revolution on the island of Santo Domingo.*

KEY DATES	
1902	Born in Alexandria, Louisiana, on October 13.
1931	Publishes *God Sends Sunday*.
1932	Begins to collaborate with Langston Hughes.
1973	Dies in Nashville, Tennessee, on June 4.

Bontemps also received the *Opportunity* magazine award for poetry and won the NAACP's *Crisis* poetry contest for the work "Nocturne at Bethesda."

Although Bontemps failed to get a publisher for his 1929 novel *Chariot in the Cloud*, he published *God Sends Sunday* two years later. This novel is considered by some critics to be the last work of the Harlem Renaissance. In 1932 he began writing *Black Thunder* (1936) and collaborating on books with Langston Hughes. The two men published *Popo and Fifina: Children of Haiti* (1932), which told the story of two black children who migrate from an inland farm to a busy fishing village. Encouraged by the book's success, Bontemps wrote several more works for children.

In 1935 Bontemps became principal of the Shiloh Academy on Chicago's South Side, where he met writer Richard Wright. Three years later Bontemps became editorial supervisor of the Federal Writers' Project of Illinois (Works Progress Administration). After completing an MA in library science at the University of Chicago in 1943, Bontemps became a librarian at Fisk University in Nashville, Tennessee, where he stayed until his retirement in 1966. Before his death in 1973 Bontemps was awarded two honorary degrees and distinguished professorial appointments at the University of Illinois, Yale University, and at Fisk as writer in residence.

Bontemps's most influential books deal with the human spirit, freedom, and a desire for social justice. He drew on folklore and history for his work, and was also influenced by jazz, spirituals, and blues.

See also: Harlem Renaissance; Hughes, Langston; Wright, Richard

Further reading: http://www.csustan.edu/english/ reuben/pal/chap9/bontemps.html (Perspectives in American Literature page on Bontemps).

BOONE, Herman
Coach

Herman Boone is a teacher and retired football coach who has worked with and motivated young people of all races. In 2000 Denzel Washington played Boone in a movie based on his life, *Remember the Titans*.

Early life

Boone was born in Rocky Mount, North Carolina, on October 28, 1935, to Frank Boone, an African American, and his wife Daisy, a Native American. He attended Abraham Lincoln Elementary School and Booker T. Washington High School, where he graduated in 1954.

Boone, or "Ike," as he became known, was an outstanding athlete. His pursuit of excellence took him to North Carolina College in Durham, where he received his BA and MS degrees. Choosing to teach and coach young people, Boone went to work at I. H. Foster High School in Blackstone, Virginia. There he coached football, basketball, and baseball; his teams achieved outstanding results, with 26 wins, six losses, and three district championships.

Three years later Boone returned to North Carolina with his wife and young family to continue coaching and teaching. He accepted a position at E. J. Hayes High School in Williamston. Over the next nine years his teams achieved a remarkable record of 99 wins and 8 losses. Among the accolades Boone received was *Scholastic Coach* magazine's recognition of his 1966 football team as "the number 1 Football Team in America." Boone also won Football Coach of the Year six times.

Racism

Despite his teams' successes, the Williamston school board informed Boone in 1969 that it was "not ready" for a black head coach. Instead, Boone became assistant football coach at T. C. Williams High School in Alexandria, Virginia.

▲ *Ever since the release of* **Remember the Titans,** *the 2000 film about his career, Herman Boone has been much in demand as a speaker across the nation.*

In 1971 Boone became the first black head coach in football when Alexandria decided to integrate its school system. He was named head coach of the Titans football team over white coach Bill Yoast, who was the local favorite and head coach of the successful white team at the former Hammond High School. Boone's appointment was seen as a gesture of goodwill to the black community but angered the white community. Boone and Yoast worked together to overcome racial tension and create a team that went on to win the state championship.

After the release of *Remember the Titans* Boone enjoyed a career as a keynote speaker and continued to coach teams, including the Native American Allstars.

See also: Washington, Denzel

Further reading: http://www.blackathlete.net/Interviews/int100201.html (Article about and short interview with Herman Boone).
http://www.71originaltitans.com/hboone.html (Titans page on Boone).

KEY DATES	
1935	Born in Rocky Mount, North Carolina, on October 28.
1971	Becomes the first black head football coach of a mixed-race team when Alexandria, Virginia, integrates its school system.
2000	The biographical movie *Remember the Titans*, starring Denzel Washington, is released.

BOSTON, Ralph
Athlete

R alph Boston was one of the top American athletes of the 1960s, taking home three medals, including a gold, from three consecutive Olympic Games. He was born on May 9, 1939, in Laurel, Mississippi (also the birthplace of Olympic gold medallist Lee Calhoun), the youngest of 10 children. His prowess in athletics emerged during his high school and college career. Although he was a top-rank high jumper and hurdler, his real talent was in the long jump.

To the Olympics
The 1960s were a decade of great achievement for Boston. In 1960, while at Tennessee A & I University (now Tennessee State), he won the long jump in the National Collegiate Athletic Association (NCAA) championship. Only two months after his NCAA win Boston broke Jesse Owens's 25-year long-jump world record with a leap of 26 feet 11¼ inches (8.21m) before heading to the 1960 Summer Olympics in Rome as part of the United States team. In Rome he took the gold medal for the long jump with a distance of 26 feet 7¾ inches (8.12m), beating fellow U.S. teammate Irvin Robertson and his Russian rival Igor Ter-Ovanesyan, who took silver and bronze respectively.

The remainder of the 1960s saw further superlative performances from Boston. He broke the world record a further six times, his achievements culminating in a huge leap of 27 feet 5 inches (8.35m) in 1965. Boston was the United States national long jump champion every year from 1961 to 1966 and broke the American distance record seven times. He also achieved the longest triple jump for an American in 1963. Boston could not repeat the gold medal success of 1960 in subsequent Olympic Games, but he still took home silver from Tokyo in 1964 and bronze

▲ *Ralph Boston competing in the 1968 Mexico City Olympics, where he took bronze.*

from Mexico City in 1968, where he was beaten by U.S. teammate Bob Beamon, who took gold with a remarkable world record. Boston's sporting honors for this time include the titles World Athlete of the Year and North American Athlete of the Year, as well as entry into the Mississippi Sports Hall of Fame.

Off the track
Boston retired from athletics in 1968 to live a busy professional life. He entered college administration at the University of Tennessee before returning to sports as a consultant to American Olympic athletes and also as a sportscaster for the Entertainment and Sports Programming Network (ESPN). Boston has also shown a flair for business, working as a partner in a television network and as a director of customer relations for the telecommunications company Ericsson. In 1985 he was elected to the U.S. Olympic Hall of Fame.

See also: Beamon, Bob; Calhoun, Lee

Further reading: Page, James A. *Black Olympian Medalists.* Westport, CT: Libraries Unlimited, 1991.
http://www.pbs.org/redfiles/sports/deep/interv/s_int_ralph_boston.htm (Interview with Ralph Boston about competing in the 1960 Summer Olympics in Rome).

KEY DATES	
1939	Born in Laurel, Mississippi, on May 9.
1960	Wins the NCAA championship, establishes a new world record, and takes gold at the Rome Olympics.
1964	Wins silver medal at Tokyo Olympics.
1968	Wins bronze medal at Mexico City Olympics; retires from Olympic level sports.
1985	Elected to the U.S. Olympic Hall of Fame.

BOUCHET, Edward
Physicist

Edward Alexander Bouchet was the first African American to hold a PhD and only the sixth person in the United States to take the qualification in physics. He was born in in 1852 in New Haven, Connecticut, to William and Susan Bouchet. His father worked as a janitor and was a church deacon. Although schooling for black children was extremely limited at the time, Bouchet found a place first at the Artisan Street Colored School and then at New Haven High School from 1866 to 1868.

Exceptional mind

At school Bouchet demonstrated excellence in the sciences, and in 1868 he was accepted at the Hopkins Grammar School, a prestigious establishment that prepared students for study at Yale University. Bouchet graduated first in his class from Hopkins in 1870 and entered Yale in the same year. At Yale Bouchet excelled in scientific and classical studies. He was the first African American to receive a degree from Yale, graduating sixth in his class in 1874. After a further two years' study Bouchet received his PhD for work on geometrical optics; it was the first doctorate awarded to an African American in the United States.

Because of his color Bouchet was excluded from teaching in any American university or college. Instead, he taught at Philadelphia's Institute for Colored Youth (ICY), the state's only high school for black students. Bouchet taught physics and chemistry to hundreds of students at ICY and remained there until 1902, when he resigned over the introduction of a new educational policy that placed industrial education above academic learning.

Final years

After leaving ICY, Bouchet taught at high schools in Missouri, Virginia, Ohio, and Texas. He also worked in several business and industrial roles, including as a hospital business manager (1903–1904) and a customs inspector (1904–1906) in St. Louis, Missouri. He returned to teaching but from 1913 became increasingly affected by heart problems and retired in 1916. Bouchet went back to New Haven and died on October 28, 1918.

▲ *Edward Bouchet had one of the best scientific minds of his generation but was denied the career opportunities of his white peers.*

KEY DATES	
1852	Born in New Haven, Connecticut, on September 15.
1868	Graduates as valedictorian from New Haven High School.
1870	Enters Yale University, graduating with a physics degree in 1874.
1876	Receives a PhD in physics and becomes the first black person in the United States to hold a doctorate.
1902	Resigns from the Institute for Colored Youth in Philadelphia.
1918	Dies in New Haven, Connecticut, on October 28.

Further reading: Sammons, Vivian O. *Blacks in Science and Education.* Washington, D.C.: Hemisphere Publishers, 1989.
http://www.princeton.edu/~mcbrown/display/bouchet.html
(African Americans in the Sciences biography and bibliography).

BOWSER, Mary Elizabeth
Civil War Spy

Mary Elizabeth Bowser is one of the great heroes of early African American history. A former slave, she operated as a spy for the Union during the Civil War (1861–1865).

Little is known about Bowser's early life. She was born into slavery around 1839 on a plantation owned by wealthy hardware merchant, John Van Lew of Richmond, Virginia. Bowser was one of many slaves freed by Van Lew's wife and daughter on his death in 1851. Van Lew's daughter Elizabeth had been schooled in Philadelphia, where she had become an enthusiastic abolitionist; she now sent Bowser to be educated in the city. Before war broke out in 1861, Bowser had returned to work for the Van Lews.

Elizabeth Van Lew

Elizabeth Van Lew (1818–1900) was an independent and outspoken woman whose neighbors nicknamed her "Crazy Bet." Throughout the war she used her reputation as an eccentric to disguise her activities in support of the Union cause. When captured Union soldiers were held in Libby Prison, Richmond, for example, she took them medicine, books, and food, while gathering information about Confederate troop movements from the prisoners, as well as hints from guards. She then sent coded messages to the Union side via her servants, who concealed them in baskets of produce or in the soles of their shoes.

A spy in the household

When Van Lew realized that war was coming, in 1860 she had recommended Bowser for a position on the staff of Confederate president Jefferson Davis. Davis and his cabinet assumed that Bowser was a stupid, illiterate slave, and so they often spoke openly in front of her about confidential matters, such as military strategy. Because they assumed that she was illiterate, Bowser was able to read confidential war dispatches and other papers that were left lying around.

Bowser passed the information she gathered to Van Lew or to Thomas McNiven, the Union's Richmond spymaster, who operated a bakery that became a major exchange point for information. In turn they would pass information in code to Union commanders, including General Ulysses S. Grant. Although Jefferson Davis became aware that someone in his household was leaking information, he never discovered who it was.

<table>
<tr><td colspan="2">KEY DATES</td></tr>
<tr><td>1839</td><td>Born in Virginia at about this time.</td></tr>
<tr><td>1850s</td><td>Goes to Philadelphia to be educated.</td></tr>
<tr><td>1860</td><td>Joins Jefferson Davis's household as a spy.</td></tr>
<tr><td>1995</td><td>Inducted into the U.S. Army Military Intelligence Corps Hall of Fame.</td></tr>
</table>

McNiven credited Bowser with being one of his best spies since she "had a photographic mind. Everything she saw on the Rebel President's desk, she could repeat word for word." The information she supplied "greatly enhanced the Union's conduct of the war," according to the account assembled by the U.S. Army Military Intelligence Corps Hall of Fame, to which Bowser was inducted in 1995.

After the Civil War ended in 1865, the government destroyed all records relating to Bowser, Van Lew, and other spies, for their protection. Grant visited Van Lew after the fall of Richmond. They drank tea together and he told her that she was "the one person who has sent me the most useful information I have received from Richmond during the war."

There is no record of what Bowser did after the war, and the date and details of her death are unknown. According to some some reports, Bowser kept papers or a diary that told her story. Some commentators say that family members destroyed the papers in case they fell into the wrong hands, others that they were lost accidentally; there are also rumors that they remain in the possession of a family that refuses to release them.

Grant rewarded Van Lew with a job as postmistress of Richmond, which she held from 1869 to 1877. She continued to live in the family mansion but was shunned by Southern society. When she lost her position, she lived on an annuity from the family of a Union soldier she had helped in Libby Prison. She probably died in 1900.

Further reading: Ryan, David D. (ed.). *A Yankee Spy in Richmond: the Civil War Diary of "Crazy Bet" Van Lew.* Mechanicsburg, PA: Stackpole Books, 2001.
http://www.lkwdpl.org/wihohio/bows-mar.htm (Biography on Women in History site).

BOYKIN, Keith
Writer, Activist, Lecturer

A lecturer, writer, and popular media figure, Keith Boykin is one of America's leading civil rights activists. Since the early 1990s he has fought to combat both discrimination against homosexuals in the African American community and racism among gay men and lesbians, among other issues. His work has made him a prominent role model for the African American community.

Rising star
Born on August 28, 1965, in St. Louis, Missouri, Boykin showed his talent as a speaker, writer, and activist from an early age, engaging in political, social, and civil rights issues. From 1983 to 1987 Boykin attended Dartmouth College in Hanover, New Hampshire, where he wrote for and edited the oldest college newspaper in the United States, *The Dartmouth*. After leaving college, he worked for 18 months as a press aide in the 1988 Democratic

▼ *Keith Boykin was the keynote speaker at the 2001 Bayard Rustin Community Breakfast, a forum created by the AIDS Action Committee to recognize the work of African Americans fighting AIDS.*

KEY DATES	
1965	Born in St. Louis, Missouri, on August 28.
1987	Graduates from Dartmouth College, New Hampshire.
1991	Announces publicly that he is homosexual.
1993	Appointed media assistant to President Clinton.
1996	Publishes *One More River to Cross*.
1999	*Respecting the Soul* wins the Lambda Literary Award.
2005	Publishes *Beyond the Down Low*.

presidential campaign of Michael Dukakis before attending Harvard Law School. While there, Boykin declared publicly that he was homosexual: The traumatic but liberating experience was the subject of his first successful book, *One More River to Cross: Black and Gay in America* (1996).

After leaving Harvard, Boykin joined the 1992 Democratic Bill Clinton–Al Gore presidential campaign in Arkansas. From 1993 to 1994 he served as special media assistant to President Bill Clinton (1993–2001), becoming the highest-ranking openly homosexual member of the White House staff.

Addressing controversial issues
Since leaving the White House in 1995, Boykin has become a respected spokesperson and writer on civil rights and gay issues. He has addressed contentious issues, such as homophobia (fear of and discrimination against lesbians and homosexuals) in religion, and AIDs and the black community. From 1995 to 1998 Boykin served as executive director of the National Black Lesbian and Gay Leadership Forum, a civil rights group; he is also president of the National Black Justice Coalition. Boykin has lectured on civil and gay rights issues around the world. He has also written two other critically acclaimed books, *Respecting the Soul* (1999) and *Beyond the Down Low* (2005).

Further reading: Boykin, Keith. *One More River to Cross: Black and Gay in America*. New York, NY: Doubleday, 1996. www.keithboykin.com (Boykin's official site).

BOYKIN, Otis
Scientist, Inventor

Otis Boykin made a number of important inventions that continue to influence the way people live. He was born on August 29, 1920, in Dallas, Texas, into a stable home environment; his mother was a housewife and his father a carpenter. As a teenager Boykin showed an inquiring mind. From 1938 to 1941 he studied at Fisk College, Tennessee, before getting his first job as a laboratory assistant at the Majestic Radio and TV Corporation in Chicago. His principal work was the testing of automatic aircraft controls. He rose to the position of foreman but left in 1944. Boykin's career path now set itself toward the activity in which he would make his name—inventing.

KEY DATES	
1920	Born in Dallas, Texas, on August 29.
1941	Gets his first job as a laboratory assistant.
1944	Sets up his own company, Boykin-Fruth Inc.
1959	Awarded his first patent on June 16 for his "wire type precision resistor."
1963	Retires from professional inventing.
1982	Dies in Chicago, Illinois.

Inventive mind

Boykin became a research engineer at the P. J. Nilson Research Laboratories in Illinois before leaving to set up his own company, Boykin-Fruth Inc., devoted to his passion for inventing. While running his own business, Boykin attended the Illinois Institute of Technology from 1946 to 1947. He never was able to finish his degree because his parents could not continue to help pay for his education.

The break in education did not stop Boykin from becoming an increasingly successful inventor. He was given his first patent on June 16, 1959, for a "wire type precision resistor." The resistor was cheaper to make and more efficient than previous ones, and soon became an important component in television sets, computers, and radios. Boykin's resistor and later refinements of it can still be found in modern electronic equipment, including in all IBM computers. He went on to make further electrical components that found a wide range of applications in both commercial and military contexts.

Boykin's work with aircraft control systems combined with his technological innovations directly influenced the development of missile guidance systems. He designed a variable resistor device that is used in infrared guided missiles, in particular a fiber optic guided missile. It uses an infrared camera in its nose to take pictures of its environment. The images are fed through a fiber-optic cable, analyzed, and sent to the weapon operator's screen. The operator can then control the direction of the missile with no delay in communication. The infrared camera gives the missile phenomenal accuracy, the cable means that the missile cannot be jammed, and the sophisticated communication system enables the missile to be retargeted. Another type of missile that uses Boykin's components is the Tomahawk, a long-range weapon that is one of the most deadly in the U.S. military arsenal.

The pacemaker

Boykin is perhaps most famous for his invention of an electrical control used in the pacemaker, an electronic device implanted in the body to regulate the human heartbeat. Typically a pacemaker has a small generator attached to the heart by wires with electrodes at their ends. Inside the generator a battery powers a small computer that monitors the heartbeat and regulates it by sending electronic pulses through the wires, stimulating the heart.

Retirement

Boykin's other inventions include a burglarproof cash register and a chemical air filter, neither of which he patented, and over 25 electronic devices with various uses. Boykin effectively retired from professional inventing in 1963. However, he worked from 1964 to 1982 as a consultant for science and engineering firms in the United States and in Europe. Boykin died in Chicago in 1982 of heart failure.

Further reading: Krapp, Kristine M. (ed.) *Notable Black American Scientists*. Detroit, MI: Gale Research, 1999. http://inventors.about.com/library/inventors/blboykin.htm (Biography).

BRADLEY, Benjamin
Inventor

Little is known about Benjamin Bradley's life; but despite being a slave and having no formal education, he became one of the first African American inventors. Although he was unable to protect his invention, the money he received for it enabled him to buy his freedom.

Childhood

Bradley was born in about 1830 in Maryland and from birth entered a life of slavery. In the early 19th century no Southern schools admitted black children, and only a handful of free public schools did in the North. However, Bradley managed to gain an education through informal means. It is possible that his master's children taught him or that he shared some of their lessons. Bradley soon demonstrated an aptitude for science and mathematics.

Early invention

By about 1846, aged about 16, Bradley was working in a printing office, but he was already inventing in his spare time. Using only a few pieces of metal and a portion of a gun barrel, he created a working model of a steam engine.

Bradley's master recognized his talent, and found him a place in the department of natural and experimental philosophy at the Naval Academy in Annapolis. Natural philosophy was the term used to describe a scientific approach to the study of nature and the physical universe before the development of modern science.

The Naval Academy

At the Naval Academy Bradley's job was to assist the professors when they conducted engineering experiments. His employers were impressed with his quick mind and inquisitive nature; a Professor Hopkins is on record as commenting that "he looks for the law by which things act." Bradley also took the opportunity to further his learning by adding algebra and geometry to his mathematical understanding.

Although Bradley was technically paid for his work, most of his wages were transferred to his master, who gave Bradley an allowance of $5 a month. With this money and the amount gained from the sale of his steam-engine model, Bradley constructed a full-scale steam engine that was powerful enough to drive a small cutter, or ship's boat, at a speed of 16 knots (16 nautical miles an hour).

Patent laws

U.S. law at the time prevented slaves from protecting their inventions by taking out a patent. A patent is a federal grant that gives its owner the right to exclude others from making, using, or selling an invention for a set term of years. Slaves, however, were not allowed to enter legal agreements. Until the Civil War (1861–1865) only free blacks were entitled to receive patents for their inventions. Few, however, had the educational opportunities, necessary skills, or experience to develop their inventive ideas or patent them. Thomas Jennings was the first known African American to be granted a patent; it was issued in 1821 for a dry-cleaning process. In 1870 the U.S. patent laws were revised so that anyone, regardless of race, could hold a patent.

Lost invention

Bradley's steam engine had exciting applications for the young U.S. Navy, but he lost all rights to exploit his work. The only positive outcome was that Bradley was paid a substantial sum of money for the steam engine. With it he was able to purchase freedom for himself and his family. No further information about Bradley is known, except that he died during the second half of the 19th century.

KEY DATES

1830   Born in Maryland at about this time.

1846   Invents a working model of a steam engine at about this time.

1847   Gains employment in the department of natural and experimental philosophy at the Naval Academy, Annapolis, at about this time.

1848   Invents a full-scale steam engine; purchases his freedom with the proceeds.

See also: Jennings, Thomas; Slavery

Further reading: Haskins, James. *Outward Dreams: Black Inventors and Their Inventions.* New York, NY: Walker & Co., 2003.
http://www.princeton.edu/~mcbrown/display/bradley.html
(Correspondence about Bradley's invention).

BRADLEY, Thomas
Mayor

Thomas Bradley became the first African American mayor of Los Angeles, California, in 1973; he held the position until 1992.

Bradley was born on a cotton plantation in Texas in 1917 and moved with his family to Los Angeles at age seven. Although his father later left the family, his parents instilled in their son the value of education, and in 1937 he won a track scholarship to attend the University of California, Los Angeles, as an education major.

However, Bradley dropped out of school three years later and joined the Los Angeles Police Force (LAPD), becoming its first black lieutenant. In 1959, while still on the police force, Bradley enrolled in Law School at Loyola University and then at Southwestern University in Los Angeles, where he gained his degree.

Political success
Bradley ran successfully for councilman in 1963. He used his victory as a stepping-stone to run in May 1973 for mayor of Los Angeles, the third-largest city in the nation and, at that time, predominantly white. Militant blacks called him "Uncle Tom" or the "white man's candidate," while others accused him of courting "black votes" and "left-wing militants." However, Bradley's victory and subsequent ability to build a "rainbow coalition" won him

▼*A smiling Tom Bradley calls the polls "very encouraging" just before his election in 1985.*

KEY DATES	
1917	Born in Calvert, Texas, on December 29.
1963	Elected councilman in Los Angeles Country.
1973	Elected mayor of Los Angeles.
1992	Announces his retirement.
1998	Dies in Los Angeles, California, on September 29.

a sizable and loyal constituency that kept him in office for decades. In 1984 he succeeded in bringing the Olympic Games to Los Angeles. Whereas the previous games had lost money, efficient management resulted in a huge financial bonanza for the city. In 1985 Bradley was reelected with 68 percent of the vote when he ran against white conservative John Ferraro. Bradley repeatedly won the contest for mayor, despite rumors in 1989 of financial wrongdoing. He was cleared of all charges but paid a civil penalty, admitting that he had made mistakes in judgment.

The riots
On April 29, 1992, four white LAPD police officers were acquitted of assault while arresting black motorist Rodney King. Riots broke out in the city in which 55 people were killed and dozens of businesses were burned or looted. A tense racial atmosphere polarized Los Angeles. Many white and black citizens held Bradley partly responsible for the unrest, especially when he did not fire his defiant chief of police, Daryl Gates. The riots signaled the end of Bradley's career as a politician, and he announced his retirement.

During his five terms as mayor Bradley presided over the expansion of Los Angeles International Airport and the Port of Los Angeles, which became the busiest in the country, the construction of the city's first subway, and the flourishing of both big and small businesses. Bradley died from a heart attack on September 29, 1998.

Further reading: Smith, Jessie Carney (ed.) *Black Firsts: 4,000 Ground-Breaking and Pioneering Historical Events.* Detroit, MI: Visible Ink Press, 2003.
http://www.rootsweb.com/~txrober2/TOMBRADLEY.htm (Robertson County biography of Bradley).

BRAGG, George Freeman, Jr.
Minister, Writer

Passionately committed to promoting the status and education of African Americans, writer and Episcopalian minister George Freeman Bragg, Jr., worked tirelessly to fulfill his civic duties.

Bragg was born in North Carolina in 1863. Two years later his family moved to Petersburg, Virginia. His grandmother had been the slave of an Episcopal minister. She and her son George Freeman helped found the St. Stephen's Episcopal Church for Negroes.

Early activism

In 1882, at age 19, Bragg founded the *Lancet*, a weekly newspaper celebrating the achievements and lives of the African American community. Asserting its independence from the major political parties, the *Lancet* supported William Mahone, leader of the Readjuster Party. A coalition of black and white Republicans and white Democrats, the Readjusters governed Virginia from 1879 to 1883. They aimed to "readjust" the state of Virginia's debt, revoke the poll tax, and boost the funding of public amenities and schools. The Readjusters also supported black suffrage, office-holding, and jury service. In 1884, shortly after his twenty-first birthday, Bragg was selected for jury duty on the Corporation Court of Petersburg.

When the Readjuster Party lost power, Bragg decided to align his newspaper with the Republican Party. In 1886, when Bragg entered the seminary to study for the priesthood, the *Lancet* became the *Afro-American Churchman*, a religious newspaper for the African American Episcopalian community that folded after a few months.

Religious career

Bragg was ordained as a deacon in 1887 and appointed as an Episcopal priest in Norfolk, Virginia, in 1888. At about the same time the governor of Virginia commissioned him as a trustee of the Hampton Normal and Agricultural Institute (founded 1868), one of the first colleges for black and Native Americans. Bragg held the position until his appointment as rector of St. James's Episcopal Church, Baltimore, in 1891. Bragg became St. James's longest-serving rector, working until his death in 1940. He founded and organized the Maryland Home for Friendless Colored Children, which took in boys aged between two and 10 when their parents were unable to afford to keep them. Bragg inspired his congregation with his

KEY DATES	
1863	Born in Warrenton, North Carolina, on January 25.
1865	Moves to Petersburg, Virginia.
1882	Founds the *Lancet*.
1888	Ordained as an Episcopal priest in Norfolk, Virginia.
1891	Becomes rector of St. James's Episcopal Church, Baltimore.
1940	Dies in Baltimore, Maryland, on March 12.

involvement in the local community and his criticism of racism within the church.

Bragg also wrote several books. The most significant were *Men of Maryland* (1914), a collection of biographical essays on significant African Americans from Maryland, and the *History of the Afro-American Group of the Episcopal Church* (1922), a detailed history of the church dating back to 1695. Bragg died in 1940.

▼ *This photograph from the 1900s shows George Freeman Bragg, Jr., at his writing desk.*

Further reading: Low, W. Augustus, and Virgil A. Clift (eds.). *Encyclopedia of Black America.* New York, NY: Da Capo Press, 1984.
http://docsouth.unc.edu/church/bragg/bio.html (Biography for and articles by George Freeman Bragg, Jr.).

BRANDY
Singer, Actor

Multitalented singer and actor Brandy Rayana Norwood—known more popularly as Brandy—is an entertainment superstar. She is internationally acclaimed in the music, film, TV, and modeling industries.

Born in McComb, Mississippi, in 1979, Brandy began her singing career in her local church choir; she performed her first solo when she was just two years old. Brandy decided that she wanted to be a singer after hearing rhythm and blues (R&B) singer Whitney Houston's hit "How Will I Know?" for the first time. Brandy signed a recording contract with Atlantic Records when she was 14.

Brandy's self-titled 1994 debut album was an immediate success, selling over four million copies. She also became the youngest artist in history to have two consecutive No. 1 songs on the music charts. Building on this success, Brandy released three more albums: *Never Say Never* (1999), *Full Moon* (2002), and *Afrodisiac* (2004), to great critical acclaim. Her music has earned her numerous awards from American Music, NAACP Image, Billboard, and BMI Pop, among others; she has also received several Grammy nominations, as well as an award in 1999.

Other avenues
Brandy also has a successful acting career. She starred in the TV sitcom *Thea* (1993) and the successful series *Moesha* (1996–2001). She also played the lead in the Emmy-nominated Disney movie *Cinderella* (1997), along with her idol Whitney Houston. Brandy was only the second African American to be cast in this role. Brandy has since starred in several hit movies, including *I Still Know What You Did Last Summer* (1998).

▲ *Singer-actor Brandy at the movie premiere of 2 Fast 2 Furious, on June 3, 2003.*

Role model
In 1997 Brandy and her family established the much-praised Norwood Kids Foundation (NK Foundation), which is dedicated to enriching the cultural life of disadvantaged eight- to 18-year-old Americans. Brandy was also named the first International UNICEF Spokesperson for Youth in 1999 and received the Martin Luther King, Jr., Award for outstanding achievements as a role model for youth from the Congress for Racial Equality.

See also: Houston, Whitney; King, Martin Luther, Jr.

Further reading: Daniels, Karu F. *Brandy: An Intimate Look.* Kansas City, MO: Andrews McMeel Publishing, 1999. http://www.foreverbrandy.com (Brandy's Atlantic Records site).

KEY DATES

1979   Born in McComb, Mississippi, on February 11.

1994   Releases *Brandy*, her debut album.

1996   Wins NAACP Image Award for Outstanding Youth Actress in Television Series.

1999   Wins Grammy Award for "Best R&B Collaboration With Vocals."

2000   Receives Governor's Award from Los Angeles Chapter of the Recording Arts and Sciences.

BRANSON, Herman
Scientist

One of the 20th century's most distinguished African American scientists, Herman Russell Branson was best known for his pioneering contributions in the fields of protein structure and sickle-cell anemia. He was also a noted educator of international standing and president of two historically black colleges.

Worms, X-rays, and proteins

Branson was born in 1914 in the town of Pocahontas, Virginia, where his father worked as a coal miner. He graduated with high honors from Virginia State University, Petersburg, in 1936, and just three years later completed his PhD in physics at the University of Cincinnati, Ohio. In 1941 Branson was invited to join the faculty of Howard University, Washington, D.C., where he became a full professor of physics in 1944.

Branson's main research interest during the early part of his career was in biophysics—then a new, rapidly changing field that applied the principles of physics to biological processes. Among his early projects, for example, was a study of the effects of X-rays on worms. From the mid-1940s Branson became interested in the physical structures of proteins, complicated chains of molecules that are often referred to as the building blocks of life.

The alpha helix

Working in collaboration with the renowned white physical chemist Linus Pauling (1901–1994), Branson discovered the alpha helix, a spiral structure common to many proteins. The Pauling research team revealed its findings in a paper published in 1951. The discovery of the alpha helix was a scientific milestone that helped Pauling win a Nobel Prize in chemistry in 1954. Many people have argued that Branson's contribution to this groundbreaking research—which helped pave the way to the discovery of DNA—has been undervalued. DNA stores all the information needed to create an organism.

However, Branson's research led him to important work on red blood cells in humans, and in particular on the inherited condition known as sickle-cell anemia, commonly found in people of African descent: Roughly 1 in every 400 African Americans suffers from the disorder.

Branson remained at Howard until 1968, when he became president of Central State University, Ohio. In

▲ *Herman Branson in 1970 when he became president of Lincoln University, Pennsylvania.*

1970 Branson became president of Lincoln University, Pennsylvania, where he served until his retirement in 1985. Branson's work as an educator often took him abroad. In 1985, for example, he became a member of the Council of the National University of Lesotho, in southern Africa.

Branson was a fellow of the American Association for the Advancement of Science (AAAS), a member of Sigma Xi, the honor society for the American Chemical Society, and Sigma Pi Sigma, the society for the American Physics Association. He was also a Rosenwald Fellow and a senior fellow at the National Research Council. He died in 1995.

KEY DATES	
1914	Born in Pocahontas, Virginia, on August 14.
1936	Graduates from Virginia State University, Petersburg.
1951	With Linus Pauling and Robert Corey publishes discovery of the alpha helix, a structure found in many proteins.
1995	Dies on June 7.

Further reading: Kessler, James H., et al. *Distinguished African American Scientists of the 20th Century*. Phoenix, AZ: Oryx Press, 1996.
www.princeton.edu/~mcbrown/display/branson.html (Biography).

BRASHEAR, Carl M.
Navy Master Diver

The story of Carl Maxie Brashear is so inspirational that in 2000 it was made into a Hollywood film, *Men of Honor*, starring Cuba Gooding, Jr., and Robert de Niro.

Brashear was born on January 19, 1931, on a farm in Kentucky, a state known for its strict racial segregation. His background was poor, but he had a loving and encouraging family, and Brashear gained an education in segregated schools and through home teaching. At age 17 he made the defining decision of his life—he decided to join the Navy.

Navy diver

Brashear enlisted in the Navy in 1948; but because the military was still segregated, the only post open to him was that of steward. He eventually managed to obtain a post as beachmaster, then a posting aboard the escort carrier (a type of aircraft carrier) USS *Palau*. Having observed Navy divers in action, however, Brashear made a request to enter diver training. Against all odds he was accepted in the course but struggled tremendously against both racist threats and the demanding academic standards. He failed the course once but eventually graduated as a First Class Diver after 26 weeks of training.

On January 17, 1966, a B-52 Stratofortress carrying four nuclear bombs collided with a refueling tanker off southern Spain. The parachutes on three of the bombs opened, and they came down safely on land. One of the bombs fell into the sea, however, and Brashear and a team of experts were sent to recover it from the seabed. They spent two and a half months searching before they located it.

Accident and amputation

During the recovery operation a cable under tension flung a pipe at high velocity into Brashear's leg, delivering a massive injury that nearly killed him from blood loss. When he finally reached a Spanish hospital, six hours after the accident, doctors originally thought he was dead but then detected a faint heartbeat. After blood transfusions that totaled 18 pints (8.5l), Brashear finally regained consciousness. He was told that his leg could be fixed but would take three years to mend. Brashear requested to be returned to the United States.

Surgeons at the Portsmouth Naval Hospital again told Brashear that his leg could be saved but confirmed that it would take three to four years and leave him walking with a brace. Brashear was determined to dive again (*see box*) and insisted that the surgeons amputate his leg. It was taken off below the knee in July 1966, and Brashear was fitted with an artificial limb. He refused to use a crutch from the moment it was fitted.

In December Brashear sneaked out of the hospital to make his first dive since the accident, making sure that he

◀ *Carl Brashear arrives at the 2000 premiere of the film* **Men of Honor** *at the Samuel Goldwyn Theater, Los Angeles.*

INFLUENCES AND INSPIRATION

When Brashear had his leg amputated, he was determined to go back to diving. During his treatment in the hospital he read books that inspired him, confirming his belief that a comeback was possible. He learned that a prosthesis can support any amount of weight.

He also read about a Canadian Air Force pilot with no legs who flew airplanes. This gave him hope that the Navy would consider returning him to active service. In interviews in 1989 and 1990 Brashear said that he had also read books that showed him that "you've got to develop

an attitude that, 'Hey, look, I'm going to accept this. I'm going to make it work.' I worked towards it."

Inspired by his reading, Brashear was determined to be positive. He told his interviewer, "I kept saying, 'I'm going to be a deep-sea diver, doggone it!'"

had photographs of the dive as evidence. He kept refusing to attend medical evaluation boards and instead reported to the second-class diving school. The Navy authorities were not sure what to do with Brashear. As one captain said, "Most of the people in your position want to get a medical disability, get out of the Navy, and do the least they can and draw as much pay as they can. And then you're asking for full duty. I don't know how to handle it."

The Navy decided to evaluate Brashear for one year before making a final decision. He dived almost every day. He also had to lead calisthenics every day and set such a pace that the other students complained. It was only after two weeks, when the class had to go swimming and Brashear went out to the pool with one leg under his arm, that the students realized he was an amputee. At the end of the year Brashear was returned to full duty and diving, again making naval history.

In interviews conducted in 1989 and 1990 Brashear admitted how tough it had been: "Sometimes I would come back from a run, and my artificial leg would have a puddle of blood from my stump. I wouldn't go to sick bay. In that year, if I had gone to sick bay, they would have written me up."

Master diver

Brashear served in Harbor Clearance Unit 2, Naval Air Station, Norfolk; Experimental Diving Unit, submarine tender *Hunley*; and in USS *Recovery*, Naval Safety Center, and Shore Intermediate Maintenance Activity, Norfolk.

In 1970 Brashear qualified as a master diver, becoming the first African American to attain the position. To do so, he undertook a physically punishing training course that many able-bodied people failed.

Brashear retired from the Navy in 1979. In 1989 he became one of only seven enlisted men to be enshrined as a "Naval Tradition Maker," and his portrait was commissioned by the Department of the Navy.

KEY DATES	
1931	Born in Tonieville, Larue County, Kentucky, on January 19.
1948	Enters the Navy as a steward.
1963	Qualifies as a Navy diver.
1966	Loses a leg after an accident.
1970	Retrains and qualifies as a master diver.
1979	Retires from Navy.
2000	*Men of Honor* released.

After the Navy

After leaving the Navy, Brashear attended college in Maryland and studied environmental science. He worked for the government, first as an engineering technician and later as an environmental protection specialist, until his retirement in 1993.

Brashear's personal life has also been eventful. In 1952 he married Junetta Wilcoxson, and they had four children. The marriage broke up in 1978. His two subsequent marriages also ended in divorce.

The film *Men of Honor* was made about his life and released in 2000. Brashear visited the set and was pleased by the final result, saying, "It was very close to the real thing."

See also: Gooding, Cuba, Jr.; Military

Further reading: Brashear, Carl M. *The Reminiscences of Master Chief Boatswain's Mate Carl M. Brashear, U.S. Navy (retired)* Annapolis, MD: US Naval Institute, 2000.
http://www.usni.org/oralhistory/B/brashear.htm
(Biography plus a long extract of an interview with Brashear).

BRAUGHER, Andre
Actor

Renowned for his integrity, the celebrated character actor Andre Braugher has consistently delivered powerful film, television, and stage performances.

Braugher was born on July 1, 1962, and raised on Chicago's West Side. He was originally drawn to acting as a means of meeting girls. However, his ambition to become an actor was awakened during a production of *Hamlet* at Stanford University, after which he changed his major to drama. Braugher went on to graduate with an MA in fine arts from the Julliard School of Drama in New York and was soon performing at the Berkeley Shakespeare Festival.

Expanding career
Braugher's move into screen acting saw him playing the role of Detective Winston Blake in the successful made-for-television film *Kojak: Fatal Flaw* in 1989. He returned in the same role for a further four *Kojak* films. On the big screen Braugher stole the show as a Harvard graduate Union soldier in the hit movie *Glory* (1989). He has gone on to develop his film career with a range of roles in movies, including *Striking Distance* (1993), *Primal Fear* (1996), *City of Angels* (1998), and *Duets* (2000). Despite his commitment to his film-acting career, Braugher turned down the role of Dr. Harry Adams in the science fiction movie *Sphere* in 1998 to spend more time with his family.

Critical acclaim
In 1993 Braugher achieved national fame in the role of Detective Frank Pembleton in the TV drama series *Homicide: Life on the Streets*. Braugher played the role for five seasons, and in 1998 his intense performance as the commanding and garrulous detective was rewarded with an Emmy for Outstanding Lead Actor in a Drama Series.

Braugher has also received critical acclaim for his theater performances. He appeared in several New York Shakespeare Festival productions, including *Much Ado about Nothing*, *King John*, and *Henry V*, for which he won an Obie (Off-Broadway Theater Award) in the lead role in 1997. In the same year he was voted one of the "Fifty Most Beautiful People" by *People* magazine. Braugher continued to be an imposing presence on television with Emmy-nominated roles in *The Tuskeegee Airmen* (1995) and the drama series *Gideon's Crossing* (2000). More recently he was lauded for his TV performances in *Hack* (2002), *Salem's Lot* (2004), and *Thief* (2005).

▲ *Andre Braugher stars on stage in the lead role in* Henry V, *for which he won an Obie award in 1997.*

KEY DATES	
1962	Born in Chicago, Illinois, on July 1.
1993	Plays Detective Frank Pembleton in the TV series *Homicide: Life on the Streets*.
1997	Wins an Obie award for his performance in *Henry V*.
1998	Wins Emmy for Outstanding Lead Actor in a Drama Series for his role in *Homicide: Life on the Streets*.

Further reading: Kalat, David. *Homicide: Life on the Street: The Unofficial Companion.* Los Angeles, CA: Renaissance Books, 1998.
http://www.tribute.ca/bio.asp?id=1103 (Biography).
http://www.tv-now.com/intervus/andre/ (2004 interview).

BRAUN, Carol
Politician

Carol Moseley Braun was the first African American woman to be elected to the U.S. Senate. She also served as the U.S. ambassador to New Zealand and Samoa.

Road to success

Born on August 16, 1947, Carol Elizabeth Moseley was the eldest of four children. The Moseley family lived in a segregated middle-class neighborhood on the South Side of Chicago, Illinois. After their parents' divorce Braun and her siblings moved into their grandmother's home. Braun attended local public schools and later studied political science at the University of Illinois at Chicago, from which she received a BA in 1969. Braun went on to study law at

▼ *Carol Moseley Braun addresses a conference in Washington, D.C., in 2003.*

the University of Chicago Law School, where she met her husband Michael Braun; she graduated in 1972.

In 1973 Braun was appointed prosecutor in the U.S. Attorney's Office, where she remained for four years. In 1978 she ran as a Democrat for a seat in the Illinois House of Representatives and won, serving in that position until 1988. Braun was the first black American and the first woman to serve as assistant majority leader in the Illinois House. She became known for her legislative leadership in sponsoring progressive bills on education and her ability to build successful coalitions.

In 1988 Braun was elected Cook County recorder of deeds, an important executive position in which she remained until 1992. That same year Braun's political career reached new heights when she won a Senate seat for Illinois, becoming the first black woman to be elected as a senator. She introduced 14 separate bills during her time as senator; more than half became law. However, she lost her attempt at reelection in 1998.

Shortly after her defeat Braun was approached by President Bill Clinton to become an ambassador to New Zealand and Samoa. After fierce opposition from conservatives in the Senate she was sworn in on December 15, 1999. She returned to the United States in 2001, briefly pursuing an academic career before returning to politics in 2003 to attempt to win the 2004 Democratic presidential nomination. She eventually withdrew from the race when her campaign ran into financial difficulties.

KEY DATES	
1947	Born in Chicago, Illinois, on August 16.
1992	Elected to the U.S. Senate.
1999	Appointed ambassador to New Zealand and Samoa.
2003	Pursues Democratic presidential nomination.

Further reading: Henderson, Ashyia N., and Ralph G. Zerbonia (eds.). *Contemporary Black Biography: Profiles from the International Black Community*. Detroit, MI: Thomson Gale, 2004.
http://bioguide.congress.gov/scripts/biodisplay.pl?index=M001025 (Biography from Congress site).

BRAWLEY, Benjamin
Educator, Writer

Benjamin Griffith Brawley was an outstanding scholar who forged a career as a highly respected teacher. He published 10 books and more than 100 newspaper articles.

A promising childhood

Brawley was born on April 22, 1882, in Columbia, South Carolina, into a well-to-do family. His father was a Baptist minister, and despite the family moving frequently during his childhood, Brawley proved to be an exceptional student. Taught by his mother until third grade, he then attended a number of schools. During his summers he studied Greek and Latin while earning money doing odd jobs.

By age 13 Brawley was so advanced in his studies that he was sent to the preparatory program at Atlanta Baptist College. Although he was younger than his classmates, Brawley soon outperformed them. He was also a talented athlete who participated in every aspect of school life. In 1901 he graduated with honors and immediately embarked on a teaching career.

Teaching career

Between 1902 and 1910 Brawley taught at Atlanta Baptist College while completing his BA (1906) from the University of Chicago and his MA (1908) from Harvard University.

Brawley considered teaching to be a "divine profession" in which he emphasized a traditional, holistic approach. He believed the student had to make as much effort as the teacher, and that teaching should not take place in a vacuum but should take account of every part of the student's life. One of his favorite methods of teaching was to have students memorize passages from classical texts.

In 1921 Brawley was ordained as a Baptist minister; but his career was short-lived, and he returned to teaching, first at Shaw University in North Carolina and then from 1931 at Howard University in Washington, D.C., where he stayed for the rest of his life.

Writing career

Later in his career Brawley started to write for publication. He wrote poems and short stories, and became one of the most prominent black historians and literary critics of the first half of the 20th century. He wrote on a variety of subjects, but the position of the African American was of particular interest to him. In 1918 he published *The Negro*

KEY DATES	
1882	Born in Columbia, South Carolina, on April 22.
1901	Graduates with honors from Atlanta Baptist College.
1908	Receives MA from Harvard University.
1912	Marries Hilda Damaris Prowd; joins Atlanta Baptist College as full-time teacher.
1921	Publishes *A Social History of the American Negro*.
1939	Dies in Washington, D.C., on February 1.

in Literature and Art and in 1921 his major work, *A Social History of the American Negro*. In the latter book he argued for the importance of the relationship between black Americans and Africa.

Brawley believed that literature should reflect every aspect of the African American experience, not just its struggles. *The Negro Genius* (1936) contained his views on the Harlem Renaissance, the flowering of black literature and culture in Harlem, New York, during the 1920s. While Brawley approved of black culture, he had reservations about the Harlem Renaissance, particularly its depiction of Harlem's crime, sexuality, and sordid element. He tended to praise the more conservative writers, such as Jessie Fauset and James Weldon Johnson, while criticizing Countee Cullen and Langston Hughes. Of Hughes's second poetry collection he said, "It would have been just as well, perhaps better, if the book had never been published." Brawley feared that writers like Hughes portrayed blacks in a way that would intensify white prejudice. Brawley died on February 1, 1939, at his Washington, D.C., home following a stroke.

See also: Cullen, Countee; Fauset, Jessie; Harlem Renaissance; Hughes, Langston; Johnson, James Weldon

Further reading: Salzman, Jack, David L. Smith, and Cornel West (eds.). *Encyclopedia of African-American Culture and History*. Vol 1. New York, NY: Simon & Schuster, 1996. http://www.poetry-archive.com/b/brawley_benjamin.html (Poetry Archive site with Brawley links).

BRENT, John E.
Architect

John E. Brent was notable as the first African American architect to practice in Buffalo, New York. Very little is known about Brent's life, although he was certainly a respected figure within both his profession and Buffalo's black community.

Brent's achievements are all the more remarkable because during the early 20th century the architectural profession was very slow to accept African Americans into its ranks. In 1930 only about 60 blacks were listed as registered architects in the United States, and many of their buildings have since been lost or radically altered. In 2004 there were 1,428 African American architects in the country out of about 37,000 architects who belong to the American Institute of Architects.

Early years
Brent seems to have been born in Washington, D.C., in 1892. If this date is correct, he showed his talents as an architect at a very early age, entering the renowned black-run Tuskegee Institute in Alabama in 1904 and graduating with a degree in architecture in 1907. He spent two years as a schoolteacher before pursuing further studies in architecture at the Drexel Institute, Philadelphia, from which he graduated in 1912.

Move to Buffalo
At this point Brent moved to Buffalo, where for the next 14 years he worked for various white architectural firms. After World War I (1914–1918) Buffalo's black community developed rapidly as thousands of African Americans migrated from the South in what became known as the Great Migration: 4,500 came to Buffalo in 1920 and 13,500 in 1930. The community, focused on the city's Lower East Side, quickly organized itself, setting up churches, numerous businesses, four newspapers, and self-help groups such as the Colored Musicians' Union of Buffalo, founded in 1917 by black musicians who had been denied membership in the white musicians' local union.

Important commission
It is within this context that Brent's 1926 commission to build the Michigan Avenue YMCA is best understood. The building was paid for with funds donated by George B. Matthews, a local white businessman and philanthropist, and was specifically commissioned to provide YMCA facilities for Buffalo's black youth. The building included a gymnasium, swimming pool, and library, as well as dormitory rooms. It opened in 1928 and over the following decades proved to be a key resource for the local black community.

Career and community involvement
The commission to erect the YMCA building enabled Brent to set up his own practice, which may have lasted until the 1950s. Nothing is known about the other buildings he may have designed.

Brent continued, however, to be active in the black community, serving, for example, as the first president of the Buffalo chapter of the National Association for the Advancement of Colored People (NAACP). He also served on the local council of the State Commission against Discrimination. He was active in St. Philip's Episcopal Church and was awarded the Bishop's Medal for meritorious service

Brent's YMCA building, although demolished in 1977, has historic significance in that it demonstrated how, by contributing to the shaping of their own urban environment, African Americans could exert greater control over the way they live. Today's cities are still largely created by white architects and are sometimes still criticized for failing to meet black needs.

Brent died in Buffalo on October 27, 1962, and was buried in Forest Lawn Cemetery.

KEY DATES

1892	Born in Washington, D.C., at about this time.
1912	Graduates from the Drexel Institute and moves to Buffalo to work as an architect.
1926	Commissioned to build the Michigan Avenue YMCA.
1962	Dies in Buffalo, New York, on October 27.

See also: Great Migration and Urbanization

Further reading: www.buffaloresearch.com/essays/brent.html
(Review of Brent's career).

BRIDGES, Sheila
Interior Designer

Sheila Bridges is one of the United States's most famous interior designers and the chief executive officer of Sheila Bridges Designs, Inc. In 2001 both CNN and *Time Magazine* named her "America's Best Interior Designer."

Early years

Sheila Bridges was born on July 7, 1964, in Philadelphia. She studied sociology at Brown University, Providence, Rhode Island, graduating in 1986. She moved to New York, where she toyed with the idea of going into advertising but instead joined the training program for retail buyers at Bloomingdale's store. She quickly became bored, however, and after responding to an ad placed by the prestigious architecture firm Shelton, Mindel & Associates, she found herself exposed to "all of these bright, exceptional people doing something I'd never even dreamed of."

Interior design

Bridges developed a particular interest in interior design, which she studied at the Parson's School of Design in New York. After finishing her course, she worked for interior designer Renny Saltzman. In 1994 Bridges decided to set up her own company. She has said that she was motivated to do so partly because most of the big interior designers were white, and she wanted to provide a service for African Americans. However, Bridges has also made it clear that she does not want to be pigeonholed by race: Her designs appeal to anyone interested in design and style.

Big break

Bridges's big break came when she heard that Andre Harrell, then president of Uptown Records, was struggling to find an apartment that he liked. She hounded Harrell for several months until he agreed to meet with her; she came away with the promise that if she could find Harrell an apartment, he would let her design the interior. Bridges succeeded, and Harrell became a long-standing client.

Bridges's client list is impressive. She designed President Bill Clinton's offices in Harlem, New York, and she has worked for hip-hop producer Sean "P. Diddy" Combs and novelist Tom Clancy.

In 1999 Bridges opened a retail shop, Sheila Bridges Home, in Hudson, New York. She has written many articles on design for prestigious journals and newspapers, such as *Time Magazine*, the *New York Times*, *Elle Decor*,

Vanity Fair, and *Harper's Bazaar*. She is also the author of *Furnishing Forward: A Practical Guide to Furnishing for a Lifetime* (2002). Bridges regularly appears on television and hosts the program *Sheila Bridges: Designer Living*.

An African American designer

Fewer than 3 percent of designers in the United States are African American. As an African American woman running her own business, Bridges said she found it challenging in the beginning to overcome stereotypes. "A lot of it had to do with not really having a mentor, who was paving a way in an industry with very few African Americans." Although she has been called "the black Martha Stewart," in an interview with CNN Bridges said, "Being African American is obviously a very big part of who I am. But I think my design is about good design." She wants people who walk into a room that she has designed to "feel comfortable, even if they don't know exactly what it is that makes them feel that way."

A connection to Harlem

At the start of the 21st century Bridges was committed to playing a part in the regeneration of Harlem. Her headquarters was in Harlem, and she worked on transforming many of the interiors of its rundown buildings. Derek Johnson, president of Harlem's Apollo Theater, observed that "There's a personal commitment on her part to see this neighborhood grow, flourish and realize all of its potential."

KEY DATES	
1964	Born in Philadelphia, Pennsylvania, on July 7.
1993	Graduates in interior design from Parsons School of Design, New York.
1994	Sets up her own company.
2001	Named America's best interior designer by *Time Magazine* and CNN.

See also: Combs, Sean; Harrell, Andre

Further reading: http://www.sheilabridges.com (Bridges's personal site).

BRIDGEWATER, Pamela E.
Diplomat

Pamela E. Bridgewater, from 2002 the United States's deputy assistant secretary for African affairs, was the nation's longest-serving diplomat in South Africa. She is also known for her role in promoting U.S. business interests across the African continent, for which she received the Charles E. Cobb, Jr., Award for Initiative and Success in Trade Development in 2002.

Education
Born in Virginia in 1947, Bridgewater grew up in a community that was still racially segregated in many respects. She attended Walker-Grant High School in Fredericksburg, studied for a BA degree in political science at Virginia State University, Petersburg, and became involved with the National Association for the Advancement of Colored People (NAACP).

Teaching career
Having achieved a master's degree, also in political science, Bridgewater—who continued to stress the important role education plays in improving lives—embarked on a career in teaching. This period included professorships in political science at Morgan State University and Bowie State University, both in Maryland, and at Voorhees College, South Carolina. She also served as a consultant to the Joint Center for Political and Economic Studies. However, after 10 years Bridgewater felt that she needed a new challenge, so she decided to enter the U.S. Foreign Service.

KEY DATES

1947   Born in Fredericksburg, Virginia.

1968   Awarded a BA in political science from Virginia State University.

1970   Embarks on a career in teaching after earning MS at the University of Cincinnati.

1980   Enters the U.S. Foreign Service.

2000   Becomes U.S. ambassador to Benin.

2002   Becomes U.S. deputy assistant secretary for African affairs.

Career diplomat
In her capacity as a foreign service officer Bridgewater has traveled the world, serving in countries such as Belgium, Jamaica, and the Bahamas. In 1993 she was named consul general in Durban, South Africa, the first woman to serve as principal officer in the posting. During her time in South Africa Bridgewater was the political officer assigned to work with Nelson Mandela and the African National Congress (ANC) in the all-important negotiations that led to South Africa becoming a democracy in 1994 under Mandela's leadership. Until then South Africa had been ruled by a white minority government that enforced a system of laws, called apartheid, that aimed to completely separate whites and blacks.

In 2000 Bridgewater became U.S. ambassador to the West African nation of Benin, where she served two years. Of her time there she said, "I receive tremendous satisfaction from working to strengthen democratic institutions in Benin; enhance quality of life for Beninese, especially women and girls; support U.S. private sector initiatives; and promote people-to-people ties between our two historically linked countries."

Deputy assistant secretary and ambassador
In 2002 Bridgewater was appointed deputy assistant secretary for African affairs in the administration of George W. Bush. In the role she managed the government's African bureau's relations with 16 countries in West Africa. Her responsibilities included economic and business policies and programs. More recently as diplomat-in-residence at Howard University Bridgewater used her knowledge of African affairs to arouse students' interest in Africa. In 2005 President George W. Bush nominated her as U.S. ambassador to Ghana.

Bridgewater remains passionate on the subject of education and worries that many young African Americans do not see education as the key to a better life. "Money, prestige, and power may wane," she said at an NAACP Freedom Fund Banquet speech in her hometown of Fredericksburg in 2004, "With knowledge, there is nothing you cannot do."

Further information: http://www.state.gov/ (Official site of the U.S. Department of State).

BRIGGS, Cyril
Journalist, Socialist

A radical journalist and socialist, Cyril Briggs prefigured 20th-century black nationalist movements with his calls for an end to racial discrimination and American imperialism. He is credited with introducing communism to the African American community.

Political thinker
Born on the Caribbean island of Nevis in 1888, Briggs was the son of a plantation overseer. He moved from Nevis to Harlem, New York City, in 1905 to begin his writing career and by 1912 was working for the black newspaper *Amsterdam News*. In 1917 he wrote an editorial entitled "Security of Life for Poles and Serbs—Why Not Colored Americans?" He argued that the principle of self-determination, which gives people organized in a national movement the right to decide whether to become a nation-state used to justify U.S. involvement in World War I (1914–1918), should also be applied to black Americans in the United States. His candid views and fervent antiwar stance eventually cost him his job.

In 1917 Briggs established the African Blood Brotherhood (ABB), a "revolutionary secret order" that sought to eliminate racial oppression, secure suffrage for southern African Americans, overthrow American imperialism, and support armed conflict to end lynching. Briggs launched the ABB's monthly journal, the *Crusader*, in 1918, emphasizing the importance of black pride and the battle for self-determination. The magazine supported the electoral campaign of Socialist Party candidate A. Philip Randolph and focused its attention on the difficulty faced by African Americans finding jobs in the northern states and the lynchings taking place in the South. After the war Briggs became disillusioned by international politics and did not believe capitalist nations intended to ensure Africa's right to self-determination.

Embracing communism
Briggs looked to communism to provide a way to ensure racial and economic equality for people of all races and nationalities. By 1919 he began criticizing capitalism and equating it to colonialism in the editorials of the *Crusader*, arguing that by joining forces, white and black workers could eradicate the oppression of African Americans. He repeated his call for a separate U.S. state for African Americans. Briggs became a member of the Communist Party in 1921 and later its first African American leader when the ABB was absorbed into the party in 1924.

In the 1920s Briggs clashed with another leading African American, Marcus Garvey. Garvey was angered by Briggs's Marxist views and accused him of trying to destroy the government and business. Garvey believed that for blacks to be respected, they had to become financially independent, and that African Americans should colonize parts of Liberia in West Africa. Garvey headed the Universal Negro Improvement Association (UNIA), which had a great following among African Americans. As both men gained more power in the black community, the dispute became more personal. Among the issues they argued about was Garvey's 1922 summit meeting with the white supremacist Ku Klux Klan (KKK), which Briggs, the ABB, and most other black leaders saw as a threat to the relationship between the black and white communities. Eventually Briggs sued Garvey for accusing him of being white. Garvey was ordered to publish an apology in his newspaper the *Negro World*. When Garvey was imprisoned in 1925 for fraud, Briggs was one of his foremost critics. Little is known about Briggs's life after this point. He died in 1966.

See also: Garvey, Marcus; Political Movements; Randolph, A. Philip

Further reading: Winston, James. *Holding Aloft the Banner of Ethiopia: Caribbean Radicalism in Early Twentieth Century America.* New York, NY: Verso, 1999.
www.tcnj.edu/~fisherc/black_and_red.html (Biography and history of communism in the United States).

KEY DATES	
1888	Born on the Caribbean island of Nevis.
1905	Moves to Harlem, New York City.
1912	Begins working for the *Amsterdam News*.
1917	Founds the African Blood Brotherhood (ABB).
1918	Launches the *Crusader*.
1921	Joins the Communist Party.
1966	Dies.

BRISCO-HOOKS, Valerie

Athlete

One of the preeminent female sprinters of the 1980s, Valerie Brisco-Hooks gained national fame for her phenomenal performance at the 1984 Summer Olympics in Los Angeles, California. It was at these games that Brisco-Hooks became the first athlete—male or female—to win both the 200-meter and 400-meter sprints at a single Olympic Games.

Born on July 6, 1960, in Greenwood, Mississippi, Valerie Brisco moved with her family to Los Angeles at age five. Brisco first demonstrated superior athletic talent as a runner in high school, following her high-school performances with national collegiate success. While attending California State University at Northridge, Brisco won the 1979 Association of Intercollegiate Athletics for Women (AIAW) 200-meter sprint championship and was part of the 4 x 100-meter relay team that won the gold medal at the Pan-American Games.

The road to Los Angeles

In 1981 Brisco married Alvin Hooks, a wide receiver for the Philadelphia Eagles football team, and the couple had a baby the following year. It appeared in the early 1980s that Brisco-Hooks had concluded her athletic career, since she planned to focus on her new family rather than continue to compete. However, with her husband's encouragement, and then management, Brisco-Hooks resumed her training in preparation for the upcoming Summer Olympic Games in Los Angeles in 1984. The hard work paid off, and Brisco-Hooks returned to her prepregnancy form, losing 40 pounds (18kg) in the process.

At the 1984 Olympics Brisco-Hooks won gold medals in the 200 meters, 400 meters, and the 4 x 400-meter relay. She clocked a time of 48.83 seconds for the 400-meter sprint, becoming the first American woman to run the event in under 50 seconds. The same year, she won the national indoor 200-meter and 400-meter titles. In 1985 Brisco-Hooks introduced shorter distances to her racing repertoire. In a personal best time of 11.01 seconds she beat top East German sprinter Marlies Gohr over 100 meters. The same day she followed up her victory by defeating East German world record holder Marita Koch in the 200 meters. At the 1987 World Championships in Rome Brisco-Hooks won a bronze medal as part of the 4 x 400-meter relay team. At the 1988 Summer Olympics in Seoul Brisco-Hooks failed to achieve a podium place in the 400

▲ *Valerie Brisco-Hooks crosses the line to win the gold medal in the women's 400-meter final at the 1984 Los Angeles Summer Olympics.*

meters; she did, however, earn a silver medal as part of the 4 x 100-meter relay team, a fitting end to a distinguished athletic career. Since retiring, among other work, Brisco-Hooks has appeared in antidrug films for use in schools.

KEY DATES	
1960	Born in Greenwood, Mississippi, on July 6.
1984	Wins gold medals in the 200 meters, 400 meters, and 4 x 400-meter relay at the Summer Olympics in Los Angeles.
1987	Wins a bronze medal in the 4 x 400-meter relay at the World Championships.
1988	Wins a silver medal in the 4 x 400-meter relay at the Summer Olympics in Seoul.

Further reading: Johnson, Anne Janette, *Great Women in Sports.* Detroit, MI: Visible Ink Press, 1996.
http://www.sporting-heroes.net/athletics-heroes/displayhero.asp ?HeroID=132 (Page on Brisco-Hooks).
http://users.skynet.be/hermandw/olymp/biobr.htm (Great Olympians).

BROCK, Lou
Baseball Player

Born in El Dorado, Arkansas, on June 18, 1939, Louis Clark Brock was raised in Collinston, Louisiana, on a cotton plantation. Brock gained an education in the Union High School in Mer Rouge, Louisiana, where he began demonstrating his skill in basketball and baseball.

Professional player
Having succeeded in math and science at school, Brock won a scholarship to Southern University in Baton Rouge, Louisiana. He dropped out at the end of the first semester owing to financial problems and low grades. However, after demonstrating his exceptional skills to the college baseball coach, he was offered a baseball scholarship.

Brock quickly made his mark on the college game. Aided by his powerful hitting and his impressive speed between bases, Southern University went all the way to the National Association of Intercollegiate Athletics (NAIA) World Series. In 1961 Brock entered professional baseball when he signed with the Chicago Cubs, playing his first season in the Northern League in 1962. His batting average of .361 convinced the Cubs to bring Brock up to the major leagues, but after a drop in his performance they traded him to the St. Louis Cardinals in 1964.

It was with the Cardinals that Brock found his place in baseball history. He played for the team from 1964 to 1979, and by the end of his career had 3,023 hits and 938 stolen bases. His impressive ability to steal bases—for which he earned the nickname "Larcenous Lou"—and a .391 career batting average helped make the Cardinals one of the most respected clubs of the time. Brock helped the Cardinals to the World Series in 1964 and 1967, breaking numerous records along the way.

Honors
Brock retired from baseball in 1979 and in 1985 was elected to the Baseball Hall of Fame. It was not his final honor. In 1999 he was named as one of the Top 100 Major League Baseball Players of the 20th century, and a statue of him was unveiled at the Cardinals' Busch Stadium in St. Louis. In 2002 Brock received the Horatio Alger Award for Distinguished Americans. Brock's connection with baseball continued as a coach for the St. Louis Cardinals. He also owns St. Louis-based Brock World Products, which is involved in marketing and promotion.

▲ *In July 1968, when this photo was taken, Lou Brock was hitting .290 with 33 runs batted in (RBIs) and had stolen 24 bases so far that season.*

KEY DATES	
1939	Born in El Dorado, Arkansas, on June 18.
1961	Signs with the Chicago Cubs.
1964	Traded to the St. Louis Cardinals; plays in his first World Series.
1974	Sets both Major League and National League records for stolen bases; *Sporting News* Player of the Year.
1979	Retires from professional baseball.
1985	Elected to the Baseball Hall of Fame.
2002	Receives the Horatio Alger Award for Distinguished Americans.

Further reading: Brock, Lou. *Stealing Is My Game.* Englewood Cliffs, NJ: Prentice-Hall, 1976.

http://www.cmgww.com/baseball/brock/index.html (Official Lou Brock site).

BROOKE, Edward
Politician

Edward Brooke was a lawyer and a politician. He became the first African American to be popularly elected to the U.S. Senate.

Edward William Brooke, III, was born in Washington, D.C., in 1919. He was educated in local public schools and took his undergraduate degree at Howard University in 1941, the year in which the United States entered World War II (1939–1945). He then joined the Army and served as a second lieutenant in the all-black 366th Combat Infantry Regiment. He saw action in the Italian campaign and was awarded the Bronze Star and promoted to captain.

A career in law
After being discharged at the end of the war, Brooke went to law school at Boston University, where he took his graduate and postgraduate law degrees in 1948 and 1949. He was also editor of the law review.

In 1948 Brooke set up as an attorney in Boston, Massachusetts, and soon built a thriving practice. In parallel with his legal career he became increasingly involved in Republican politics. His choice of party seemed strange to many other African Americans, many of whom were traditionally Democrat since the 1930s, but Brooke explained his allegiance thus: "My father and my mother both voted Republican because it was the party of Lincoln. They were staunch Republicans because it was the party of African Americans and minorities, and the party of hope."

African Americans and the Republican Party
Brooke is a reminder that until the 1930s most African Americans were registered Republicans. In the early 1960s it was still not unusual for Republican candidates to get 30 percent of the black vote. The party's relationship with African Americans declined sharply from 1964, when it chose Senator Barry Goldwater, an archconservative from Arizona, as its presidential candidate. Only 6 percent of blacks voted for him. Since then Republicans have never received more than 15 percent of the black vote; in 2004 George W. Bush polled 8 percent of African American votes.

Involvement in politics
In 1950 Brooke ran for a seat in the Massachusetts legislature. His campaign was a failure, however; and when he missed out again in the 1952 election, he decided that he would abandon all hope of public office.

By 1960 he had changed his mind. He returned to the fray but failed in his bid to become the Massachusetts secretary of state. The following year he was appointed chairman of the Boston Finance Commission, a municipal watchdog, where he led a vigorous campaign to stamp out corruption in city politics. His efforts made him well known and popular. As a result, in 1962 he was elected attorney general of Massachusetts.

Attorney general
In his new post Brooke stepped up the crusade against abuses of civic power. He was so successful that in 1964 he was reelected by the largest margin received by any

▼ *Edward Brooke in 1966 when he became the third black U.S. senator.*

Republican in the state's history, despite a national swing to the Democrats in the wake of the assassination of President John F. Kennedy in November 1963.

Brooke became a champion of standards in public life, and his tireless efforts to weed out corruption led to the indictment of more than 100 officials, private citizens, and corporations on charges of graft and bribery.

Senator

In 1966 Brooke ran for a seat in the U.S. Senate. During the campaign his book *The Challenge of Change: Crisis in Our Two-Party System* was published. In it Brooke distanced himself from right-wing Republicans such as Goldwater and condemned Republicans who opposed desegregation in an attempt to lure conservative Southern whites away from the Democrats. In Brooke's view true Republicans were motivated by compassion, not by racism.

In the 1966 senatorial election Brooke polled nearly half a million votes more than his Democratic opponent and thus became the United States's first popularly elected African American senator. Brooke was the third black American in the U.S. Senate but the first to win a seat in a popular election.

On Capitol Hill Brooke quickly acquired a reputation as a moderate and became the effective leader of the progressive wing of his party. In 1968 there was even talk that he might run for vice president with George Romney, the governor of Michigan. Nothing came of it, however, and the names on the winning Republican ticket were those of Richard M. Nixon and Spiro T. Agnew. Brooke was overwhelmingly reelected to the Senate in 1972.

Brooke was a champion of peace and rights for the poor. He strongly opposed escalation of the Vietnam War (1964–1973). He also fought proposals that would have expanded nuclear arsenals. In 1969 Brooke was the author of the "Brooke Amendment," which ensured that tenants in public housing paid no more than 25 percent of their income for housing.

KEY DATES	
1919	Born in Washington, D.C., on October 26.
1948	Begins practicing law.
1962	Elected attorney general of Massachusetts.
1966	Elected to U.S. Senate.
1972	Reelected with increased majority.
1978	Loses Senate seat.
2004	Awarded the Presidential Medal of Freedom.

Losing his seat

In 1972, some months before the presidential election, five men were caught breaking into the headquarters of the Democratic National Committee in the Watergate Building in Washington, D.C. The resulting scandal, known as Watergate, eventually forced the resignation of President Nixon in 1974. The news media were quick to pounce on any wrongdoing by Republican politicians. The general disrepute into which the party fell during this period undermined Brooke when he went through a messy divorce and himself came under suspicion of financial misdeeds. His poll ratings dropped, and in 1978 he lost his bid for a third term of office.

On leaving the Senate, Brooke went back to his law practice and became chairman of the National Low-Income Housing Coalition. In retirement he divided his time between homes in Virginia and Florida. In 2004 he was awarded the Presidential Medal of Freedom.

Further reading: Cutler, John Henry. *Ed Brooke: Biography of a Senator.* Indianapolis, IN: Bobbs-Merrill Company, 1972.
http://bioguide.congress.gov/scripts/
biodisplay.pl?index=B000871(Congress page on Brooke).

BROOKS, Avery
Actor

Esteemed actor, singer, director, and professor Avery Brooks has dedicated his career to celebrating African American culture and fighting stereotypes.

Avery Franklin Brooks was born on October 2, 1948. He grew up singing jazz and developing his impressive operatic bass voice. While at Oberlin College, Ohio, he became a part of the African American students' theater group Psukay. Brooks became the first African American to graduate with an MA in fine arts in acting and directing from Rutgers University, New Jersey. His fruitful association with Rutgers continued when he was appointed professor of theater at the Mason Gross School of the Arts in 1972, a position he still holds.

On stage and screen

Following his graduation, Brooks worked mainly in theater, winning leading roles in Shakespeare's *Othello* and *A Midsummer's Night Dream* and singing the role of Malcolm

KEY DATES	
1948	Born in Evansville, Indiana, on October 2.
1982	Premier of his one-man show *Paul Robeson*.
1985	Debuts as Hawk in ABC's *Spenser: For Hire*.
1992	Debuts as Captain Benjamin Sisko in *Star Trek: Deep Space Nine*.

X in Anthony Davis's opera *X: The Life and Times of Malcolm X*. Brooks won critical acclaim in 1978 playing Paul Robeson in *Are You Now or Have You Ever Been* both on and off Broadway. In 1982 Brooks reprised the role of Robeson, this time in the one-man show *Paul Robeson*. Since the play was revived in 1988, Brooks has toured the United States delivering more than 300 performances.

Brooks launched his career in television in 1984 with a starring role in the TV movie *Solomon Northrup's Odyssey*, and in 1985 he achieved national fame as the streetwise Hawk in ABC's popular crime-fighting drama *Spenser: For Hire*. For four seasons Brooks fought against stereotyping in his role and improvised more realistic dialogue. The character proved popular, and Brooks starred in a spinoff series, *A Man Called Hawk*. Brooks gained further renown and was twice nominated for a best actor Image Award for the role of Captain Benjamin Sisko in *Star Trek: Deep Space Nine*, which he played from 1992 to 1999. He also directed a number of episodes for the series.

In 1993 Brooks became artistic director of the National Black Theater Arts Festival in Atlanta, Georgia. He has been awarded several honorary doctorates and was inducted into the College of Fellows of the American Theater in 1994. Brooke continues to teach and work in film, television, and theater.

▼ *Avery Brooks in the role of Captain Benjamin Sisko in* **Star Trek: Deep Space Nine.**

See also: Malcolm X; Robeson, Paul

Further reading: Erdmann, Terry J., and Paula M. Block. *Star Trek: Deep Space Nine Companion*. New York, NY: Pocket Books, 2000.
http://www.startrek.com/startrek/view/series/DS9/cast/69054.html (Official *Star Trek Deep Space Nine* site with a biography of Brooks).

BROOKS, Gwendolyn
Poet

One of the greatest American poets of the 20th century, Gwendolyn Brooks was the first African American to win the Pulitzer Prize for poetry.

Early life

Although born in Topeka, Kansas, on June 7, 1917, Gwendolyn Elizabeth Brooks grew up on Chicago's South Side, a vibrant, largely poor black neighborhood to which thousands of African Americans from the South were moving at the time. Encouraged by her educated, middle-class parents, Brooks developed a talent for poetry at a very early age. She published her first poem, "Eventide," in the *American Childhood Magazine* in 1930; at age 17 she was already contributing to a weekly poetry column in the *Chicago Defender*, the leading national black newspaper.

During the 1930s Brooks became involved in Chicago's black arts scene, which brought her increased self-awareness as a black writer and led her to focus her work on the everyday life she saw around her. Brooks

▼ *Gwendolyn Brooks in May 1950 after winning the Pulitzer Prize in poetry for* **Annie Allen,** *a series of poems about black life in Chicago.*

met the Harlem poet Langston Hughes, who introduced her to the experimental poetry of white writers such as T. S. Eliot and W. H. Auden. During this time Brooks began to develop her own rich, powerful style.

The poet of Bronzeville

In 1945 the mainstream New York publisher Harper & Row published Brooks's first collection of poetry, *A Street in Bronzeville*. Praised by both black and white critics, the first part of the book describes the hardships and discrimination faced by the people of "Bronzeville," an affectionate nickname for Chicago's South Side. In "The Ballad of Chocolate Mabbie," for example, Willie Boone rejects the title character Mabbie because her skin is too dark. The second part of the book, "Gay Chaps at the Bar," is a powerful treatment of the experiences of black soldiers during World War II (1939–1945).

Brooks's next collection, *Annie Allen* (1949), a sequence of poems about a black girl growing up in Chicago, was even more widely praised and won her critical acclaim. The poems were more experimental than her earlier work, using an intensely lyrical and allusive language that Brooks herself later termed "poetincense" and "language-flowers." In 1950 Brooks became the first African American poet to win the Pulitzer Prize.

A black awakening

During the 1950s Brooks became increasingly dissatisfied with her work. Moved and angered by such events as the racist murder of black teenager Emmett Till in 1955 (*see box*), Brooks increasingly came to believe that "…black poets should write as blacks, about blacks, and address themselves to blacks."

In pursuit of this new ideal Brooks's language became more direct and forceful, as seen in her 1960 collection *The Bean Eaters*, which included poems about Till as well as other events that contributed to the rise of the civil rights movement. One of Brooks's best-known poems, "We Real Cool," a short, blues-inspired poem about a group of young black pool players, comes from the collection.

The Bean Eaters and subsequent collections brought Brooks to the forefront of the black arts movement, sometimes called the artistic wing of the black power movement. The black arts movmement struggled to raise black pride and consciousness, and included prominent

INFLUENCES AND INSPIRATION

Although Brooks drew her inspiration from a wealth of literary influences—from Paul Laurence Dunbar, the first black American poet to gain a national reputation, and the writers of the Harlem Renaissance in the 1920s to writers of the black arts movement, including Amiri Baraka—her main creative source was the world in which she lived. Many of her ideas were inspired by her beloved Chicago and the people she saw each day or events reported in the press.

Brooks was both enraged and politicized—as were many other African Americans—by the brutal and senseless murder of a 14-year-old Chicago boy, Emmett Till, who was killed while visiting relatives in Money, Mississippi. A prank in a grocery store resulted in Till's kidnapping, beating, and shooting by the white store owner and an accomplice. Till's mangled body was displayed in an open casket during his Chicago funeral. An all-white Mississippi jury found his killers not guilty.

The event inspired two of Brooks's finest poems, both published in *The Bean Eaters* (1960). In "A Bronzeville Mother…" Brooks explored Till's murder from the viewpoint of the wife of the grocery-store owner; she describes the woman's hatred of "a blackish child/Of fourteen, with eyes still too young to be dirty." In contrast "The Last Quatrain of the Ballad of Emmett Till" looks at the grief of Till's mother, sitting alone at home after her son's funeral.

black writers such as Amiri Baraka (formerly LeRoi Jones), Nikki Giovanni, Lorraine Hansberry, and Sonia Sanchez.

One of Brooks's angriest and most overtly political books was *In the Mecca* (1968). The collection included poems about discrimination such as "Boy Breaking Glass," whose protagonist "has not Congress, lobster, love, luau/the Regency Room, the Statue of Liberty"; others were about black heroes, such as Malcolm X.

In the late 1960s Brooks's commitment to the black arts movement resulted in her leaving Harper & Row and publishing her work through small African American-run companies, such as the Broadside Press, and sometimes publishing her own work. She also became more involved in education, teaching creative writing courses at Columbia College, University of Chicago, Northeastern Illinois University, and Clay College, New York. Brooks was particularly interested in making poetry accessible to ordinary people. Much like the poet Haki Madhubuti, whom she treated like a son, she visited schools and held public readings and poetry workshops. In 1990 Madhubuti was successful in getting a center named for Brooks at Chicago State University, where she had her offices in her later years.

By the time of her death in December 2000 Brooks had received many honors. In 1968 she was named poet laureate of Illinois, and in 1985 she was appointed the consultant in poetry to the Library of Congress. Brooks was also awarded more than 50 honorary degrees.

Despite her involvement with the black arts movement, Brooks's enduring literary legacy is not just as a protest poet but as an acute, unblinking, and uncompromising recorder of African American urban life. As one critic wrote in the late 1960s, Brooks's poetry "grips the strong stuff of life and squeezes a kind of bloody beauty from it."

KEY DATES

1917   Born in Topeka, Kansas, on June 7.

1945   Publishes first poetry collection, *A Street in Bronzeville.*

1950   Becomes the first African American poet to be awarded the Pulitzer Prize.

1960   Publishes *The Bean Eaters.*

1968   Becomes poet laureate of Illinois.

1987   Publishes *Blacks*, a selection of her work.

2000   Dies in Chicago, Illinois, on December 3.

See also: Baraka, Amiri; Dunbar, Paul Laurence; Giovanni, Nikki; Hansberry, Lorraine; Harlem Renaissance; Hughes, Langston; Madhubuti, Haki; Malcolm X; Political Movements; Sanchez, Sonia

Further reading: Melhem, D.H. *Gwendolyn Brooks: Poetry and the Heroic Voice.* Lexington, KT: University Press of Kentucky, 1987.
http://www.poets.org/poet.php/prmPID/165 (Academy of American Poets page on Brooks).

BROOKS, Tyrone
Activist, Politician

Tyrone Brooks has been influential in helping change the racial politics of the United States. Born on October 10, 1945, in Warrenton, Georgia, he attended school in Warrenton and high school in Keysville, Georgia. In the 1940s Georgia was a deeply segregated state with racism at the highest levels of state institutions. From an early age Brooks responded by involving himself in political activity.

Resisting racism

At age 15 Brooks became an activist for the Southern Christian Leadership Conference (SCLC), an organization fighting for black rights in the South. Among the leaders of the SCLC were some of the great names of the 1960s civil rights movement—Martin Luther King, Jr., Fred Shuttlesworth, Joseph E. Lowery, and Ralph Abernathy. By 1967 Brooks was a full-time staff member with the SCLC. His constant activism opposing injustices ranging from black poverty through to the apartheid system in South Africa—he was arrested while protesting outside the South African Embassy in 1976—made him numerous enemies. He was arrested 65 times during the 1960s and 1970s; meanwhile, however, his work pushed him higher and higher up the political ladder.

In 1980 Brooks was elected to the Georgia House of Representatives, where he became a tireless activist. He helped the passage of numerous pieces of legislation, from antiterrorism laws to the removal from the flag of Georgia the image of the Confederate battle flag, which was offensive to the African American community because of its historic links with slavery.

▲ *Tyrone Brooks outside the offices of the Southern Christian Leadership Conference in 1975, when he was national communication director.*

Honors

Brooks has gained numerous honors in recognition of his civil rights work. The John Marshall Law School awarded him an honorary degree in 2001, and he received a Public Servant Award from Atlanta City Council. The National Association for the Advancement of Colored People (NAACP) inducted Brooks into their Hall of Fame.

See also: Abernathy, Ralph; King, Martin Luther, Jr.; Shuttlesworth, Fred

Further reading: Hampton, Henry, and Steve Fayer. *Voices of Freedom: An Oral History of the Civil Rights Movement from the 1950s through the 1980s.* New York, NY: Bantam Books, 1991.
http://www.affirmativeaction.org/awards/Tyrone_Brooks.html (Biography).

KEY DATES	
1945	Born in Warrenton, Georgia, on October 10.
1960	Joins the Southern Christian Leadership Conference.
1967	Becomes a full-time member of staff of the SCLC.
1976	Arrested during an anti-apartheid protest at the South African Embassy in Washington, D.C.
1980	Elected to the Georgia House of Representatives.
2001	Awarded an honorary degree from the John Marshall Law School in Atlanta, Georgia.

BROWN, Bobby
Musician, Singer

Bobby Brown's musical career begain in his early teens with the rhythm and blues (R&B) group New Edition. As a solo artist Bobby Brown was a pioneer of the music movement known as new jack swing. In the late 1980s and early 1990s he was one of the most commercially successful R&B superstars in the United States.

A rising star

Born on February 5, 1969, in the Roxbury neighborhood of Boston, Massachusetts, Robert Baresford Brown began singing with school friends Michael Bivins and Ricky Bell in 1978. In the early 1980s the group became New Edition and was discovered by producer Maurice Starr, who signed them to his Streetwise label and cowrote their first hit "Candy Girl." That single and two others reached No.1 on the R&B chart, and New Edition fired Starr and signed a new deal with MCA.

An innovative album

Brown, however, became dissatisfied with New Edition's teen pop image. He left the band in 1986 to pursue a solo career, releasing the album *King of Stage* that same year; it achieved only minimal success. For his second album, *Don't Be Cruel* (1988), Brown brought in new producers L. A. Reid, Babyface, and Teddy Riley to make his sound more distinctive. With singles such as the No. 1 hit "My Prerogative" and "Every Little Step," the album introduced new jack swing (a blend of soul, urban funk, and hip-hop) to mainstream music. It sold a massive seven million copies and made Bobby Brown one of the biggest R&B stars of the decade. In 1992 Brown married the singer and actor Whitney Houston and released his third solo album, *Bobby*. Although the album provided several hit singles, Brown's success was beginning to wane as the R&B audience's tastes moved on.

For much of the 1990s Brown's troubled personal life rather than his music dominated the headlines. In early 2005 the TV channel Bravo aired *Being Bobby Brown*, a series chronicling his attempts to clean up his life.

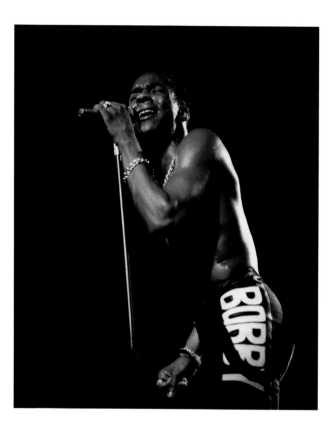

▲ *Bobby Brown performs live on stage during his 1989 American tour.*

See also: Houston, Whitney

Further reading: Parish, James Robert. *Whitney Houston.* London: Aurum Press, 2003.
http://www.allmusic.com/cg/amg.dll?p=amg&uid=MIW040503300901&sql=11:7aq3g4attv4z~T1 (Biography).

KEY DATES

1969	Born in Boston, Massachusetts, on February 5.
1978	Begins singing with schoolmates and forms the group New Edition.
1986	Releases his first solo album, *King of Stage*.
1988	Reaches No. 1 with "My Prerogative."
1992	Marries singer Whitney Houston on July 18.
1995	Checks into Betty Ford Clinic to overcome drug and alcohol problems.
2005	Appears in reality TV show *Being Bobby Brown*.

BROWN, Charlotte Hawkins
Educator

An innovative and courageous educationalist, Charlotte Hawkins Brown revolutionized education for countless African Americans.

She was born Lottie Hawkins in Henderson, North Carolina, in 1883. Her parents were former slaves. In 1888 the family moved to Cambridge, Massachusetts, to escape the discrimination of the South. Hawkins displayed leadership potential at an early age. At age 12, she organized a kindergarten at her church.

Finding a mentor

In 1899, while in high school, Hawkins attracted the interest of Alice Freeman Palmer, the first woman president of Wellesley College, following a chance meeting. Impressed by Hawkins's commitment to her education, Palmer took on financial responsibility for her further education. Palmer also introduced Hawkins to many important members of Boston society, whom she would later approach to help with her school.

Hawkins changed her name to the more professional Charlotte Eugenia in 1900, shortly before enrolling in Salem Teachers' College. In October 1901 Hawkins accepted a teaching position at the Bethany Institute, Sedalia, North Carolina, with the American Missionary Association (AMA), but the impoverished school was closed in early 1902.

The Palmer Memorial Institute

With the backing of the local community the 18-year-old established her own school in a blacksmith's shed in October 1902. Hawkins named the school the Palmer Memorial Institute, in memory of her mentor, and rapidly secured the money from friends and associates in New England to build a new campus with two buildings and more than 200 acres (81ha) of land.

Ignoring the widespread conviction of the time that African Americans should only be educated to the most basic level, Hawkins progressively developed Palmer's curriculum until it was exclusively academic, providing college preparatory instruction, liberal arts courses, and personal development training. She also introduced the study of African American history before any other high school in North Carolina.

Hawkins returned to Cambridge each summer to study and raise money for her school. In 1911 she married Edward S. Brown, a teacher. In 1927 Hawkins Brown took a

year off to travel. In Europe she met Mary McLeod Bethune and Nannie Helen Burroughs. The three African American women became known as the "Three Bs of Education."

Hawkins Brown helped create the first state school for delinquent African American girls and in 1937 convinced Guildford County officials to open the nation's first public rural high school for African Americans. In 1952 Hawkins Brown retired after 50 years as Palmer's president but remained on the school's board of directors until her death.

Civil rights

A fervent civil rights campaigner, Hawkins Brown lectured on interracial issues and against lynching. She helped found numerous associations for the advancement of African Americans, including the National Council of Negro Women, and became president of the North Carolina Association of Colored Women's Clubs.

Hawkins Brown published the first of her two books in 1919; her second, an etiquette guide entitled The Correct Thing to Do, to Say, to Wear (1944), won her the Mark Twain Award and earned her the title of "First Lady of Social Graces." She received three honorary master's degrees and four honorary doctorates in acknowledgment of her contributions to education and society.

See also: Bethune, Mary McLeod; Burroughs, Nannie Helen

Further reading: Silcox-Jarrett, Diane. *Charlotte Hawkins Brown: One Woman's Dream*. Winston-Salem, NC: Bandit Books, 1996.
http://www.ah.dcr.state.nc.us/sections/hs/chb/chb.htm (Charlotte Hawkins Brown Museum site featuring a comprehensive biography).

BROWN, Clara
Pioneer, Businesswoman

Known as "Aunt Clara," Clara Brown was born a slave but became one of the first black pioneers and a successful businesswoman.

Clara was born on a plantation near Fredericksburg, Virginia, in 1800 or 1803. In 1809 she moved with her owner, Ambrose Smith, to Logan County, Kentucky. In 1818 she was married to Richard, also a slave of Smith's, with whom she had four children. Following Smith's sudden death in 1835, Clara was sold to George Brown and separated from her husband and children, who were also sold. In 1857, following the death of her third master, she was set free.

A pioneer businesswoman

Brown moved from Kentucky to Leavenworth County, Kansas, where she opened a laundry. She then decided to move to Colorado. To get to Denver, Brown worked as a cook, nurse, and launderer on a wagon train of gold prospectors headed for Pike's Peak, Colorado, on a 600-mile (965-km) prairie journey. Brown was forced to join the wagon train because even though she could afford the fare, blacks were forbidden to use the stage coach.

Brown ended up in Central City, Colorado, a booming gold town where she opened another laundry business, while at the same time investing in real estate and mining. By the 1860s she had accumulated $10,000.

From 1810 Brown was a devout Christian. She raised funds for several churches, fed the hungry, welcomed migrants to her home, searched for employment for others, took care of children, and delivered babies. Brown also constantly kept looking for her own children, especially her daughter Eliza Jane, traveling as far as Tennessee (where some sources say she was born). She

▲ *This photograph of Clara Brown was taken when she was about 70 years old.*

is said to have brought back to Colorado 34 relatives and 16 freed African Americans, employing some and helping others find employment and housing.

As Brown grew older and fell sick, she suffered several misfortunes. In 1864 floods destroyed some of her properties in Denver, and she lost all her ownership papers. Nine years later fire destroyed three of her properties in Central City. In 1874 her home on Lawrence Street was burned to the ground. She was so admired, however, that people helped her build a new cottage.

Brown never gave up looking for Eliza Jane. In 1882 Brown found her daughter in Council Bluffs, Iowa. She returned home with granddaughter Cindy, who took care of her until her death in 1885.

In 1880 Brown was honored as the first black woman pioneer by Denver's Pioneers Association, which made her its first "Negro" member. In 1977 a stained-glass window of her was placed in the rotunda of the Colorado State Capitol. In 2003 *Gabriel's Daughter*, an opera depicting her life, was performed in Central City.

Further reading: Lowrey, Linda. *One More Valley, One More Hill*. New York, NY: Random House, 2002.

KEY DATES	
1800	Born in Virginia at about this time.
1874	Her home burns down.
1882	Finds her daughter, Eliza Jane.
1885	Dies in Denver, Colorado, in October.
2003	Opera depicting her life performed in Denver.

BROWN, Clifford
Musician

The jazz trumpeter Clifford Brown was renowned for his innovative style. During his short career he played with some of the greatest names in the jazz world. His work has continued to be influential since his death in an automobile accident in 1956.

A phenomenal talent

Brown was born on October 30, 1930, in Wilmington, Delaware, and was given his first trumpet by his father when he started high school. His musical ability quickly became evident, and he began to play with college and youth bands. Brown soon experimented with jazz, and by his late teens his musical skill had attracted the attention of some of the leading names in the genre, including trumpeters Dizzy Gillespie, Miles Davis, and Fats Navarro.

Brown received a scholarship to study music at Maryland State College in 1948, although he actually majored in math. While there he played with musicians such as Max Roach and Fats Domino. Brown transferred to Maryland State University in 1949 and played in its orchestra. In 1950 Brown was involved in a serious car accident (the first of three in his short life), which resulted in his spending almost a year in the hospital. Once he had recovered, however, he began to immerse himself in music. In 1952 he played in a rhythm-and-blues band with Chris Powell and also recorded with pianist Tadd Dameron.

In fall of 1953 Brown went to Europe as a member of Lionel Hampton's big band. Despite contractual obligations, many of Hampton's band moonlighted on various recordings, Brown among them. When Hampton found out, he fired Brown. Brown then joined drummer Art Blakey in early 1954, recording two live albums with him. Later that year Brown teamed up with Max Roach again to form the Clifford Brown–Max Roach quintet. They quickly gained recognition as one of the outstanding groups in contemporary jazz, with Brown as a major trumpeter and composer. However, on June 26, 1956, Brown and another quintet member, pianist Richie Powell, were killed in a road accident while driving between engagements during a nationwide tour.

Like his friend and source of inspiration Fats Navarro, Brown was remarkably technically proficient and developed a rich, full, and frequently beautiful tone. He felt equally at home playing at scorching tempos or on languorous ballads. While Brown was enormously and brilliantly

▲ *Trumpeter Clifford Brown performs live in 1954, the year in which he recorded some of his finest work.*

inventive, his search for original ideas was never pursued at the expense of his music. In all his work Brown displayed great emotional depths. His playing was only one aspect of his talent, however; he was also a fine composer, creating many works, such as "Joy Spring" and "Sandu," that have become modern jazz standards.

Although his career was brief, Brown's spirit lived on in the work of fellow trumpeters Lee Morgan and Freddie Hubbard, both of whom were heavily influenced by him. Brown's own genius was captured in a number of live and studio recordings.

KEY DATES	
1930	Born in Wilmington, Delaware, on October 30.
1953	Travels to Europe with Lionel Hampton's big band.
1954	Forms group with Max Roach.
1956	Dies on June 26.

See also: Blakey, Art; Davis, Miles; Domino, Fats; Gillespie, Dizzy; Morgan, Lee; Roach, Max

Further reading: Catalano, Nick. *Clifford Brown: The Life and Art of the Legendary Jazz Trumpeter.* New York, NY: Oxford University Press, 2001.
http://abel.hive.no/oj/musikk/trompet/clifford (Biography and links).

BROWN, Dorothy L.
Physician

Dorothy Lavinia Brown was the first female African American surgeon in the South and the first woman to serve in the Tennessee state legislature.

Brown was five months old when her mother put her in an orphanage in Troy, New York in 1919. She remained there until she was 13, when her mother returned to claim her. Brown was unhappy with her mother and ran back to the orphanage on five occasions.

Pursuing a dream

When Brown was five, she had her tonsils removed and decided that she wanted to be a physician. Aged 15, she ran away to Troy High School. When the principal realized she had no home, he found foster parents for her.

When Brown graduated at the top of her class in 1937, the Troy Conference Methodist Women sponsored her on a four-year scholarship to Bennett College in Greensboro, North Carolina. She graduated second in her class in 1941 and worked as an inspector in the Rochester Army Ordinance Department during World War II (1939–1945). In 1944 her ambition to be a physician came closer when she started at Meharry Medical College in Nashville, Tennessee. She graduated four years later. After completing a year internship at Harlem Hospital, she specialized in surgery.

In the United States in the 1940s there were few female surgeons and no African American women in surgery in the South. Against opposition from his staff, Dr. Matthew Walker at Meharry Medical College accepted Brown into the surgery program, and by 1954 she had completed her residency. She became assistant professor of surgery in 1955 and was the first African American woman to be made a fellow of the American College of Surgeons.

▲ *Dorothy Brown overcame a troubled childhood to become a professor of surgery.*

In 1956 Brown became the first single woman to legally adopt in the state of Tennessee when one of her unmarried patients begged her to take her newborn daughter.

From 1957 to 1983 Brown was chief of surgery at the Riverside Hospital in Nashville, clinical professor of surgery at Meharry Medical College, and educational director for the Riverside-Meharry Clinical Rotation Program.

In 1966, when redistricting in Tennessee permitted a black candidate to run for office, Brown agreed to run for the state legislature and won. She became the first African American woman in the Tennessee state legislature.

In later years Brown was honored for her achievements and continued teaching and practicing into the early 1990s. She died of heart failure on June 13, 2004.

KEY DATES

1919   Born in Philadelphia, Pennsylvania, on January 7.

1948   Becomes the first female African American surgeon in the South.

1956   Becomes the first single woman in Tennessee to legally adopt a child.

1966   Becomes the first African American woman to serve in Tennessee state legislature.

2004   Dies in Nashville, Tennessee, on June 13.

Further reading: Hine, Darlene Clark (ed.). *Black Women in America.* New York, NY: Oxford University Press, 2005. http://www.nlm.nih.gov/changingthefaceofmedicine/physicians/biography_46.html (Biography).

BROWN, H. Rap
Civil Rights Activist, Black Panther, Religious Leader

Rap Brown came to prominence in 20th-century American politics through his involvement in the student wing of the civil rights movement. His beliefs grew more radical when he became a leading member of the Black Panther Party. In the early 1970s he converted to Islam and changed his name to Jamil Abdullah al-Amin.

Early years

Brown was born Hubert Gerold Brown in Baton Rouge, Louisiana, on October 4, 1943. He earned the nickname "Rap" because of his quick thinking and ability with words. From 1960 to 1964 he attended Southern University, Louisiana. In 1964 he moved to Washington, D.C., and became involved with the Student Nonviolent Coordinating Committee (SNCC). In 1967 Brown succeeded Stokely

▼ **Black Power advocate H. Rap Brown is arrested on July 27, 1967.**

Carmichael as the organization's chairman. He became chairman at a time when the black student movement, heavily influenced by the anti-Vietnam War movement and the violent white extremist backlash against desegregation in the South, was moving away from the Christian pacifist approach advocated by Martin Luther King, Jr. After King's assassination in Memphis in 1968, the movement toward more radical political positions accelerated.

Black Panther Party

Brown was arrested on charges of "incitement to riot" after giving a speech at a rally in Cambridge, Maryland, in 1967. In 1968 the leaders of the SNCC merged with the more radical nationalist Black Panther Party. J. Edgar Hoover, head of the FBI, declared that the Black Panthers represented "the greatest threat to the internal security of the U.S." and pledged to close them down.

Brown was famous, or notorious, for fiery speeches attacking the injustices and hypocrisy of American society, once commenting that "violence is as American as cherry pie." In 1969 he published his political autobiography *Die Nigger Die!,* in which he outlined his views on the position of black people in America in the 1960s. Brown's view of society was that "There are three basic categories: they are white america, negro america and Black America… Color is the first thing Black people become aware of." He concluded: "The biggest difference between being known as a Black man or a negro is that if you're Black, then you do everything you can to fight white folks. If you're a negro, you do everything to appease them."

By 1970 Brown was justice minister of the Black Panther Party, on the FBI's Ten Most Wanted List, and on the run for failing to appear in court on charges of incitement to riot and carrying a gun across state lines. By then almost all of the leadership of the Black Panther Party was either dead, in jail, living in hiding, or in exile.

Prison and Islam

In late 1971 Brown was shot and seriously wounded in a running gun battle with police outside a New York City bar, following which he was convicted of armed robbery and sentenced to 5 to 15 years in Attica State Prison in upstate New York. In prison Brown converted to the Islamic faith and changed his name. The conversion marked a major shift in his political and personal philosophy. When he

INFLUENCES AND INSPIRATION

Brown's major early influence was his older brother Ed, who directed his reading toward the classics of black American political protest such as W. E. B. DuBois, Frederick Douglass, Marcus Garvey, and Richard Wright. The racial injustices Brown saw as he grew up in Louisiana and his student experiences in the sit-ins, marches, and voting rights campaigns radicalized his feelings toward the American state. As he relates in his political autobiography *Die Nigger Die!*, he had come to see that racism was too fundamental to American life to be ended by legal reforms alone, and that violent revolutionary changes in the nature of the American state and its institutions were necessary. His second book, *Revolution by the Book* (1993), reflects his conversion, while in prison, to Islam and promotes a personal, moral revolution based on Sunni Islamic principles.

emerged from jail in 1976, al-Amin made the Hajj pilgrimage to Mecca, a religious obligation for all Muslims. He settled in Atlanta, Georgia, where his older brother Ed (*see box*) was a prominent community activist. Al-Amin founded an Islamic congregation in the city and became their imam, or religious leader. He supported himself by running a small community grocery store and Islamic cultural center. He published a second book, again addressing the situation of black people in America, entitled *Revolution by the Book*.

In this book al-Amin did not abandon his previous concerns about individuals changing society but reevaluated his views from an Islamic perspective. He continued to emphasize the need for major dramatic change in American society but from an orthodox Sunni Islamic perspective, in such passages as: "When you understand your obligations to God then you can understand your obligations to society. Revolution comes when human beings set out to correct decadent institutions. We must understand how this society has fallen away from righteousness and begin to develop, Islamically, the alternative institutions to those that are in a state of decline around us."

Further clashes with the law

By 1980 al-Amin had become head of the National Ummah group of Dar-ul Islam, which has over 30 Islamic centers around the United States. However, his clashes with the law enforcement agencies did not end. After the 1993 bombing of the World Trade Center he was arrested on suspicion of involvement but released without charge. In 1995 he was arrested and charged with an Atlanta shooting, but charges were dropped when the victim withdrew his identification, claiming that he had been pressured to identify al-Amin as his assailant.

On March 16, 2000, two Fulton County sheriff's deputies attempted to serve an arrest warrant on al-Amin on charges of impersonating a police officer and receiving stolen property. Both were shot, one fatally, in the ensuing gun battle near his mosque in Atlanta. Two years later a jury convicted al-Amin of the deputy's murder but rejected prosecution calls for the death penalty. He was sentenced to life imprisonment without parole. He continues to declare his innocence, and his brother Ed has vowed to continue to fight to clear his name.

KEY DATES

1943   Born in Baton Rouge, Louisiana, on October 4.

1967   Appointed chairman of the SNCC.

1968   Joins the Black Panther Party.

1969   Publishes political autobiography *Die Nigger Die!*; put on FBI's most wanted list.

1971   Shot and captured during an armed robbery in New York City; later sentenced to 5 to 15 years in Attica State Prison.

1976   Paroled from prison, where he had converted to Islam and taken the name Jamil Abdullah al-Amin.

2000   Accused of shooting two sheriff's deputies, fatally wounding one, during an attempt to serve a warrant on him.

2002   Found guilty of murder and 13 other charges; sentenced to life imprisonment without parole.

See also: Carmichael, Stokely; Civil Rights; Douglass, Frederick; DuBois, W. E. B.; Garvey, Marcus; King, Martin Luther, Jr.; Political Movements; Wright, Richard

Further reading: Brown, H. Rap. *Die Nigger Die! A Political Autobiography*. Chicago, IL: Lawrence Hill Books, 2002. http://www.historychannel.com/speeches/archive/speech_397.html (History Channel page, including a speech).

BROWN, Hallie Quinn
Educator, Lecturer, Activist

Hallie Quinn Brown was one of America's most influential educators of the late 19th and early 20th centuries. She worked tirelessly to improve educational opportunities for African Americans, particularly women.

The daughter of former slaves, Brown was born on March 10, 1850, in Pittsburgh, Pennsylvania. Her parents were strong believers in education, and Brown and her five siblings were heavily influenced by them. From an early age Brown showed an interest in and passion for public speaking, which she used to great benefit later in her life.

In 1870 Brown enrolled at Wilberforce University, Ohio, graduating with a BS in 1873. She then moved south and started to teach in schools and plantations in Mississippi and South Carolina, beginning her lifelong involvement in the education of disenfranchised groups, particularly former slaves.

Public speaking

During her time in the South Brown became involved in the lyceum movement, which promoted adult education through traveling programs of lectures and concerts. Her confident style of public speaking drew large audiences, and by the 1880s Brown was touring full time. As her reputation grew, so did her employment offers, and in 1885 she accepted the job as dean of the historically black Allen University in South Carolina. She stayed in the post until 1887, when she returned to Ohio to teach. She moved to Alabama when she was appointed lady principal (dean of women) of Tuskegee Institute, working with the legendary educator Booker T. Washington from 1892 to 1893.

From 1893 Brown began to travel and lecture on education and temperance. A great believer in equal rights for all, Brown supported the suffrage movement and equal

▲ *Hallie Quinn Brown dedicated much of her life to the education of African Americans.*

rights for African Americans. Brown was an energetic promoter of the Colored Woman's League and also represented the United States at the International Congress of Women, which met in London, England, in 1899. Brown fought vehemently against anything she thought was unfair or unjust. In 1922 she lobbied President Warren Harding to outlaw lynching and fought against a bill that would have made interracial marriages illegal.

Following her retirement from teaching, Brown served as president of the National Association of Colored Women from 1920 to 1924. She died on September 16, 1949.

See also: Washington, Booker T.

Further reading: Hine, Darlene Clark. *Black Women in America.* New York, NY: Carlson Publishers, 1993.
http://voices.cla.umn.edu/vg/Bios/entries/brown_hallie_quinn.html (Biography).

KEY DATES	
1850	Born in Pittsburgh, Pennsylvania, on March 10.
1873	Graduates with a BS from Wilberforce University.
1892	Appointed as lady principal of Tuskegee Institute.
1920	Appointed president of the National Association of Colored Women.
1949	Dies in Wilberforce, Ohio, on September 16.

BROWN, James
Musician

Legendary singer and songwriter James Brown is known as the "Godfather of Soul." Brown was instrumental to two revolutions in 20th-century popular music—the development of rhythm and blues (R&B) into soul and turning soul music into funk. A consummate performer, an impressive dancer, and a brilliant and influential musician, Brown once said that if people wanted to get to know him, all they had to do was listen to his music.

Early life

James Joe Brown, Jr., was born in a shack just outside of Barnwell, South Carolina, on May 3, 1933. His parents, Joe and Susan, were extremely poor. His father used to sing the young Brown blues songs and gave his son his first musical instrument, a harmonica.

When Brown was four, his parents separated, and he went to live with his aunt, who ran a brothel in Augusta, Georgia. Brown sang in the local church, and he taught himself to play the organ when he was eight years old. He also experimented with other instruments, including the guitar, bass, and saxophone. He danced on the streets for money; but his life was full of hardship, and he began to commit petty crimes such as shoplifting. In 1948 Brown was caught breaking into a car and was sentenced to 8 to 16 years in the Georgia Juvenile Training Institute. He sang in the gospel choir; he also met Bobby Byrd in 1952 during a prison basketball game. Following his release after four years Brown went to live with Byrd's family and joined Byrd's four-man group, the Gospel Starlighters. Under Brown's guidance the band abandoned gospel music in favor of the more popular R&B; they also changed their name to the Famous Flames. Their vibrant, intense performances soon gained them public recognition.

In January 1956 producer and talent scout Ralph Bass signed the group for Cincinnati-based King Records. A month later James Brown and the Famous Flames recorded "Please, Please, Please," which went straight to No. 5 on the R&B charts. In 1958 "Try Me," the band's next single, reached No. 58 on the pop charts and No. 1 on the R&B charts, making the band one of a number of black artists to cross over to appeal to mainstream white audiences.

▼ *James Brown on stage in 2004, still active after 50 years of performing.*

INFLUENCES AND INSPIRATION

Among the people whom James Brown has influenced is the civil rights and political activist Reverend Al Sharpton, who refers to Brown as his "surrogate father." Born in Brooklyn in 1954, Sharpton delivered his first sermon in the Pentecostal church at age four and was a fully ordained minister by the time he was 10. Sharpton's preaching helped support his family after his father left them.

Sharpton met Brown when he was 16. Brown agreed to do some benefit work for the youth group that Sharpton was running. The two men became close friends, and Brown began to take Sharpton on tour with him. Sharpton said in a 1999 interview with *Salon* magazine that Brown "would talk to me the way a father talked to a son: 'Watch this on the road, don't deal with these kind of girls, dress like this, eat this.' I mean, literally, like a father. And I guess because I'd never had that kind of relationship with anybody, he became the father [that] I never had."

The success of the second single came at an opportune time: King Records had threatened to cancel the band's contract if it did not have another hit.

The master

Brown was always famous for his onstage performances and was a master of every dance craze that came along in the 1950s and 1960s. He was primarily a creative musician who fused jump blues, gospel, jazz, and Latin rhythms with his raw, often desperate and screaming lyrics in a way that was completely new and exciting.

Brown quickly became a star in his own right. In October 1962, against the wishes of King Records, he paid for and recorded what was to become a landmark album, *The James Brown Show Live at the Apollo,* a recording of a live performance at the Harlem Theater in New York City. The album sold one million copies and established Brown as one of the top African American musicians of the time.

In 1965 Brown released "Papa's Got a Brand New Bag," which topped the R&B charts for eight weeks, reached No. 8 on the pop charts, and won a Grammy. It was followed by R&B No. 1 and pop No. 3 "I Got You."

During the 1960s and 1970s Brown's music focused increasingly on rhythm rather than harmony. His music was key to the development of funk. He said, "I was hearing everything, even the guitars, like they were drums." The 1967 song "Cold Sweat," for example, emphasized rhythm and had Brown delivering lyrics in a voice closer to speaking than singing; it also contained long sections in which there were no chord changes.

Brown increasingly used his music to promote black consciousness as songs like the 1966 "Don't Be a Drop Out" (aimed at keeping black children in school) and the hugely successful 1968 song "Say It Loud—I'm Black and I'm Proud" illustrate. From the mid-1960s he also played benefit concerts for black civil rights organizations.

Between 1966 and 1974 Brown had more than 40 R&B chart hits, including 32 Top 10 hits. In 1974 alone Brown had three No. 1 hits with "Payback," "My Thang," and "Papa Don't Take No Mess (Part 1)." By the end of the 1970s his career was in decline, however.

In the 1980s the increasing popularity of hip-hop brought Brown back into fashion as bands like Public Enemy sampled his music. Some music critics argue that hip-hop would not have become so popular without Brown. In 1986 "Living in America," commissioned by actor Sylvester Stallone for the movie *Rocky IV*, reached No. 4 on *Billboard*'s Hot 100 chart. Brown was also inducted into the Rock and Roll Hall of Fame in that year.

See also: Belafonte, Harry; Sharpton, Al

Further reading: Brown, James, and Bruce Tucker. *James Brown: The Godfather of Soul.* New York, NY: Publishers Group West, 2003.
http://www.godfatherofsoul.com (Discography and excerpt).

KEY DATES

1933	Born in Barnwell, South Carolina, on May 3.
1956	Releases "Please, Please, Please."
1963	Pays for and releases *The James Brown Show Live at the Apollo;* the album sells one million copies.
1968	Releases "Say It Loud."
1974	Has three No. 1 hits.
1986	Records "Living in America" for *Rocky IV*; inducted into the Rock and Roll Hall of Fame.

BROWN, Jesse L.
Navy Pilot

Jesse Leroy Brown was the first African American to fly a plane for the Navy and the first black naval officer to be killed in combat during the Korean War.

The son of a poor farmer, Brown grew up in a home in rural Mississippi without electricity, water, or sanitation. His mother had been a teacher, and she was determined that her children would go to college. When Brown graduated from public school in Hattiesburg, he decided against enrolling at a blacks-only college in Mississippi and opted instead for Ohio State University, where fewer than 1 percent of students were black. He worked his way through college by loading boxcars at night.

Navy

In 1946 Brown enlisted in the Naval Reserve, joining the regular Navy as a midshipman the following year. He had always wanted to fly, so he attended the Navy's preflight school in Ottumwa, Iowa, and went on to flight training at Pensacola and Jacksonville, Florida, where he was the only black serviceman among 600 cadets. On October 21, 1948, Brown was awarded his wings, becoming the Navy's first black pilot.

▲ **Jesse L. Brown in the cockpit of an F4U-4 Corsair fighter in about 1950.**

KEY DATES	
1926	Born in Hattiesburg, Mississippi, on October 13.
1943	Enters Ohio State University.
1946	Joins Naval Reserve.
1948	Qualifies as pilot.
1950	Killed in action on December 4.

In 1949 Midshipman Brown was promoted to ensign aboard USS *Wright*. In 1950 his squadron sailed aboard the aircraft carrier USS *Leyte* to Korea.

The Korean War (1950–1953) began when the armed forces of the Democratic People's Republic of Korea invaded the Republic of Korea on June 25, 1950. Sixteen nations, led by the United States under the flag of the United Nations (UN), sent military forces to South Korea's defense. In October Brown's squadron joined Fast Carrier Task Force 77 in support of the UN forces.

War hero

As a pilot in Fighter Squadron 32, Brown became a section leader and won the Air Medal for bravery during raids on Wonsan, Chongjin, Songjin, and Sinanju. On his 20th combat mission on December 4, 1950, while providing air cover for U.S. Marines near Chosin Reservoir, his Corsair aircraft was hit by enemy fire and crashed into the side of a snow-covered mountain. Although Brown survived the impact, he was trapped in the wreckage. Lieutenant Thomas J. Hudner crash-landed his own plane and tried to free his comrade, but his efforts were in vain. Although a rescue helicopter arrived, its crew was also unable to free him. Brown died, aged 24. His body was never recovered.

After his death Brown was awarded the Distinguished Flying Cross. In 1951 Hudner was awarded the Medal of Honor. On March 18, 1972, the Navy named a new destroyer USS *Jesse L. Brown* in Brown's honor.

Further reading: Taylor, Theodore. *The Flight of Jesse Leroy Brown.* New York, NY: Avon Books, 1998.
http://www.history.navy.mil/photos/pers-us/uspers-b/j-brown.htm (Naval Historical Center page on Brown).

BROWN, Jim
Football Player, Actor

Recognized by ESPN as football's Player of the Millennium, Jim Brown remains, nearly 40 years after his retirement, one of the greatest ever running backs.

At 6 feet 2 inches (1.8m) and 230 pounds (104kg), Brown combined size, speed, athleticism, and toughness to become the National Football League's dominant back between 1957 and 1965. During his nine seasons Brown led the league in rushing eight times while never missing a game due to injury. When he retired at age 30, still in his prime, Brown owned all of the game's major rushing records including 12,312 rushing yards and 106 rushing touchdowns; in 2005 his career averages of 5.2 yards per carry and 104 yards per game remained unsurpassed.

Early years

James Nathaniel Brown was born on February 17, 1936, on St. Simons Island off the southern coast of Georgia. His father abandoned the family two weeks after the baby was born. When he was two, his mother left to take a job as a maid on Long Island, New York. Brown was raised by his great-grandmother until age eight, when he joined his mother in Long Island. It was the first time they had seen each other since she left.

Brown earned 13 varsity letters at Long Island's Manhasset High School, playing football, basketball, lacrosse, and baseball, and running track. He took his athletic skills to Syracuse University, where he starred in football, basketball, and lacrosse. During his senior year at Syracuse, Brown was named first team All-American in both football and lacrosse. His excellence in intercollegiate athletics helped make Brown the only player ever to be inducted into the Pro Football, College Football, and Lacrosse halls of fame.

Professional football

Drafted in the first round by the Cleveland Browns, Brown became the NFL's Rookie of the Year in 1957, leading all running backs with 942 yards. In 1958 he was the NFL's Most Valuable Player, leading the league in rushing with 1,527 yards and touchdowns with 18. In 1959 and 1960 he led NFL rushers with 1,329 and 1,257 yards. In 1961 he led again, with 1,408 yards. Tensions between Brown and coach Paul Brown meant that Brown missed the rushing title in 1962. Brown told the owner that either Paul Brown had to quit or he would. Paul Brown was fired.

Brown had his best season in 1963, rushing for a then-record 1,863 yards, making him the first back to run for more than a mile. He also scored 12 touchdowns and averaged 6.4 yards per carry.

In 1964 Brown led his team to the NFL championship game, where they defeated the Baltimore Colts 27–0. The following year, in Brown's last game as a professional, the Browns returned to the title game but lost 23–12 to Vince Lombardi's Green Bay Packers. Brown, however, earned MVP, leading the league with 1,544 yards and scoring 21 touchdowns.

Aged 30, Brown stunned the football world by resigning at the peak of his career. He closed his career with three touchdowns in the 1966 Pro Bowl. According to *Sporting News*, "He was, simply, the greatest pure runner

▼ *Jim Brown, football's Player of the Millennium, film actor, and founder of the Amer-I-Can foundation.*

INFLUENCES AND INSPIRATION

One of Brown's main inspirations was singer, actor, football star, and activist Paul Robeson. Robeson played football for Rutgers University, New Jersey, from 1915 to 1918. He helped Rutgers to a 7–1 record in his freshman year and was named first on the roster for the All-American college team in 1918.

He graduated with 15 letters in sports. Robeson went on to play professional football to earn his school fees while attending Columbia Law School. In 1928 he embarked on a highly successful singing and acting career. Robeson was one of the first African American athletes to speak out against racism. His

comments about the oppression of blacks and his praise for the Soviet Union led to him being branded a communist. In 1950 the U.S. government canceled his passport, and he was banned from concert halls. Robeson continued to speak out and regained his passport in 1958. He died in 1976.

KEY DATES

1936   Born on St. Simons Island, Georgia, on February 17.

1963   Finishes season with 1,863 yards, an NFL record that stands for a decade, on December 15.

1964   Wins NFL Championship, Cleveland Browns vs Baltimore Colts on December 27.

1966   Final professional game, NFL Championship Game; Green Bay Packers 23 Cleveland Browns 12

1971   Inducted into the Pro Football Hall of Fame in July.

1988   Sets up the Amer-I-Can Foundation.

2002   Spike Lee's film *Jim Brown: All American* released.

in the history of the NFL." Larry Schwartz of ESPN said, "Jim Brown is to running backs what Superman is to cartoon heroes." The Pro Football Hall of Fame page calls him "a superb craftsman."

Film career

Before he retired, Brown had landed a major role in the war movie *The Dirty Dozen* (1967), and he wanted to devote more time to his acting career. He appeared in a total of 39 movies, including *Rio Conchos* (1964), *Ice Station Zebra* (1968), *100 Rifles* (1969), *Slaughter* (1972), and *Any Given Sunday* (1999). According to film historian Donald Bogle, Brown made movie history by becoming the first black man to convey a strong, highly sexual image. In an interview in 2002 director Spike Lee said, "He really blazed a trail for other black action heroes." That same year Brown became the star of a documentary directed by Lee, *Jim Brown: All American*, which explored all aspects of his life, including the more controversial side.

Brown's personal life has often been troubled. He has been accused of several assaults on women, and in 1999 he was convicted of smashing his wife's car window. When Brown refused to do community service, he was sentenced to six months in jail but was released in July 2002 after serving less than four months.

Civil rights

Throughout his career Brown has been an outspoken advocate of civil rights and racial justice. He strongly believed that African American athletes had a duty to be involved with the African American community.

During the 1960s Brown founded the Negro Industrial Economic Union to assist African American businesses. In a 1968 interview he said its aim was "helping black people acquire the green power they need to make life, liberty, and the pursuit of happiness a tangible reality."

In 1988 Brown started the Amer-I-Can Foundation, a life-management skills and human-development program that operates in 13 U.S. cities. It was set up to help turn gang members toward more productive activities by developing their self-esteem and changing their attitude from "I can't" to "I can."

In 2005 two Syracuse University alumni set up two scholarships in Brown's name to honor his achievements: the Jim Brown Endowed Football Scholarship and the Jim Brown Endowed Lacrosse Scholarship.

See also: Lee, Spike; Robeson, Paul

Further reading: Brown, Jim, and Steve Delsohn. *Out of Bounds.* New York, NY: Kensington Publishing Corporation, 1989.
http://espn.go.com/classic/biography/s/Brown_Jim.html (Biography).
http://www.amer-i-can.org/v1/program.html (Amer-I-Can site).

BROWN, Lawrence
Musician

Famed for the 30 years he spent with Duke Ellington, Lawrence Brown was underrated as a musician in his own right. His reputation as a balladeer combined with his upright nature earned him the nickname "the Deacon."

Early years
Born in Kansas in 1907, Brown was the son of a minister. He had a strict upbringing and grew up an abstemious individual. Throughout his career he never smoked, drank, or gambled, although such activities were a major part of the jazz scene.

After moving to California when he was seven, Brown learned to play piano, violin, and tuba, before settling on the trombone. It was an unusual choice, as was his modeling his sound on that of a cello; Brown later claimed, "I wanted a big, broad tone, not the raspy tone of a tailgate."

By now Brown was studying medicine and with his father eager that he continue his studies, combined school with moonlighting with local bands until 1926. When he decided to pursue a career in music full time, his father threw him out of the family home. Brown played and recorded with Paul Howard (1929–1930) and Louis Armstrong (1930) in and around Los Angeles before joining Duke Ellington in 1932.

KEY DATES

1907   Born in Lawrence, Kansas, on August 3.

1926   Abandons studying medicine for a career in music.

1932   Begins playing with Duke Ellington and His Orchestra.

1960   Rejoins Duke Ellington.

1970   Retires from music.

1988   Dies in Los Angeles, California, on September 5.

Duke Ellington and His Orchestra
The addition of Brown and his trombone to the Duke Ellington Orchestra caused controversy among Ellington's fans, who were used to his aggressive "jungle" sound. Despite criticism that Brown's melodic, lyrical style did not fit in, he was to remain with Ellington for nearly two decades as fans and fellow musicians came to recognize him for the gifted player he was.

Brown left Ellington in 1951 to join a new band led by Johnny Hodges, another of Ellington's former sidemen. He stayed until the group split in 1955, when he traveled to New York to work as a freelancer and as a session musician for CBS. Not long after the monotony of studio work caused Brown to resign, he received a call from Ellington. He rejoined Ellington's orchestra in 1960 for another decade, eventually retiring from music in 1970 to work as a business consultant before fully retiring in 1974.

A morose character, Brown remained unconvinced of his own considerable talents. He resisted attempts to persuade him back into music, claiming to have left his trombone at an aunt's house soon after leaving Ellington. As far as he was concerned, it could stay there. Brown died in California in 1988.

See also: Armstrong, Louis; Ellington, Duke; Hodges, Johnny

Further reading: Hasse, John Edward. *Beyond Category: The Life and Genius of Duke Ellington.* New York, NY: Da Capo Press, 1995.
http://www.mp3.com/lawrencebrown/artists/6706/biography.html (Artist page on MP3).

▲ *Lawrence Brown (left), together with fellow jazz greats Coleman Hawkins (seated center) and clarinettist Buster Bailey (right), at a 1950s recording session.*

BROWN, Ron
Politician

Ron Brown was a leader in foreign economic relations. He promoted international trade agreements by negotiating with corporate and political leaders. As secretary of commerce he helped create new jobs with a strategy of "commercial diplomacy." In 1970 Congressman Charles Rangel called him an "American champ."

Early years
Born in Washington, D.C., in 1941, Ronald Harmon Brown demonstrated his abilities early, reading the newspaper by age five. The family moved to New York City, where Brown helped his father manage a hotel in Harlem that drew top entertainers and celebrities such as Ray Charles and Billie Holliday. An active teenager, Brown played sports, proved to be intellectually gifted in school, and modeled in Pepsi commercials.

He attended Middlebury College in Vermont, where he broke the color barrier when he pledged the all-white fraternity Sigma Phi Epsilon and developed an interest in John F. Kennedy's (1961–1963) campaign for president.

Graduating in 1962, Brown joined the army, married his college sweetheart, Alma Arrington, and enrolled in law school. He was promoted to captain during tours of duty in Germany and Korea but left the military in 1967 to complete his legal studies. He returned to Washington, D.C., to work with the National Urban League as an

▼ *Ron Brown at a press conference in 1995 when he was secretary of commerce.*

KEY DATES	
1941	Born in Washington, D.C., on August 1.
1963	Becomes a captain in the Army.
1970	Gains law degree from St. John's University, New York.
1976	Becomes National Urban League executive.
1989	First African American to chair the Democratic National Committee.
1993	First African American appointed secretary of commerce.
1996	Dies in plane crash in Croatia on April 3.

advocate for fair housing and civil rights. By 1976 he was the league's deputy executive director for programs and government affairs. Brown left the league to work as deputy campaign manager for Edward Kennedy in his 1980 bid for the Democratic presidential nomination.

Career highs
Brown established a series of firsts for African Americans: the first law partner at a prestigious law firm; the first to chair the Democratic National Committee; and the first secretary of commerce.

Brown's public charisma, commitment to the voting process, and business acumen helped transform the Democratic Party into a powerful, unified organization. His innovative leadership was partly responsible for the election of President Bill Clinton (1993–2001), who later described him as a team player "determined that American workers and companies would get a fair shake around the world."

During a trip to Croatia in 1996 to orchestrate trade agreements, Brown and 33 corporate leaders were mysteriously killed in a plane crash, provoking a number of conspiracy theories that have yet to be disproved.

Further reading: Brown, Tracy. *The Life and Times of Ron Brown: A Memoir.* New York, NY: William Morrow & Co., 1998.
http://www.loc.gov/loc/lcib/0011/rbrown.html
(Library of Congress page on Brown).
http://www.arlingtoncemetery.net/rbrown.htm (Arlington National Cemetery page on Brown).

BROWN, Sterling A.
Poet, Critic, Academic

Eminent poet, literary critic, academic, and folklorist, Sterling Allen Brown was devoted to establishing a genuine African American folk literature peopled by authentic black folk heroes.

Early years

Brown was born on the campus of Howard University in Washington, D.C, on May 1, 1901. His father was a pastor and professor of religion, and Brown grew up surrounded by many prominent black intellectuals, including Alain Locke and W. E. B. DuBois. He was educated first at Washington's Dunbar High School, then at Williams College in Williamstown, Massachusetts, and Harvard University, where he earned an MA in 1923. After graduation Brown began teaching at the Virginia Seminary and College in Lynchburg. Immersing himself in the rural African American southern community, Brown began collecting the stories and songs he heard, and was inspired to write poetry of his own, employing phonetic spelling to accurately convey the southern black dialect. Brown left Lynchburg in 1926 and went to teach at Fisk University in Nashville, Tennessee, and Lincoln University in Jefferson City, Missouri. In 1929 he became professor of English at Howard University.

The Black Renaissance

The 1920s and 1930s saw a burgeoning of African American art and culture in Washington that was known as the Black Renaissance and was part of the wider Harlem Renaissance movement in New York. Among Brown's contributions to the movement was his first collection of poetry, *Southern Road*, which appeared in 1932 to widespread acclaim. Exploring ideas of race and identity, Brown's poetry was indebted to the blues, jazz, work songs, and spirituals. With the continuing Great Depression Brown's second book of poetry went unpublished, and he concentrated on his work as a teacher and critic.

Both as a teacher and in his own work Brown encouraged realism, disparaged writing that perpetuated black stereotypes, and recognized the importance of folklore to African American art and literature. He expressed his views in a monthly column in *Opportunity* magazine, "The Literary Scene: Chronicle and Comment," which he wrote for 10 years, and in his groundbreaking studies *The Negro in American Fiction* (1937) and *Negro Poetry and Drama* (1937). Brown was also national editor of *Negro Affairs* for the Federal Writers' Project from 1936 until 1940 and coedited *The Negro Caravan*, an anthology of African American literature, in 1941.

Brown spent 40 years at Howard University, during which time he spent semesters at Vassar College, Atlanta University, and New York University. He also returned to Harvard in the early 1930s (it was from there that *Southern Road* was published). Among the students that Brown mentored at Howard University were Stokely Carmichael, Ossie Davis, and Amiri Baraka.

After retiring from Howard University in 1969, Brown focused on poetry once more. He published a second collection, *The Last Ride of Wild Bill*, in 1975 and his *Collected Poems* in 1980. Celebrated for his profound influence on African American literature, Brown was selected for the Academy of American Poets and appointed poet laureate of the District of Columbia in 1984. Brown died of leukemia on January 13, 1989, in Takoma Park, Maryland.

See also: Baraka, Amiri; Carmichael, Stokely; Davis, Ossie; DuBois, W. E. B.; Locke, Alain

Further reading: Brown, Sterling Allen. *The Collected Poems of Sterling Allen Brown.* (Selected by Michael S. Harper). New York, NY: Harper & Row, 1980. www.english.uiuc.edu/maps/poets/a_f/brown/brown.htm (Modern American Poetry site featuring biography, poetry, and essays).

KEY DATES	
1901	Born in Washington, D.C., on May 1.
1929	Begins teaching at Howard University, Washington, D.C.
1932	Publishes first volume of poetry, *Southern Road*.
1969	Retires from Howard University to concentrate on writing poetry.
1975	Publishes *The Last Ride of Wild Bill*.
1989	Dies in Takoma Park, Maryland, on January 13.

BROWN, William Wells

Writer, Educator, Abolitionist

A leading intellectual of 19th-century America, William Wells Brown was a writer, physician, historian, and antislavery lecturer. During his groundbreaking career he became the first African American to publish a novel and a play. His commitment to the antislavery cause made him an inspirational figure during the civil rights era of the 20th century.

A new name

Born in about 1814, the son of a black slave woman and a white plantation owner, Wells grew up as a slave on a plantation near Lexington, Kentucky. In 1834 he escaped and made his way to Canada. During his escape he was helped by a Quaker named Wells Brown, whose name he adopted to show his gratitude. For nine years Brown worked as a steward on a steamship on the Great Lakes, using his position to help fugitive slaves escape to freedom. He devoted his spare time to educating himself. In 1834 he married Elizabeth Spooner, a free black woman, with whom he had three daughters.

In 1843 Brown met the celebrated African American abolitionist Frederick Douglass, who inspired him to join the Western New York Anti-Slavery Society as a lecturer and writer. Like other former slaves, Brown wrote an account of his life to help publicize the antislavery cause. His *Narrative of William W. Brown, a Fugitive Slave* was published to much acclaim in 1847. Unlike some abolitionists, Brown opposed violence as a means of ending slavery.

The first African American novelist

In 1849 the American Peace Society chose Brown as their representative to the Peace Congress in Paris, France, where Brown became friends with some of the leading European intellectuals, including French novelist Victor Hugo (1802–1885). The passing of the 1850 Fugitive Slave Law—which allowed slave owners to hunt down fugitive slaves in the United States—forced Brown to settle for a time in London, England. In England Brown published his only novel, *Clotel; or The President's Daughter*, a daring,

◀ **The 19th-century writer William Wells Brown documented his life as a slave to promote the antislavery cause.**

melodramatic story that drew on rumors that President Thomas Jefferson (1743–1826) had children by his black mistress, Sally Hemmings. The novel marks the beginning of a long tradition of African American writing.

Brown was able to return to the United States in 1854, when friends raised enough money to purchase his freedom. He continued to campaign and write on various causes, including antislavery, woman's suffrage, and temperance (abstinence from alcohol). His published works from the period include a play, *The Escape, or a Leap for Freedom* (1858), and innovative studies on black history, such as *The Black Man: His Antecedents, His Genius, and His Achievements* (1863). Brown eventually settled in Boston, where he practiced as a physician. He died in Chelsea, Massachusetts, on November 6, 1884.

KEY DATES	
1814	Born near Lexington, Kentucky, at about this time.
1834	Adopts the name Wells Brown from a Quaker who helps him escape from slavery.
1847	Publishes autobiography *Narrative of William W. Brown, a Fugitive Slave*.
1853	Publishes novel *Clotel; or The President's Daughter*.
1884	Dies in Chelsea, Massachusetts, on November 6.

See also: Civil Rights; Douglass, Frederick; Slavery

Further reading: Brown, William Wells, and M. Guila Fabi (ed.). *Clotel; or The President's Daughter*. New York, NY: Penguin, 2004.
docsouth.unc.edu/brownw/menu.html (Biography and excerpts from Wells's work).

BRUCE, Blanche K.
Senator

Blanche Kelso Bruce was born into slavery but became a U.S. senator. He was the first African American to serve a full senatorial term.

Bruce was born in 1841 to a family that worked for a slave owner near Farmville, Virginia. As he grew up, he worked in the fields and later as a printer's apprentice, but he also received an education from his master's son, who acted as his tutor.

When the Civil War (1861–1865) started Bruce escaped from slavery and applied unsuccessfully to the Union Army. Instead he went through a number of jobs, including steamboat porter and teacher: In 1864 he helped establish the first state school for blacks in Hannibal, Missouri. In 1869 he made the career shift that would define his adult life when he entered politics.

Political rise

Bruce's political career began in Mississippi. He worked in local politics in a range of positions, including registrar of voters, tax assessor, and education supervisor. Having acquired influence and amassed wealth, he bought a plantation in Floreyville, Mississippi. In 1874 the Mississippi legislature elected Bruce to the U.S. Senate, where he served from March 5, 1875, to March 3, 1881, as one of 22 black representatives in Congress during Reconstruction, the time following the Civil War when former slaves were attempting to establish themselves. In 1878 Bruce married educator Josephine Willson.

While in the Senate, Bruce took on many of the human rights issues of the day. He campaigned for an increase in

▲ *This double portrait photograph of Blanche K. Bruce was taken early in his political career.*

land allocation to blacks and also attacked segregation in the Army. He advocated better treatment of Native Americans and helped reclaim money for 61,000 people defrauded by the Freedman's Savings and Trust Company, a bank for former slaves that failed in 1874 because of corruption and mismanagement.

After the Senate

The end of Bruce's service in the Senate did not end his political career. He rejected an offer to work as an ambassador to Brazil, a slave-owning nation, and instead worked as registrar of the Treasury, where he served two terms from 1881 to 1885 and 1895 to 1898. In the period between Bruce lectured, wrote, and was recorder of deeds for the District of Columbia from 1889 to 1895. He died in Washington, D.C., on March 17, 1898.

See also: Emancipation and Reconstruction; Slavery

Further reading: Rabinowit, Howard (ed.). *Southern Black Leaders of the Reconstruction Era.* Urbana, IL: University of Illinois Press, 1982.
http://bioguide.congress.gov/scripts/biodisplay.pl?index=B0009681900/reconstruction/bruce.htm (Biography).

KEY DATES	
1841	Born near Farmville, Virginia, on March 1.
1861	Freed at the beginning of the Civil War.
1869	Moves to Mississippi and becomes involved in local politics.
1875	Begins a six-year term as a Republican senator.
1881	Senatorial career comes to an end.
1898	Dies in Washington, D.C., on March 17.

BRYANT, Kobe
Basketball Player

Kobe Bryant was born on August 23, 1978, and found fame in the late 1990s as one of the top professional basketball players of his generation. He is the son of Joe "Jellybean" Bryant, who played for the Philadelphia 76ers, the San Diego Clippers, and the Houston Rockets. In 1984 Bryant's father signed with a team in Rieti, Italy, where the family lived for the next seven years.

The Bryants returned to the United States in 1991, when Joe took the assistant coaching job at La Salle University in Philadelphia. Kobe, now aged 13 and 6 feet 6 inches (1.98m) tall, enrolled at Lower Merion High School in Philadelphia and soon emerged as a court star. With 2,883 points in his final year Bryant became the leading scorer in southeastern Pennsylvania history. At 16 he turned pro with the Charlotte Hornets and signed lucrative sponsorship deals with Adidas and Sprite.

The LA Lakers

In 1997 the Hornets traded Bryant to the Los Angeles Lakers, with whom he signed a three-year $3.5 million contract. Shortly afterward he became the youngest National Basketball Association (NBA) player to debut in the league. In that year's Rookie Game Bryant scored 31 points and had 8 rebounds, a new record for the game. He also won the Slam Dunk Championship at the 1997 NBA All-Star Weekend. In 1998–1999 Bryant was the only Lakers player to start all 50 of the season's games. In 2000 he helped the team to the first of three consecutive NBA Championship titles. His play was outstanding, although he was often criticized for not sharing the ball enough. The only other Laker whose achievements and star-quality rivaled those of Bryant was Shaquille O'Neal, who was traded to the Miami Heat in 2004.

A fall from grace

In 2003 Bryant's career suffered a major setback when he was charged with sexual assault. Although the case was dropped in 2004, the bad publicity and the pressure of fighting his case had an adverse effect on both his court play and his previously huge power to attract sponsorship deals. Bryant admitted that he did have a consensual relationship with his accuser, but his wife stood by him as he attempted to resurrect his career with the Lakers.

▼ *Kobe Bryant on court for the Los Angeles Lakers in July 2004.*

See also: O'Neal, Shaquille

Further reading: Bradley, Michael. *Kobe Bryant.* New York, NY: Benchmark Books, 2003.
http://www.nba.com/playerfile/kobe_bryant/index.html?nav=page
(Bryant page from the LA Lakers' official site).

KEY DATES	
1978	Born in Philadelphia, Pennsylvania, on August 23.
1994	Becomes professional basketball player.
1997	Joins the LA Lakers.
2000	Wins the first of three consecutive NBA championships.
2001	Marries Vanessa Laine.
2003	Is charged with sexual assault.
2004	The charges and court case are dropped.

BUBBLES, John
Dancer, Entertainer

One of the most innovative tap dancers of the 20th century, John Bubbles was famous as one half of the 1920s and 1930s song-and-dance duo Buck and Bubbles. Honored as the "father of rhythm tap," Bubbles created exuberant dance steps that still inspire dancers today.

Star of vaudeville

Born in Louisville, Kentucky, in 1902, John William Sublett showed his prodigious talents as a tap dancer at an early age. In about 1913 he met the musician Ford Lee Washington (1903–1955), and together they formed the vaudeville act Buck and Bubbles, in which Washington ("Buck") played jazz piano and Bubbles danced, sang, and clowned. At the time vaudeville—light-entertainment theater that included dancers, magicians, singers, and comedians—was at the height of its popularity.

▼ *This publicity photo of John Bubbles dates from 1964, a decade after he began his solo career.*

Buck and Bubbles's witty, fast-paced act met with huge success. By 1919 the duo had moved to New York City, where they appeared at Broadway's Palace Theater, the most prestigious vaudeville theater in the country. They topped the bill throughout the 1920s and 1930s, playing largely for white audiences and sometimes even appearing in "blackface" (black minstrel makeup). They also appeared either together or individually in motion pictures, including *Varsity Show* (1937) and *A Song Is Born* (1948).

Amazing moves

Bubbles amazed audiences with his unconventional tap moves. One of his most celebrated innovations was the spectacular double over-the-top, in which he appeared repeatedly to almost trip over as he danced in a figure-eight. His virtuoso dancing and singing caused the composer George Gershwin to cast him as the New York gambler Sportin' Life in the opera *Porgy and Bess* in 1935.

Buck and Bubbles continued to perform together until 1953. Bubbles then went on to pursue a solo career and was the first black person to appear on *Johnny Carson Tonight*. He gave his last performance in 1980 in the revue *Black Broadway*. Bubbles died in 1986.

KEY DATES	
1902	Born in Louisville, Kentucky, on February 19.
1917	Forms Buck and Bubbles with the musician Ford Lee Washington.
1919	Moves to New York City to appear at the Palace Theater.
1935	Stars in George Gershwin's opera *Porgy and Bess*.
1953	The Buck and Bubbles partnership splits.
1986	Dies in Louisville, Kentucky on May 18.

See also: Washington, Buck

Further reading: Frank, Rusty E. *Tap! The Greatest Tap Dance Stars and Their Stories, 1900–1955.* New York, NY: Da Capo Press, 1995.
http://www.ukjtd.force9.co.uk/Timestepsite/Bubbles.htm (Biography and video clips).

BUCHANAN, Buck
Football Player

Junious "Buck" Buchanan, who went on to become one of the great football players of the 1960s and early 1970s, was born on September 10, 1940, in Gainesville, Alabama. By his teenage years and aided by a formidable physique—at the height of his career he was 6 feet 8 inches (2m) tall and weighed up to 300 pounds (136kg)—Buchanan was already showing power and skill on the football field. He was fortunate enough to be talent spotted at the right time, and his big break came at the A. H. Parker High School in Birmingham, Alabama, in the late 1950s. His potential was spotted by Eddie Robinson, an expert coach at Grambling State University, Louisiana, and Buchanan was awarded one of the few university scholarships available to black students at that time.

Power player

At Grambling Buchanan showed his professional skills and extreme speed on the field—he could run the 100 meters in 10.2 seconds. He was talented on both offense and defense, and Robinson called him "the finest lineman I've ever seen."

Buchanan soon moved into the American Football League (AFL). He was drafted by the Dallas Texans (who later became the Kansas City Chiefs) in 1963, the first player selected in that year's draft. In the National Football League (NFL) he made his mark as a defensive lineman and helped the Kansas City Chiefs rise to new heights of success, including Super Bowl games in 1966 and 1969. Buchanan played professional football until 1975. In his 13-year career he demonstrated impressive physical stamina by missing only one game of the 182 played by his team. The Chiefs twice named Buchanan their Most

▲ *Kansas City Chiefs' defensive lineman Buck Buchanan in action in 1967.*

Valuable Player (in 1965 and 1967) and each year between 1964 and 1971 he was selected as an AFL All-Star or for an NFL Pro Bowl game.

Success after retirement

Buchanan retired from professional football in 1975 but remained as a coach for three years. He also became involved in business, running a construction enterprise and an advertising company in Kansas City. In 1990 he was inducted into the Pro Football Hall of Fame. Buchanan died of lung cancer on July 16, 1992, at the age of 51.

See also: Robinson, Eddie

Further reading: Ashe, Arthur. *A Hard Road to Glory: A History of the African American Athlete: Football.* New York, NY: Amistad Press, 1993.
http://www.cmgworldwide.com/football/buchanan (Buchanan's official site).

KEY DATES	
1940	Born in Gainesville, Alabama, on September 10.
1963	Goes into professional football, joining the Dallas Texans.
1975	Retires from football, moving into coaching and various business activities.
1990	Is inducted into the Pro Football Hall of Fame.
1992	Dies on July 16.

BULLARD, Eugene Jacques
Fighter Pilot

Eugene James (Jacques) Bullard was the first African American combat pilot. His heroism in two world wars was recognized by France but ignored in his homeland until recent times.

Early years
Bullard was born on October 9, 1894, in Columbus, Georgia. As a boy he witnessed the lynching of his uncle and an attempted lynching of his father. His father had told him that black people were treated fairly in France, so at the age of eight Bullard ran away from home with the aim of getting to Europe. He spent two years effectively on the run in the southeastern states. When he was 10, he stowed away on a steamer that took him to the United Kingdom. There he found more acceptance, earning money as a street performer, then, by his late teens, as a welterweight boxer, winning fights in England, France, and North Africa. When he was 18, he moved to France, settling in the capital, Paris.

▼ *Eugene Jacques Bullard was one of 200 Americans who flew for France in World War I.*

KEY DATES

1894	Born in Columbus, Georgia, on October 9.
1904	Moves to the United Kingdom.
1912	Moves to Paris, France, and joins the Foreign Legion at the outbreak of war in 1914.
1917	Qualifies as a fighter pilot in the French air force.
1940	Serves in the French Resistance during World War II.
1959	Receives France's Légion d'Honneur.
1961	Dies in Harlem, New York, on October 12.

To the skies
In 1914 World War I broke out in Europe. Bullard enlisted in the French Foreign Legion. He fought bravely and was both decorated and wounded before he volunteered for pilot training in 1916. On May 17, 1917, he qualified, becoming the world's first black combat pilot. Bullard flew 20 missions and downed at least one German plane. When the United States entered the war in 1917, he was barred from joining the U.S. forces as a pilot because of his race. Instead, he served in the 170th French Infantry Regiment.

Bullard left military service in October 1919, a year after the war's end. He lived on in Paris, married a countess, had two daughters, and opened a nightclub.

During World War II (1939–1945) France was invaded by Germany in 1940, and Bullard joined the Resistance movement. He was wounded in fighting near Orleans and smuggled out of France to Spain. From there he returned to the United States, where his remarkable story was ignored. In 1954, with two other French war heroes, Bullard was given the honor of relighting the eternal flame of the Tomb of the Unknown Soldier in Paris. He died on October 12, 1961, and was buried in the French War Veterans Cemetery in Flushing, New York, with full French military honors.

Further reading: Carisella, P. J. *The Black Swallow of Death—The Incredible Story of Eugene Jacques Bullard, the World's First Black Combat Aviator.* New York, NY: Marlborough House, 1972.
http://afehri.maxwell.af.mil/pages/EnlistedPilots/EugeneBullard.htm (Includes magazine articles, biographies, and timelines).

BULLINS, Ed
Playwright

During the course of his lengthy career Ed Bullins has written plays, poetry, essays, and a novel. All of his work has been political in nature, attacking racism and promoting black culture.

Edward Artie Bullins was born into a middle-class family on July 2, 1935, in Philadelphia, Pennsylvania. While a teenager he moved to the downtown Franklin High School and joined a street gang. He was once stabbed during a fight, and his heart stopped beating momentarily. Bullins later dropped out of high school and enlisted in the Navy, where he served between 1952 and 1955. While in the Navy he started to read widely.

Writing career

After he left the Navy, Bullins moved to Los Angeles, where he started to write, attending classes part time at Los Angeles City College. In 1964 he moved to the San Francisco Bay Area. Bullins enrolled in a college writing program and began to write plays, motivated by the realization that it was the best way to reach as large an African American audience as possible.

During this period Bullins was influenced by the plays of his contemporary LeRoi Jones, later known as Amiri Baraka. Baraka was an African American poet and playwright who gained a great deal of critical acclaim when his play *Dutchman* opened Off-Broadway in 1964. Inspired by Baraka's success, Bullins founded an African American theater group. Black Arts/West took its name from a similar organization, the Black Arts Repertory Theatre/School (BARTS), founded in New York by Baraka. Black Arts/West functioned between 1965 and 1967. During his time in California Bullins also became involved with

the Black Panther Party. He was briefly its minister of culture in California, but a disagreement about beliefs led to him leaving the post.

Bullins's playwriting career began in 1965 with the production of a trio of one-act plays: *How Do You Do?*, *Dialect Determinism (or The Rally)*, and *Clara's Ole Man*. In 1967 he moved to New York and began an association with the New Lafayette Theatre in Harlem that lasted until 1973. The theater was the venue for Bullins's first full-length play, *In the Wine Time* (1968). The play was the first in a series known as the Twentieth-Century Cycle; others included *The Corner* (1968), *The Duplex* (1970), and *The Fabulous Miss Marie* (1971). While working at the New Lafayette Theatre, Bullins headed its Black Theatre Workshop and also edited the magazine *Black Theatre*.

The Taking of Miss Janie, arguably Bullins's best-known play, opened in 1975. The play examines interracial relationships among a group of 1960s political activists and revolves around the rape of a liberal white woman by a black man. Bullins intended the rape to symbolize the folly of blacks trying to integrate with white society. The play provoked criticism by feminists but earned a number of awards, including a Drama Critics Circle Award for best American play and an Obie (Off-Broadway Theater Awards), presented by the *Village Voice* newspaper.

Academic career

In the 1970s and 1980s Bullins worked with numerous writers' groups and theaters, including the American Place Theatre. He also reentered the world of academia, earning a BA degree in liberal studies from Antioch University in 1989. He went on to complete an MA in playwriting at San Francisco State University in 1994 and in 1995 gained a permanent position, distinguished artist-in-residence, at Northeastern University. During this period he continued to write, completing the play *Boy x Man* in 1995. He remained at Northeastern University into the early 21st century, simultaneously working on a musical, *Hot Feet*.

KEY DATES	
1935	Born in Philadelphia, Pennsylvania, on July 2.
1952	Joins Navy.
1965	Founds Black Arts/West.
1975	*The Taking of Miss Janie* earns New York Drama Critics Circle Award.
1994	Completes MA in playwriting.
1995	Takes up permanent post at Northeastern University.

See also: Baraka, Amiri

Further reading: Hay, Samuel. *Ed Bullins: A Literary Biography.* Detroit, MI: Wayne State University Press, 1997.
http://www.edbullins.com (Bullins's official site).

BUMBRY, Grace

Singer

Internationally renowned singer Grace Melizia Ann Bumbry is considered to have one of the finest voices in opera. Like her contemporary Shirley Verrett, Bumbry first began her career as a mezzo-soprano—a range of the female singing voice lower than a soprano, which is the highest female singing voice—but later expanded her vocal range to include soprano.

Born in St. Louis, Missouri, on January 4, 1937, Bumbry displayed musical talent at an early age. She studied piano with her mother from the age of seven and aged 11 began singing in public in the Union Memorial Methodist Church choir in Missouri. In 1954 she was a winner on the *Arthur Godfrey Talent Scouts* television show, and she was awarded a scholarship to Northwestern University.

Bumbry became a student of the celebrated German opera singer Lotte Lehmann (1888–1976), who was teaching an MA course at Northwestern. Lehmann quickly recognized Bumbry's unique talent and took her under her wing. In 2004 Bumbry acknowledged that Lehmann's influence lay in getting her to understand "that you have to go beyond yourself when performing."

Achieving a dream

In 1958 Bumbry won several competitions. Using her prize money, Bumbry traveled to Europe to pursue her dream of becoming an opera singer. She made her concert debut in London in 1959; one year later she made her operatic debut as Amneris in *Aida* with the Paris Opera Company. She was an immediate success and was invited to join the Basel Opera in Switzerland, where she impressed the grandson of the German composer Richard Wagner so much that he invited her to play Venus in a new production of *Tannhauser* at the Bayreuth Festival, Germany's annual Wagner festival. Bumbry was the first black opera singer to

▲ *Grace Bumbry performs in Bizet's* **Carmen** *at the Metropolitan Opera, New York, in December 1967.*

receive the honor and was called the "Black Venus of Bayreuth." She also won the esteemed Wagner Medal.

In 1962 Bumbry toured the United States. Her performances at the Royal Opera House, London (1963), and La Scala Opera House, Milan, Italy (1964), helped establish her reputation as a brilliant singer. Since then Bumbry has sung all of the great mezzo-soprano roles, including Carmen. In 1997 she made her last operatic appearance and established the Grace Bumbry Black Musical Heritage Ensemble, which teaches Lehmann's vocal tradition. Bumbry has received many awards; she is also a United Nations Scientific and Cultural Organization (UNESCO) goodwill ambassador.

See also: Verrett, Shirley

Further reading: http://www.musicacademy.org/ Alumni/RecipientInterview.html (Interview).

KEY DATES

1937 Born in St. Louis, Missouri, on January 4.

1960 Makes her operatic debut in Paris, France.

1961 Becomes the first black singer to perform at the Bayreuth Festival, Germany.

1997 Gives last operatic performance in Lyons, France; establishes Grace Bumbry Black Musical Heritage Ensemble.

BUNCHE, Ralph
Academic, Diplomat

More than a decade before Martin Luther King, Jr., won the Nobel Peace Prize, Ralph Bunche was the first African American man to be honored in this way. Bunche's impressive record of black public service "firsts," much of it compiled before the era of civil rights and black power, is in many ways unrivaled, even today.

Humble beginnings

Ralph Johnson Bunche was born in Detroit, Michigan, in 1904 into what was then regarded as a not-quite-middle-class family: his mother, Olive, was a musician, and his father, Fred, was a barber. His most influential relative by far was his grandmother Lucy Johnson. A light-skinned black woman who could have easily passed for white, Nana (as she was called) instilled in Bunche a fierce sense of racial pride, humility, self-respect, and honesty. She taught him to stand his ground when he was right and never to allow himself to be limited by his race.

Finding steady work sufficient to support a family proved challenging to Bunche's father, so the family moved frequently as they searched for the right place in which to settle. Their economic status deteriorated significantly after a move from Tennessee to Ohio left Bunche's father without work and the family in a poorly heated, single-room home. The move was to set in motion a series of events that resulted in Ralph's father's departure from the family, his mother's early death, and his uncle's suicide. Out of this series of tragedies was to come a small ray of hope as the family achieved some measure of stability with a move to Los Angeles, where Bunche was to remain until he graduated from college.

Foundation in challenge and achievement

As a young man, Bunche worked early and hard to earn money, selling newspapers, laying carpet, and working in a bakery. He encountered a number of incidents of racial discrimination, which he mostly took in stride with the support of his grandmother. A talented athlete and outstanding student in high school, Bunche was excluded from the local honor society because of his race. Momentarily disheartened (he considered leaving school), he went on to be class valedictorian, only to discover in a conversation with the principal that because of his level of achievement, he was never really considered "a Negro." His grandmother then

▲ *Ralph Bunch's outstanding public record culminated in the 1950 Nobel Peace Prize.*

helped the principal see the insult he had caused to a family "as American as everyone else" who had "no shame in being Negroes."

Bunche went on to attend the University of California, Los Angeles, on a football scholarship, but his football career ended prematurely with an injury to his left leg that was to trouble him for the rest of his life. Bunche switched to basketball but continued his established habit of working hard outside of school to make ends meet. Bunche again excelled academically and as the top student in his graduating class delivered the valedictory address. So impressive was his address that several members of the audience raised or directly contributed money to help meet his graduate school expenses. In 1928 Bunche was awarded an MA in government (political science) from Harvard University. He was about to begin work toward his doctorate when he was recruited to establish the first political science department at Howard University.

Bunche was now a member of an elite black faculty, a group that included Alain L. Locke, Carter G. Woodson, and Charles Hamilton Houston. During his time at Howard Bunche met and married Ruth Harris, returned to Harvard to complete work on his doctorate, traveled to Africa and Europe for fieldwork in support of his dissertation, and began to formulate a consciousness that included the colonized people of Africa as well as the black Americans.

INFLUENCES AND INSPIRATION

Bunche was influenced by W. E. B. DuBois, James Weldon Johnson, and Carter G. Woodson, although he did not necessarily share their emphasis on race as the primary factor around which all strategies for uplifting the condition of blacks should be organized. Bunche initially emphasized much more strongly the effect of class on the struggling people of all races, but he was not inclined to align himself as readily with the Communist Party as did some black intellectuals. As his career developed, Bunche worked closely with and was influenced by three Swedes: academic Gunnar Myrdal, UN negotiator Count Folke Bernadotte, and Dag Hammarskjöld, UN secretary general.

Bunche taught a number of African Americans who went on to illustrious careers in law, public service, and social sciences, including Kenneth Clark (psychology), former D.C. mayor Walter Washington, and former Health, Education and Welfare (Health and Human Services) secretary Patricia Roberts Harris.

Martin Luther King, Jr., and Bunche worked very effectively together. Bunche formulated policy, while King carried out the practical organization on the streets. The two men admired and supported each other.

Making history

Bunche moved onto the national stage when he was selected to work with Swedish academic Gunnar Myrdal on a study commissioned by the Carnegie Corporation on black life and race relations in the United States. The completed work, *An American Dilemma: The Negro Problem and American Democracy*, was about 15,000 pages long (3,000 of which Bunche authored). It was considered the authoritative study of the American Negro for the mid-20th century. Through his field research Bunche uncovered a long list of voting abuses against blacks in a disorganized but effective movement to prevent them from voting.

Just before the United States was forced into World War II (1939–1945) by the Japanese bombing of Pearl Harbor, Bunche was asked to serve as an African specialist in the Office of Strategic Services. Bunche and his colleagues were to provide the president and the military with information needed to fight the war and to counter the propaganda of the enemy. Bunche quietly crafted the output of his office to reflect policies that would emphasize the importance of black manpower to a successful military campaign. In this way he advanced the cause of civil rights while providing exemplary service to his country.

As a result of his war service, Bunche moved into the arena where he was to do the work for which he is best known. First, as the director of the Trusteeship Division of the newly created United Nations, his work paved the way for colonies, especially those in Africa, to achieve independence. After the 1948 assassination of Folke Bernadotte, chief United Nations' mediator in Palestine, Bunche was thrust into the position of prime negotiator of the 1949 Arab-Israeli peace agreement, a peace that was to last nearly 20 years, and that earned him the Nobel Peace Prize in 1950. As a result Bunche was offered numerous faculty appointments at elite institutions, awarded scores of honorary degrees, and suggested as a candidate for office within both the Democratic and Republican parties. Bunche remained at the United Nations for nearly 25 years, mediating sometimes violent changes in government in several nations, including Zaire (former Belgian Congo), Cyprus, and Yemen. Bunche died in 1971.

KEY DATES

1904 Born in Detroit, Michigan, on August 7.

1944 Completes work on *An American Dilemma*.

1949 Negotiates Arab-Israeli armistice agreements; awarded NAACP Spingarn Medal.

1950 Receives Nobel Peace Prize for 1949 armistice agreements.

1963 Awarded the Presidential Medal of Honor.

1971 Dies in New York on December 9.

See also: Clark, Kenneth; DuBois, W. E. B.; Harris, Patricia Roberts; Houston, Charles Hamilton; Johnson, James Weldon; King, Martin Luther, Jr.; Locke, Alain; Woodson, Carter. G.

Further reading: Urquhart, Brian. *Ralph Bunche: An American Odyssey.* New York, NY: WW Norton & Co., 1998.
http://nobelprize.org/peace/laureates/1950/bunche-bio.html (Nobel Prize page on Bunche).

BURGESS, John Melville
Bishop

John Melville Burgess rose from humble beginnings to become the twelfth bishop of Massachusetts and a leading force within the American Episcopal Church.

Early years

Burgess was born on March 11, 1909, in Grand Rapids, Michigan, the son of Ethel and Theodore Burgess. His father supported the family by working as a waiter in the dining car of a train on the Pierre Marquette Railroad.

Burgess showed two key characteristics during youth —a deep Christian faith, which had emerged by his late teens, and a strong academic mind. As a young adult these traits took him first to the University of Michigan, where he earned his BA in 1930 and his MA in 1931, and then to the Episcopal Theological School in Cambridge, Massachusetts, where he prepared for a life as a priest. He graduated from the theological school in 1934. He was ordained as a priest in 1935 and returned to Grand Rapids to hold his first ministry.

Religious career

Between 1935 and 1969 Burgess had a busy religious career, moving through various communities and roles but bringing his messages of social equality and compassion to them all. His first position was at St. Phillip's Church in Grand Rapids. He then became the priest to the Mission of St. Simon of Cyrene in Woodlawn, near Cincinnati, Ohio. It was an impoverished community where Burgess also administered a social services center, a day school, and a medical clinic, and became involved with labor affairs in the auto industry, helping workers fight for integration. His activism was the first step in a lifelong concern for the urban poor and the problems of working people.

In 1945 Burgess married Esther J. Taylor, an activist who was one of a group jailed in 1964 when they refused to eat in the kitchen rather than the restaurant of a Florida motel.

From 1946 to 1956 Burgess was the first denominational chaplain at Howard University, Washington, D.C., from 1951 to 1956 serving also as a canon of Washington Cathedral. He began his career in Massachusetts as archdeacon of Boston's missions and parishes and superintendent of Boston City Mission, which he reorganized and renamed the Episcopal City Mission so that it could work in urban centers outside of Boston.

KEY DATES	
1909	Born in Grand Rapids, Michigan, on March 11.
1934	Graduates from theological school.
1962	Becomes a bishop.
1969	Elected bishop of Massachusetts.
2003	Dies in Vineyard Haven, Massachusetts, on August 24.

In 1962 Burgess was elected bishop at Trinity Church in Copley Square, Boston, becoming the first African American bishop to preside over a white congregation in the history of the Episcopal Church.

Senior figure

Seven years after he was first made bishop, Burgess was elected bishop of the diocese of Massachusetts, a position that he held until 1975. With the new authority came new responsibilities, which included work with the National Council of Churches, the Church Society for College Work, and the Boston Committee on Foreign Relations.

The latter position indicated a real commitment to overseas work; Burgess was also vice president of the Overseas Mission Society and a representative of the World Council of Churches.

When Burgess retired in 1975, the groundbreaking Joint Urban Fund he had set up to give grants to local community groups was renamed the John Melville Burgess Urban Fund in his honor. After retirement Burgess taught at Yale's Divinity School, in New Haven, Connecticut. He also acted as assisting bishop to several dioceses, was mentor to many young clergy, and wrote a book, *Black Gospel/White Church* (1982). Burgess died on August 24, 2003.

See also: Demby, Edward T.

Further reading: Beary, Michael J. *Black Bishop: Edward T. Demby and the Struggle for Racial Equality in the Episcopal Church.* (Studies in Anglican History). Champaign and Urbana: University of Illinois Press, 2001.
http://thewitness.org/agw/burgess082903.html (Lengthy obituary of Burgess).

BURLEIGH, Harry T.
Singer, Composer

Harry Thacker Burleigh, born on December 2, 1866, has an important place in the history of American music. He was the first composer to arrange Negro spirituals for solo voice and piano accompaniment, taking them out of the oral tradition and into the concert hall.

Burleigh's main influence was from his mother's family, who encouraged his musical talents. His maternal grandfather, Hamilton Waters, was a former slave who had educated his children, and his mother, Elizabeth Burleigh Elmendorf, was a graduate from Avery College in Pennsylvania. As a child Burleigh had piano lessons and sang in a church choir.

Burleigh won a scholarship to study at the National Conservatory of Music, New York, in 1892. The Czech composer Antonín Dvořák (1841–1904) was then director of the conservatory; Dvořák was a nationalist composer who argued that a vocabulary for American music was to be found in African American and Native American traditions rather than in the German model popular at the time. Although Burleigh was not formally Dvořák's pupil, Dvořák took an interest in his voice and repertoire of African American songs. Their relationship inspired Dvořák's Symphony no. 9 ("From the New World") and String Quartet in F Major ("America"), which both include African American themes.

A prolific career

Burleigh's career was busy and diverse. His first major break came when he sang at the World's Columbia Exposition in Chicago in 1893. His main and longest engagements were as a baritone soloist at the two wealthiest churches in the United States, both in New York. He sang at Saint George's Episcopal Church from 1894 to 1949 and Temple Emanu-El synagogue from 1900 to 1925. He was also music editor for the music publisher Ricordi

▲ *Harry T. Burleigh in 1927, when he was the baritone soloist at St. George's.*

from 1911 until his death. Burleigh established his fame as a composer with his arrangement of the spiritual "Deep River" (1916), but his catalog of music included 141 art songs and religious songs, 73 albums of spiritual and Negro folk songs (including the 187 arrangements of spirituals for choir, published as *Old Songs Hymnal* in 1929), and three instrumental works for violin and piano.

Awards

During his career Burleigh received several awards, including the Spingarn Achievement Medal from the National Association for the Advancement of Colored People in 1917 and honorary degrees from Atlanta University and Howard University, Washington, D.C., in 1920. Most of his works were published, and his spiritual arrangements for both solo and choir are still in print. Burleigh died, aged 82, in Stamford, Connecticut.

Further reading: Simpson, Anne Key. *Hard Trials: The Life and Music of Harry T. Burleigh.* Metuchen, NJ: Scarecrow Press, 1990.
http://www.afrovoices.com/burleigh.html (Biography).

KEY DATES	
1866	Born in Erie, Pennsylvania, on December 2.
1892	Enters the National Conservatory of Music, New York.
1916	Writes the art song "Deep River," based on a spiritual.
1949	Dies in Stamford, Connecticut, on September 12.

BURRELL, Leroy
Athlete

Leroy Burrell ranks among the finest sprinters in recent U.S. history, a preeminence he attained despite enduring serious injury setbacks.

Early career
Burrell was born on February 21, 1967, and grew up in Lansdowne, Pennsylvania. Suffering from poor eyesight, the young Burrell struggled with ball sports at school and was dropped from the junior high school baseball team in three consecutive seasons. However, he excelled on the track and almost singlehandedly pushed Penn Wood High School to a state title in 1985. Burrell won the 100 meters, 200 meters, long jump, and triple jump.

Burrell went on to study at the University of Houston, where he emerged as a world-class athlete. In 1986, his freshman year, he made a long jump of 26 feet 9 inches (8.15m), a freshman record at the university. However, later in the year he suffered a major knee injury at the Southwest Conference (SWC) Outdoor Championships. Many observers feared that the injury might end Burrell's career. However, he underwent a diligent rehabilitation program and entered competitions again in 1988.

Burrell was soon picking up medals. In 1989 he took gold at the Mobil Outdoor Championships, where he won the 100 meters in 9.94 seconds. The following year he won both the 100 meters and 200 meters at the SWC Outdoor Championships. Burrell's success continued after the end of his college career. He beat Olympic champion Carl Lewis in the 100 meters at the Goodwill Games in Seattle in 1990 and again at the U.S. National Championships in New York in 1991, where Burrell broke the 100-meter world record with a time of 9.9 seconds. Another highlight of Burrell's

▲ *Leroy Burrell competes in the 200 meters at the 1991 World Championships in Tokyo, Japan.*

career was the 1992 Olympic Games in Barcelona, where he was part of the U.S. 4 x 100-meter relay team that won gold. A further individual 100m world record of 9.85 seconds followed in 1994.

Injuries
From the mid-1990s onward Burrell's career was increasingly hampered by injuries, and he retired from competitive sports in 1998. Burrell went on to become a coach, a role in which he has helped both collegiate and professional teams to great success. He is married to Michelle Finn, an Olympic sprinter, with whom he has two sons.

See also: Lewis, Carl

Further reading: Hunt, Donald. *Great Names in Black College Sports*. Indianapolis, IN: Masters Press, 1996.
http://uhcougars.collegesports.com/sports/w-track/mtt/burrell_leroy00.html (Extended biography of Burrell).

KEY DATES

1967	Born in Lansdowne, Pennsylvania, on February 21.
1985	Almost singlehandedly wins a state championship for Penn Wood High School.
1991	Sets a world record of 9.9 seconds in the 100-meter sprint at the U.S. National Championships.
1992	Wins a gold medal at the Olympic Games as part of the U.S. 4 x 100-meter relay team.
1998	Retires from competitive sports.

BURRELL, Thomas J.
Advertising Executive

Thomas J. Burrell is the chairman and chief executive officer of Burrell Communications Group, a powerful advertising agency with annual earnings of about $200 million. Burrell was born on March 18, 1939, on the South Side of Chicago. Having done well in school, he attended Chicago Roosevelt University from 1957, completing a three-year BA in English and discovering an ambition and enthusiasm for advertising.

From mailroom to boardroom

Burrell's first job after leaving the university in 1960 was working in the mailroom of Wade Advertising in Chicago. In 1961 he was promoted to the position of copywriter ("copy" is the term used for advertising text) within the agency. He left in 1964 to join the Leo Burnett Co., agency as a copy supervisor. Other moves came quickly, including a year spent with Foote, Cone, and Belding in London, England, before a return to Chicago to work for Needham, Harper, and Steers.

By the early 1970s Burrell sensed that African Americans were being underserved by advertising. In a bold move he left his job and set up his own company, Burrell Communications Group, in 1971 to target the African American market. Starting with only three people in the company, Burrell developed his new business and began to attract major new clients, including the fast-food chain McDonald's in 1972. The 1980s dawned with Burrell Communications as the largest African American agency in the United States. In 1986 Burrell was given the Advertising Person of the Year Award in Chicago and also received the Albert Lasker Award for Lifetime Achievement in Advertising. From the 1980s to today Burrell has driven his agency to ever-greater heights, acquiring clients that include Proctor and Gamble, Coca-Cola, Jack Daniel's, and Sears, Roebuck, and Co.

Recognition

Burrell has gathered numerous honors besides those for his work in advertising, including the Missouri Honor Medal for Distinguished Service in Journalism in 1990. In 2003 he also received the HistoryMaker Award from Chicago's DuSable Museum of African American History. As well as involving himself in the advertising world, Burrell gives much of his time to charitable and educational activities.

▼ *Thomas Burrell, seen here in 1997, gained success in advertising by marketing to African Americans.*

KEY DATES

1939 Born in Chicago, Illinois, on March 18.

1960 Graduates with a degree in English from Chicago Roosevelt University.

1961 Becomes a copywriter at Wade Advertising, Chicago.

1971 Founds Burrell Communications Group.

1986 Receives the Albert Lasker Award for Lifetime Achievement in Advertising.

1990 Receives the Missouri Honor Medal for Distinguished Service in Journalism from the University of Missouri's School of Journalism.

2003 Receives the HistoryMaker Award from DuSable Museum of African American History in Chicago.

Further reading: Moss, Janice Ward. *The History and Advancement of African Americans in the Advertising Industry, 1895–1999.* Lewiston, NY: Edwin Mellen Press, 2003. www.burrell.com (The Burrell Communications Group site).

BURROUGHS, Margaret
Artist, Writer

Margaret Taylor Burroughs had a diverse career as an artist in several media, a writer, a teacher of art history, and a civil rights activist. She and her second husband, Charles Gordon Burroughs, founded the Ebony Museum of Negro History in Chicago, Illinois, the first museum of African American history and culture.

Margaret Taylor was born in Louisiana in 1917 but moved with her family to Chicago when she was five. She graduated from Chicago Teachers' College in 1937 and gained a BA and an MA (1948) in art education from the Art Institute of Chicago. In 1939 she married artist Edward Goss, but they divorced. Burroughs taught art history at DuSable High School in Chicago for 21 years.

Artist and writer

Burroughs recognized the link between art and politics in the work of the 20th-century Mexican muralists Diego Rivera and Clemente Orozco, and like them used her art as a vehicle for social awareness and change. Her art is figurative, but her preferred media of carved stone and lithography, a type of printing, give it an abstract

▼ *Margaret Burroughs is an accomplished visual artist and a pioneer in the black cultural movement.*

appearance reminiscent of African art. Her writings mirror her art as a vehicle for social awareness, fusing folk traditions with contemporary issues. Her first book was for children, *Jasper, the Drummin' Boy*, and was published in 1947. Later books include *Did You Feed My Cow? Rhymes and Games from City Streets and Country Lanes* (1955), a book of poems for children, *What Shall I Tell My Children Who Are Black?* (1968), and a second volume of poems *Africa, My Africa* (1970).

As African heritage became a source of pride in the 1960s, Burroughs and her husband founded the Ebony Museum in their home on the South Side of Chicago in 1961. The museum grew in importance; on her retirement in 1968 Burroughs transferred it to the DuSable Museum in Washington Park.

Awards and recognition

Burroughs has received many awards and honors for her achievements, including a doctorate of humane letters from Lewis University, Illinois, and honorary degrees from the Art Institute of Chicago, Chicago State, and Columbia colleges. In 1980 she was one of 10 black artists honored by President Jimmy Carter, in 1982 she received an Excellence in Art Award from the National Association of Negro Museums, and in 1986 Chicago's mayor Harold Washington (1922–1987) made February 1 "Dr. Margaret Burroughs Day" in the city. Burroughs remains actively involved in the institutions she founded.

Further reading: Leininger, Theresa A. "Margaret Taylor Burroughs" in *Notable Black American Women*. (Edited by Jessie Carney Smith.) Detroit, MI: Gale Research, 1992. http://www.teenchicago.org/documents/558_M_Burroughs.pdf (Interview with Burroughs).

BURROUGHS, Nannie Helen
Educator

Nannie Helen Burroughs fought for civil rights, women's suffrage, and an end to lynchings and discrimination. She was an educator and an innovative leader of black women's issues.

Burroughs was born in Virginia in 1879. When her father died, her mother moved to Washington, D.C., in 1883 so her daughter could get a better education. In 1896 Burroughs graduated with honors from high school. Denied a post as a domestic science teacher because of her race, she found a job in Philadelphia as an assistant editor for the *Christian Banner*, a Baptist newspaper. In 1886 she joined the National Baptist Convention.

At age 21 Burroughs gave a speech entitled "How the Sisters Are Hindered from Helping." The speech helped galvanize support for the formation of the Women's Convention (WC), which became the nation's largest black women's organization. Burroughs served as its recording secretary (1900–1948) and president (1948–1961). In her first year she raised $1,000 by asking members for 50 cents each. Donations soon grew to $50,000.

▼ *This undated photograph shows Nannie Helen Burroughs as a young woman.*

KEY DATES	
1879	Born in Orange, Virginia, on May 2.
1900	Becomes recording secretary of the Women's Convention of the National Baptist Convention.
1909	Becomes founding president of the National Trade and Professional School for Women and Girls.
1922	Becomes president of National Association of Wage Earners.
1948	Becomes president of Women's Convention Auxiliary.
1961	Dies in Washington, D.C., on May 20.

Burroughs's activism was encouraged by meeting influential women like Margaret Washington (wife of Booker T. Washington) and Mary McLeod Bethune. In 1907 Burroughs started the National Trade and Professional School for Women and Girls in Washington, D.C. The school began as a stable, barn, and houses with no plumbing or electricity but was transformed and ready to open in 1909, after Burroughs raised $6,500.

Fundraising had become second-nature to Burroughs, who claimed to specialize "in the wholly impossible." She did not draw a salary. Student scholarships and teachers' salaries were paid from public donations. Public endorsements from educators like Carter G. Woodson and politicians like Adam Clayton Powell drew support. The school's curriculum combined vocational training with subjects such as Latin, drama, and black history. Burroughs called it the school of the three B's: the Bible, the Bath, and the Broom.

In 1907 Burroughs was awarded an honorary MA from Kentucky's Eckstein-Norton University. She died in 1961. In 1964 her school was renamed after her. In 1975 the mayor of Washington, D.C., named May 10 Nannie Burroughs Day in the District of Columbia.

See also: Bethune, Mary McLeod; Powell, Adam Clayton; Washington, Booker T.; Woodson, Carter G.

Further reading: Easter, Opal V. *Nannie Helen Burroughs.* New York, NY: Taylor & Francis Inc. 1995.
http://www.toptags.com/aama/bio/women/nburroughs.htm (Biography).

BURTON, Annie L.
Writer

Born into slavery in about 1858, Annie L. Burton is remembered for her account of her childhood spent on a plantation near Clayton, Alabama, during the Civil War (1861–1965). The work, *Memories of Childhood's Slavery Days*, provides an important record of Southern life and the disruption suffered by both black and white southerners immediately after the Emancipation Proclamation of 1863, which freed the slaves in the South.

Plantation life

Little about Burton's life is known beyond the account she herself provided in her memoirs. Her father was a white man who had been born in Liverpool, England. Her mother was the household's cook, who had grown up together with her mistress. One day they had an argument, and Burton's mother was whipped for the first time in her life. She ran away from the plantation, abandoning her children.

Burton describes her life on the plantation as "happy." "Our days were spent roaming about from plantation to plantation, not knowing or caring what things were going on in the great world outside our little realm."

However, she also describes the poverty and injustices suffered by the slaves, and the frequent whippings to which both adults and children were subjected. She relates how one man was hanged "for killing a blood hound and biting off an overseer's ear." Nonetheless, the abolition of slavery causes Burton to regret the passing of "the beautiful, proud Sunny South." For many liberated African Americans freedom brought with it insecurity, uncertain job prospects, and different kinds of racism from slavery.

Later life

Burton's mother returned in 1865 and demanded the return of her children. When her former mistress refused she threatened to report her to the authorities and the children were allowed to leave. The family went to live on a

▲ *This photograph of Annie L. Burton is likely to have been taken about 1909, when her book was published.*

neighboring plantation and then moved to Clayton. Burton found work as a nursemaid, and her employer, a music teacher, taught her to read, write, sew, and cook. After her mother's death Burton took care of the three younger children and in 1879 moved to Boston to work as a family cook. Later she set up a restaurant in Jacksonville, Florida. Business was good, but the summer temperatures drove her back to Boston. In 1888 she married Samuel Burton, who worked as a valet in Braintree. Burton began writing her memoirs at the suggestion of the headmaster of Franklin Evening School, where she attended classes. *Memories of Childhood's Slavery Days* was published in 1909. There is no record of when Burton died.

See also: Slavery

Further reading: Davis, Charles T., and Henry Louis Gates, Jr. *The Slave's Narrative.* New York, NY: Oxford University Press, 1985.
docsouth.unc.edu/burton/burton.html (Free, downloadable edition of Burton's work).

KEY DATES	
1858	Born near Clayton, Alabama, about this time.
1865	Burton goes to live with her mother.
1879	Moves to Boston, Massachusetts.
1909	Publishes *Memories of Childhood's Slavery Days*.

BURTON, LeVar
Actor, Director, Producer, TV Host, Writer

Winner of numerous awards, LeVar Burton is recognized for his exceptional talents as an actor, director, producer, TV host, and writer.

Early career

Levardis Robert Martyn Burton, Jr., was born on February 16, 1957, in Landstuhl, West Germany, where his father was posted on United States military duty. At age 13 he entered a Catholic seminary to study for the priesthood. After four years, realizing that his talents were in theater, he went to the University of South Carolina School of Theater on a full scholarship. In his second year he got the role of Kunta Kinte in the celebrated TV series *Roots* (1977). Burton has since had starring roles in several highly rated movies, including *One in a Million: The Ron LeFlore Story* (1978), the Emmy-nominated *Dummy* (1979), *Roots: The Gift* (1988), *Parallel Lives* (1994), and *Ali* (2001). He is, perhaps, most famous for his role as Geordi La Forge, the blind lieutenant in the *Star Trek* series.

Hosting and writing

Burton has produced and hosted the Emmy-award winning children's series *Reading Rainbow* since 1983. He is also the voice of Kwame in the animated children's series *Captain Planet*, which educates children about the environment. Burton's directorial credits include several episodes of *Star Trek* and the biographical feature film *The Tiger Woods Story* (1998), which was nominated for three Emmys. In 1997 Burton published his first novel, *Aftermath*, a science fiction story set in the year 2019.

▲ **After becoming a successful screen star, LeVar Burton turned his hand to directing and writing.**

Burton's achievements have been widely recognized. In 1990 he received a star on Hollywood's Walk of Fame. From 1996 to 1997 he was a member of the National Commission on Library and Information Sciences (NCLIS) to advise the government on electronic information policy. In 2000 he received a Grammy for narrating the talking book *The Autobiography of Martin Luther King, Jr.* For *Reading Rainbow* Burton received awards from the National Association for the Advancement of Colored People (NAACP) in 1994, 1996, 1999, 2002, and 2003.

Burton is married to Stephanie Cozart Burton. They have a daughter, Michaela.

See also: King, Martin Luther, Jr.; Woods, Tiger

Further reading: http://www.startrek.com (Official Startrek website with biographies).

KEY DATES	
1957	Born in Landstuhl, West Germany, on February 16.
1977	Makes acting debut in the role of Kunta Kinte in *Roots*.
1983	Becomes TV host of *Reading Rainbow*.
1990	Awarded a star in Hollywood's Walk of Fame.
1993	Makes directorial debut with *Star Trek*.
2000	Wins Grammy for *The Autobiography of Martin Luther King, Jr.*
2002	Directs first feature film, *Blizzard*.

BUSTA Rhymes
Rapper, Actor

Famed for his quirky personality, rasping vocals, and distinctive ragga-inspired delivery—an influence of his Jamaican heritage—New York rapper and occasional actor Busta Rhymes was born Trevor Smith, Jr., on May 20, 1972, in East Flatbush, Brooklyn. He spent his early childhood in Uniondale, where he met MCs Charlie Brown, Dinco D., and Cut Monitor Milo, before his family moved to Long Island in 1983. Smith reunited with his former high school friends as the group Leaders of the New School, and the four signed with Elektra Records in 1990. It was Chuck D. from Public Enemy—the inspirational pioneers of hip-hop and fellow Long Islanders—who gave Busta Rhymes his stage name. Leaders of the New School released two albums and were much respected in the hip-hop underground by the time they broke up in 1994.

Solo success

Busta Rhymes worked with artists such as Boyz II Men, Mary J. Blige, and TLC before signing with Elektra as a solo artist. In 1996 he released his hugely successful debut album, *The Coming*, and the Top 10 single "Woo-Hah! Got You All in Check." With his innovative, word-twisting vocal style, Busta Rhymes became the toast of the hip-hop community and an international star. Albums that followed included *When Disaster Strikes* (1997), *Extinction Level Event: The Final World Front* (1998), and *Anarchy* (2000), which yielded such chart hits as "Put Your Hands Where My Eyes Could See" (1997), "Gimme Some More" (1999), and "What's It Gonna Be?!," a 1999 collaboration with Janet Jackson.

After a decline in musical success and several movie projects, including a remake of the classic blaxploitation movie *Shaft* (2000), Rhymes signed with the new label J Records in 2001. His fifth studio album, *Genesis* (2001), featuring production by legends Dr. Dre and the Neptunes, represented a return to form with the hits "Break Ya Neck" and "Pass the Courvoisier." Rhymes's second album on J Records in 2002, *It Ain't Safe No More*, was a commercial disappointment but did feature a duet with Mariah Carey, "I Know What You Want," that reached the Top 10.

Following months of speculation and rumor, Busta Rhymes signed with Dr. Dre's Aftermath Entertainment label in February 2004, joining such notables of the hip-hop world as Eminem and 50 Cent. His debut with the label, "The Big Bang," was released in 2005.

KEY DATES	
1972	Born in Brooklyn, New York, on May 20.
1990	Leaders of the New School sign with Elektra Records.
1996	Releases his debut solo album, *The Coming*.
2000	Involved in movie projects, including *Finding Forrester* and the remake of *Shaft*.
2001	*Genesis* is released on J Records.
2004	Signs with Dr. Dre's label Aftermath Entertainment.

▼ *Busta Rhymes performs in concert at the Zenith in Paris, France, in December 2003.*

See also: Black Identity and Popular Culture; Dr. Dre; 50 Cent; Jackson, Janet

Further reading: Bogdanov, Vladimir, Chris Woodstra, Stephen Thomas Erlewine, and John Bush. *All Music Guide to Hip-Hop: The Definitive Guide to Rap and Hip-Hop*. San Francisco, CA: Backbeat Books, 2003.
http://www.allmusic.com/cg/amg.dll?p=amg&sql=11:ez5uakok5m3m~T1 (Biographical information and discography from the All Music site).

CALIVER, Ambrose
Educator, Public Servant

A leading black educator of the early and mid-20th century, Ambrose Caliver fought for better educational opportunities for African Americans and was an early supporter of the emerging adult education movement.

Fighting for African American education

Caliver was born in Saltsville, Virginia, on February 25, 1894. He attended public schools in Virginia and Tennessee, and graduated from Knoxville College in 1915. He earned an MA from the University of Wisconsin in 1920 and in 1930 a PhD from Columbia University. Meanwhile he had also launched a career in education, becoming the first African American dean of the historically black Fisk University, Nashville, Tennessee, in 1927. In 1930 Caliver became specialist in black education in the federal Office of Education in Washington, D.C.

Caliver was passionate about black education at a time when education in the United States was almost entirely segregated. Black schools and colleges often received far

▼*Ambrose Caliver addressed racial inequality in the education system in the United States.*

KEY DATES

1894   Born in Saltsville, Virginia, on February 25.

1915   Graduates from Knoxville College, Tennessee.

1927   Becomes the first African American dean of Fisk University, Nashville, Tennessee.

1930   Becomes specialist in Negro education in the federal Office of Education.

1955   Becomes chief of the Adult Education Section of the Office of Education.

1962   Dies in Washington, D.C., on January 29.

less financial support than their white counterparts. His tireless research while at the Office of Education resulted in numerous articles and reports in which he addressed racial inequalities throughout the American education system. His work led to the establishment of several federal bodies charged with the development of black education, including the National Advisory Committee on the Education of Negroes (1930–1950).

Educating adults

During his later career Caliver became increasingly concerned with the level of illiteracy among American adults, particularly in the African American population. As director of the Project for Literacy Education from 1946 and chief of the Adult Education Section of the Office of Education from 1955, Caliver was able to coordinate research into illiteracy and to develop specific educational programs aimed at adults. In 1961 his work was honored when he was elected president of the Adult Education Association of the United States.

See also: Historically Black Colleges and Universities; Segregation and Integration

Further reading: Wilkins, Theresa. "Ambrose Caliver: Distinguished Civil Servant," *Journal of Negro History*, Spring 1962, pp. 212–214.
www. 2souls.com/main/Knowledge%20Warehouse/Caliver/caliver.htm (Biography).

CALLIER, Terry
Musician

Terry Callier is a popular folk–jazz artist whose musical career falls into two parts: initial success in the 1960s and 1970s and a revival in the 1990s.

Born on Chicago's North Side on May 24, 1945, Callier grew up in the Cabrini Green housing projects, which are notorious for gangs, drugs, murder, and misery. At an early age he displayed an interest in and love of music. He began to play the piano when he was three years old, and by 11 he was writing his own songs and appearing in doo-wop groups. He later learned to play the guitar in college.

Determined to succeed, Callier hounded Chess Records, an independent label producing some of the best blues, rhythm and blues (R&B), and jazz in Chicago. Aged 17 he was given a contract and recorded four tracks; one of them, "Look at Me Now," became his 1962 debut single.

Folk–jazz

In 1965 Callier recorded *The New Folk Sound of Terry Callier* for Prestige; but the master tapes were lost, and the album's release was delayed until 1968. Meanwhile Callier became popular on the Chicago club scene.

In 1970 Callier signed on with childhood friend Jerry Butler's Chicago Songwriters Workshop. Callier had a hit in 1972 when he cowrote with Larry Wade "The Love We Had Stays on My Mind" for the Dells. Cadet offered him a contract. With producer Charles Stepney, Callier released three albums over the next three years that showcased his unique blend of jazz, soul, and folk: *Occasional Rain*, *What Color Is Love?*, and *I Just Can't Help Myself*. The last two albums brought him acclaim from R&B audiences, and Callier went on national tour, performing with George Benson and Gil Scott-Heron among others; but his records did not sell well, and Cadet dropped him.

KEY DATES	
1945	Born in Chicago, Illinois, on May 24.
1962	Receives a contract with Chess Records.
1981	Gives up music to become a computer programmer.
1998	Releases *TimePeace*.
2004	Goes on sellout international tour.

▲ *Terry Callier was not desperate to get back into music and has been surprised by his recent success.*

Callier recorded *Fire on Ice* and *Turn to Love* with Elektra's Jazz Fusion label in 1978 and 1979, and he had a pop chart hit with the single "Sign of the Times." He was, however, dropped by Elektra; and when he gained custody of his only daughter in 1981, he decided to give up recording for a more steady job. He became a computer programmer and went back to college to study sociology.

A second chance

In the early 1990s Callier's music career received a kickstart when acid jazz fans began to listen to his earlier recordings. Eddie Pillar, head of UK label Acid Jazz, asked permission to rerelease Callier's 1983 single "I Don't Want to See Myself (Without You)," which became a hit on the British club scene. Callier recorded three songs with Beth Orton and released a new album, *TimePeace*, on her label in 1998. In 1999 *Lifetime* was rereleased. Playing to new audiences at festivals and touring internationally, Callier began to receive the acclaim he deserved.

See also: Benson, George; Scott-Heron, Gil

Further reading: http://www.vh1.com/artists/az/ callier_terry/artist.jhtml (Page on Callier on Vh1 site).

CALLOWAY, Cab
Bandleader, Composer, Musician

Ebullient jazz composer, bandleader, singer, and entertainer Cab Calloway influenced a generation of jazz singers and thrilled audiences with his inventive, energetic scat technique.

Cabell Calloway III was born in New York in 1907. After graduating from high school in Baltimore, Calloway toured with the revue show *Plantation Days* to Chicago, where he attended law school and sang with the Alabamians. Calloway quickly realized his passion for performance and dropped out of law school to lead the band. Moving back to New York, Calloway led a number of bands and sang in Fats Waller's musical *Connie's Hot Chocolates* before taking over the swing band the Missourians. In 1930 they opened at Harlem's Cotton Club and changed their name to Cab Calloway and His Cotton Club Orchestra. He led the band for 18 years; it became the highest paid band of the era.

The Hi-di-Ho Man

Charismatic with a distinctive voice, Calloway was famous for bounding around the stage as he performed. A legendary scat singer, Calloway would rapidly improvise sounds such as "skeeten, scaten, hi de ho," to a melody; he also invented his own dialect using Harlem street language. Calloway and his orchestra began recording in 1930 and hit the big time with "Minnie the Moocher," one of a series of songs written by Calloway about Harlem that featured the fictional characters Minnie the Moocher and Smoky Joe. By 1932 a combination of regular live broadcasts from the Cotton Club, extensive touring, and hit records ensured that Calloway was a household name. His fame was increased by several animated appearances in Betty Boop cartoons, where he sang "Minnie the Moocher" and "St. James Infirmary Blues."

KEY DATES	
1907	Born in Rochester, New York, on December 25.
1930	Becomes leader of the Harlem Cotton Club Orchestra.
1931	Records "Minnie the Moocher."
1980	Has supporting role in *The Blues Brothers*.
1994	Dies in Hockessin, Delaware, on November 18.

As the age of the big band drew to a close, Calloway toured Europe and the United States with *Porgy and Bess* from 1952 to 1954. He also was featured in a number of movies, including *Stormy Weather* (1943), *The Cincinnati Kid* (1965), and *The Blues Brothers* (1980). Calloway died in 1994 and the following year was inducted into the International Jazz Hall of Fame.

▼ *Cab Calloway (right) sings with the Cotton Club Orchestra in 1934.*

See also: Waller, Fats

Further reading: Shipton, Alyn. *The Hi-de-Ho Man: The Life of Cab Calloway.* New York, NY: Oxford University Press, 2005 http://www.cabcalloway.cc/timeline.htm (Timeline).

CAMPANELLA, Roy
Baseball Player

Baseball legend Roy Campanella, nicknamed "Campy," established the African American presence within major league baseball. He was born on November 19, 1921, in Homestead, Pennsylvania, his last name coming from his Italian father. By his early teens he was demonstrating a natural aptitude for baseball, and at age 15 he was signed to play for the Baltimore Elite Giants of the Negro National League. Although he was able to play only on weekends because of school commitments, Campanella became a rising star of the league.

Professional player

In 1938 Campanella began playing for the Giants full time, and his formidable power as batter, fielder, and catcher helped them to championship titles in 1939. Campanella played with the Giants until 1947, apart from an interlude of nearly two years between 1942 and 1943 when he played in the Mexican League. During this period his talent was spotted by the Brooklyn Dodgers, and he became a member of their International League team in 1947. In the same year he received his second Most Valuable Player (MVP) award. He took his full position in the Dodgers in 1948 and remained with the team for nearly a decade.

In the 1950s Campanella reached the peak of his career; he was named the National League MVP in 1951, 1953, and 1955, and played in five World Series between 1949 and 1956—he was a key ingredient in the Dodgers' World Series championship in 1955. In 1953 alone Campanella scored 103 runs, including 41 home runs.

▼ *In 1953, when this picture was taken, Dodgers' star Roy Campanella was enjoying his greatest season.*

Tragedy

In January 1958, with his career going strong, Campanella drove his car home from the liquor store he owned and ran when not playing baseball. The roads were icy, and he lost control of the car, which smashed into a telephone pole. Although he survived the crash, Campanella suffered major spinal injuries and was left severely and permanently disabled. The baseball world was shocked by the accident. In 1959 the Yankees and the Dodgers held an exhibition game at Los Angeles Coliseum to honor his achievements in front of a record crowd of more than 93,000 spectators. Despite being paralyzed from the chest down and confined to a wheelchair, Campanella worked for the Dodgers as a special coach of young catchers. In 1974 his autobiography, *It's Good to Be Alive,* was made into a movie. He died of a heart attack in Woodland Hills in 1993.

Further reading: Campanella, Roy. *It's Good to Be Alive.* Lincoln, NE: University of Nebraska Press, 1995.
http://www.roycampanella.com (Official Roy Campanella site).

KEY DATES	
1921	Born in Homestead, Pennsylvania, on November 19.
1936	Begins playing for the Baltimore Elite Giants while still in school.
1947	Moves to the Brooklyn Dodgers.
1953	Scores National League best with 142 RBIs.
1958	Disabled in an automobile accident.
1969	Inducted into the Baseball Hall of Fame.
1993	Dies in Woodland Hills, California, on June 26.

CAMPBELL, Milt
Athlete

No list of the great all-around athletes in the history of sports would be complete without Milton Gray Campbell of Plainfield, New Jersey, who was born on December 9, 1933. During the 1950s Campbell won Olympic gold and silver medals in the decathlon, played professional football, and posted a world record in the high hurdles. A big, strong, fast, and remarkably versatile athlete, Campbell has been inducted into 10 different athletic halls of fame and is the only member of both the National Track and Field and the International Swimming and Diving halls of fame.

An outstanding career

Few could have foreseen the extraordinary athletic future of Campbell as a tall and lanky youth. "No one ever thought I would make it," Campbell said, "no one except for me." By high school he had blossomed physically and earned All-American honors as a swimmer. At age 18 he qualified to represent the United States as a decathlete at

▼ **Milt Campbell crosses the line during the decathlon at the 1956 Summer Olympics.**

the 1952 Summer Olympic Games in Helsinki, Finland. Campbell took home the silver medal when he finished second to two-time champion and fellow American Bob Mathias. The next year Campbell won the decathlon at the National Track and Field Championships. After finishing high school, he enrolled at Indiana University.

In 1956 Campbell competed in his second Olympics in Melbourne, Australia, where he became the first African American to win a gold medal in the decathlon. The 7,937 points he scored in the competition's 10 events established a new Olympic record and put him ahead of fellow African American Rafer Johnson, who finished second. The following year Campbell set a world record when he ran the 120-yard high hurdles in 13.4 seconds; later he also established a world indoor best by running the 60-yard high hurdles in 7.0 seconds.

Campbell spent the fall of 1957 playing in the National Football League as a halfback with the Cleveland Browns and later played for the Montreal Alouettes in the Canadian Football League. He was elected to the United States Olympic Hall of Fame in 1992 and in 2000 was voted the greatest New Jersey athlete of the 20th century.

Since his days in athletics Campbell has been involved in local politics and inner-city youth programs, and is highly regarded as a motivational speaker.

See also: Johnson, Rafer

Further reading: Ashe, Arthur. *A Hard Road to Glory: A History of the African-American Athlete since 1946.* New York, NY: Amistad Press, 1993.
http://www.blackathletesportsnetwork.net/Track&Field/tf052701.html (Black Athlete Sports Network article).

CARA, Irene
Actor, Singer, Dancer

Award-winning actor, singer, dancer, and songwriter Irene Cara was born to an African Puerto Rican father and Cuban American mother on March 18, 1959. By the age of eight Cara had made her Broadway debut in the musical *Maggie Flynn* and recorded her first album in Spanish. By age 10 Cara had starred both on and off Broadway and performed with Stevie Wonder, Sammy Davis, Jr., and Roberta Flack. In 1971 Cara played a member of a rock group in the educational television series *The Electric Company* alongside Bill Cosby, Rita Moreno, and Morgan Freeman. Making her film debut at 16, Cara starred in *Aaron Loves Angela* (1975) and the cult musical *Sparkle* (1976). Further significant roles followed in the critically acclaimed mini-series *Roots: The Next Generation (1979)* and *The Guyanna Tragedy: The Story of Jim Jones* (1980).

An international star

The 1980s brought Cara international stardom. Her performance as Coco Hernandez in the hit musical *Fame* (1980) saw her nominated for two Grammys and a Golden Globe. The film's soundtrack went multiplatinum, and Cara notched hit singles with "Fame" and "Out Here on My Own." She recorded a solo album, *Anyone Can See*, and won a National Association for the Advancement of Colored People Image Award for Best Actress for the NBC movie *Sister, Sister* in 1982. Cara reached the pinnacle of her success when she was invited to cowrite and sing the title track for the movie *Flashdance* (1983). The resulting single, "Flashdance… What a Feelin'," spent six weeks at No. 1 and won Cara two American Music Awards, two Grammys, a Golden Globe, a People's Choice Award, and an Academy Award for Best Original Song.

▲ *Irene Cara, pictured here at a film premiere in 2001, is best known for her 1980s hit singles "Fame" and "Flashdance… What a Feelin'."*

Cara continued to make music in the mid-1980s, releasing two further albums and scoring several hit singles. She starred opposite Clint Eastwood and Burt Reynolds in the gangster comedy movie *City Heat* (1985) and toured extensively throughout Europe and Asia. Cara had a Europe-wide hit in 2000 after teaming up with DJ Bobo to remake "Flashdance… What a Feelin'." After her success in the 1980s Cara has written a screenplay, *A Waltz with Destiny*, and began to manage the all-female band Hot Caramel, of which she is a member.

KEY DATES

1959   Born in New York City on March 18.

1980   Stars as Coco Hernandez in the movie *Fame*.

1983   Cowrites and sings the award-winning "Flashdance … What a Feelin'" from the movie *Flashdance*.

2000   Has a Top Five European-wide hit with DJ Bobo with a remake of "Flashdance…What a Feelin'."

See also: Cosby, Bill; Davis, Sammy, Jr.; Freeman, Morgan; Wonder, Stevie

Further reading: Bronson, Fred. *The Billboard Book of Number One Hits*. New York, NY: Billboard Books, 2003. http://www.irenecara.com/bio.htm (Cara's official site).

CAREW, Rod
Baseball Player

Rodney Cline Carew was born—on a train—on October 1, 1945, in Gatun in the Panama Canal Zone, a territory within Panama that was controlled by the United States until 1999. Carew's early interest in baseball was encouraged by his family, who fashioned balls out of taped-up wads of paper, and he was soon progressing up through the school teams. In 1961 Carew moved with his mother and siblings to live in New York City, close to Yankee Stadium, and it was here that his sporting abilities really began to take shape.

Playing for the Twins

In 1967 Carew was signed to play for the Minnesota Twins, beginning as a second baseman but quickly moving on to other positions while demonstrating undeniable skill with the bat. His first professional year culminated in his being voted American League Rookie of the Year; he continued to add to his awards throughout the 1960s, despite losing some significant periods of playing time through military service and injury.

▼ *In 1983, when this picture was taken, Rod Carew started the season with a batting average of .500.*

KEY DATES	
1945	Born in Gatun, Panama Canal Zone, on October 1.
1967	Plays professionally with the Minnesota Twins.
1977	Attains a .388 season batting average.
1979	Traded to the California Angels.
1983	Begins the season with a .500 batting average.
1986	Retires from professional baseball.
1991	Inducted into the Baseball Hall of Fame.

By the beginning of the 1970s Carew had established himself as one of baseball's foremost batters; he maintained a batting average of over .300 for 15 consecutive seasons. A batting average of .300 is the mark of a top player, while a .400 average is rarely achieved. Carew had won all the major batting titles between 1972 and 1975, but his outstanding year was 1977, when he came close to achieving the .400 average. He fell short by just eight hits and achieved an average of .388 with 128 runs. Carew also won the American League's Most Valuable Player in 1977 and was named to 18 straight All-Star teams.

Moving on

Carew served the Twins well until a dispute over pay led to his being traded to the California Angels in 1979. Initially the spectacular performances he had given while playing for the Twins continued with the Angels, and he maintained his batting average at over .300. However, as the 1980s went on injuries began to plague Carew. Although he got his 3,000th hit on August 4, 1985, his batting average had dropped to .280. He retired in 1986 and entered the Baseball Hall of Fame in 1991. After retiring as a professional player, Carew became a hitting coach for the California Angels and the Milwaukee Brewers.

Further reading: Carew, Rod. *Carew.* New York, NY: Simon & Schuster, 1979.
http://www.thebaseballpage.com/past/pp/carewrod/default.htm (Extensive game and biographical information).

CARMICHAEL, Stokely
Civil Rights Activist, Black Panther

Stokely Carmichael was a civil rights activist and a leader of the Black Panther Party. From 1969 he became known as Kwame Toure. He is most famous as the originator of the slogan "black power."

Early years
Carmichael was born in Port of Spain, Trinidad, in 1941. In 1952 he immigrated to the United States with his parents, Adolphus and Mabel Carmichael. The family settled in New York, where Carmichael graduated from the Bronx High School of Science in 1960. He turned down scholarships from several white universities to attend the historically black Howard University in Washington, D.C. He graduated in 1964 with a BS in philosophy.

While in college Carmichael became active in the civil rights movement and participated in numerous sit-ins and other protests against segregation. He became a leader of the Non-Violent Action Group (NAG), a militant student protest organization, and was also involved with the Congress of Racial Equality (CORE). In 1961 he was one of several Freedom Riders who traveled through the South challenging segregation laws on interstate transportation. For his participation he was arrested and jailed for 50 days in Jackson, Mississippi.

Carmichael was rapidly losing faith in the capacity of civil disobedience to deliver the desired changes in American society. Throughout the United States he saw that peaceful rallies were being broken up by violence, beatings were increasingly common, and several civil rights activists had been murdered. In an interview in *Life* magazine he explained his change of attitude: "When I first heard about the Negroes sitting in at lunch counters down South, I thought they were just a bunch of publicity hounds. But one night when I saw those young kids on TV, getting back up on the lunch-counter stools after being knocked off them, sugar in their eyes, ketchup in their hair—well, something happened to me. Suddenly I was burning."

SNCC and "black power"
Carmichael had not yet given up hope of achieving his aims without violence, however, and in 1964 he joined the Student Nonviolent Coordinating Committee (SNCC), which supported the peaceful approach to desegregation advocated by Martin Luther King, Jr. In the summer of that year Carmichael went with a SNCC delegation to

▲ *Kwame Toure (Stokely Carmichael) in 1984, in Conakry, Guinea, where he moved in 1969.*

Alabama, where he helped run the Lowndes County Freedom Organization, an independent political party that adopted as its emblem an image of a black panther.

On his election as national chairman of the SNCC in June 1966 Carmichael immediately introduced a separatist policy and ousted whites from the organization. During a march in Greenville, Mississippi, he and his friend Willie Ricks encouraged fellow demonstrators with the cry "black power!" The slogan became the most popular rallying cry of the civil rights era and soon gave birth to a movement of the same name. It alarmed whites, however, many of whom blamed Carmichael for the riots that broke out in many cities during the summer of 1966.

Some black power aims—racial pride and political and economic self-determination for African Americans—were

INFLUENCES AND INSPIRATION

In interviews after Kwame Toure's death Mike Miller, a former SNCC member, collected reminiscences from people inspired by him. Black Panther Assata Shakur said, "As a young woman, Kwame was one of the people who changed my life. He helped give me the strength and courage to throw off the mental burden of white supremacy and to begin the long journey home, back to my African roots."

Hardy Frye, who joined CORE and SNCC, said Carmichael had "forced me to confront the whole thing of blackness in the movement." Phil Hutchings, SNCC national program secretary (1968–1969), said, "I think his enduring contribution is his life, which was a model of how to struggle, how not to sell out, how to maintain your principles through different time periods—from the civil rights period to now... his life is a model, an inspiration."

KEY DATES

1941 Born in Port of Spain, Trinidad, on June 29.

1952 Moves to the United States.

1966 Becomes national chairman of the Student Nonviolent Coordinating Committee (SNCC).

1968 Joins Black Panthers; marries singer Miriam Makeba.

1969 Moves to Guinea, West Africa; changes name to Kwame Toure.

1998 Dies in Conakry, Guinea, on November 15.

not substantially different from those of King and his followers, but many members of the new group were extremists who rejected white America and were prepared to counter violence with violence.

Carmichael then traveled to North Vietnam, China, and Cuba, where he spoke out against the political and economic repression of African Americans and denounced U.S. involvement in the Vietnam War (1964–1973). On his return to the United States the U.S. government confiscated his passport, which it held for 10 months.

In 1968 Carmichael left SNCC and joined the Black Panther Party, an urban black revolutionary organization founded two years previously in Oakland, California, and headed by Huey P. Newton and Eldridge Cleaver. Its name had been inspired by Carmichael's work in Alabama. The Black Panthers made Carmichael their honorary prime minister, in which role he called unsuccessfully for unity among the Southern Christian Leadership Conference (SCLC), the National Association for the Advancement of Colored People (NAACP), and the Nation of Islam so that they could work together in their struggle for civil rights and equality.

Carmichael's extremism marginalized him: He was feared by nearly every group in U.S. society regardless of its race or color. Moderate African Americans saw him as detrimental to the civil rights cause. Carmichael strongly defended his militancy: "No one ever talked about 'white power' because power in this country is white... the furor over 'black power' reveals how deep racism runs and the great fear which is attached to it."

Move to Africa

In 1969 Carmichael and his wife, the South African singer Miriam Makeba, left the United States and moved to Guinea, West Africa. There he changed his name to Kwame Toure in honor of two early socialist advocates of pan-Africanism, Ghanaian Kwame Nkrumah, who had led his country to independence from Britain, and Guinean Sékou Toure, his own mentor and patron.

Kwame Toure helped establish and then lead the All-African People's Revolutionary Party, an international political organization dedicated to pan-Africanism and the fight against racism toward people of African descent no matter where in the world they now lived. In 1971 he wrote *Stokely Speaks: Black Power Back to Pan-Africanism*.

In 1998, at age 57, Toure died in Guinea from complications of prostate cancer, which he had had treated in New York. To the end of his life he always answered the telephone with the words: "Ready for the Revolution."

See also: Civil Rights; Cleaver, Eldridge; King, Martin Luther, Jr.; Newton, Huey; National Organizations; Political Movements; Segregation and Integration

Further reading: Carmichael, Stokely, and Charles V. Hamilton. *Black Power: The Politics of Liberation in America*. New York, NY: Vintage, 1992.
http://www.interchange.org/KwameTure (Site dedicated to Kwame Toure).

CARNEGIE, M. Elizabeth
Nurse, Author, Activist

The pioneering work of Mary Elizabeth Carnegie helped pave the way for the equal recognition and treatment of African American nurses in the United States. In addition to holding posts in nursing, education, administration, and publishing, Carnegie wrote an acclaimed 150-year history of black nurses.

Born Mary Elizabeth Lancaster on April 19, 1916, in Baltimore, Maryland, Carnegie grew up in a segregated community and spent much of her childhood with her aunt and uncle following her parents' divorce. After her graduation from Dunbar High School she was forced to move to New York when she found few work opportunities close to home. There in 1934 she was accepted in a diploma program at Lincoln Hospital School of Nursing.

Groundbreaking achievements

Carnegie's early nursing education was followed by a period studying sociology at West Virginia State College, where she gained a BA in 1942. The following year, as assistant director of nursing, she initiated the first baccalaureate nursing program in Virginia at the historically black Hampton University, where the archives are now named in her honor.

In 1945 Carnegie was appointed dean and professor of the school of nursing at Florida A&M University. In the same year she became the first African American nurse to be appointed to the board of the Florida Nurses Association. However, Carnegie remained merely a courtesy member of the board until she became an official elected member in 1949. As Carnegie later noted: "Up until then, we were limited to [attending] maybe one business meeting...[full status] was the main thing I fought for."

From 1953 until 1978 Carnegie was employed at the *American Journal of Nursing*, where she continued to champion the cause of black nurses. During this period she also received a doctorate in administration from New York University. After officially retiring in 1978, Carnegie continued to hold a series of prestigious positions. In 1978 she was elected president of the American Academy of Nursing, while in 1988 she became chair of the American Nurses Association's Minority Fellowship Program Advisory Committee, a position that she held until 1999. She was also visiting professor at the schools of nursing at Hampton University, the University of North Carolina at Greensboro, and Pennsylvania State University.

The Path We Tread

Carnegie was also a prolific writer, contributing to nearly 20 books. Her most famous work was the award-winning *The Path We Tread: Blacks in Nursing Worldwide, 1854–1994*, the third edition of which was published in 1995. The book chronicles the experiences of African American nurses from the mid-19th century to the late 20th century. Carnegie used the work to celebrate the lives of such pioneers as Mary Seacole, a Jamaican nurse who tended to British troops in the Crimean War (1853–1856), and Susie King Taylor, who served with an all-black regiment, the First South Carolina Volunteers, in the Civil War (1861–1865). The book also tells the stories of the establishment of nursing colleges at black institutions and the struggles of black nurses during the civil rights era.

Despite her advancing age, Carnegie continued to work in the early 21st century, serving as editor emeritus of *Nursing Research*.

See also: Taylor, Susie King

Further reading: Carnegie, Mary Elizabeth. *The Path We Tread: Blacks in Nursing Worldwide, 1854–1994*. New York, NY: National League for Nursing Press, 2000
http://www.nursingworld.org/hof/carnegie.htm (Biography from American Nursing Association Hall of Fame).

KEY DATES

1916   Born in Baltimore, Maryland, on April 19.

1934   Enrolls at Lincoln Hospital School of Nursing.

1943   Initiates first BA nursing program in Virginia at Hampton University.

1945   Becomes dean of the school of nursing at Florida A&M University.

1953   Begins work at the *American Journal of Nursing*, where she remains for 25 years.

1995   Third edition of *The Path We Tread: Blacks in Nursing Worldwide* is published.

CARNEY, Harry
Musician

Harry Howell Carney first made the baritone saxophone popular as a solo instrument while playing as a lifetime member in the Duke Ellington Orchestra. For many years he was the major baritone saxophone soloist in jazz.

Learning his trade
Carney's family provided private musical training for him as a child first on the piano, then the clarinet, and later the alto saxophone. From the age of 13 he played in bands in Boston, meeting Duke Ellington when he played there in 1926. He moved to New York in 1927, where he joined the Duke Ellington Orchestra. The orchestra departed from the standard formula of dance bands by emphasizing the different sections of the band, so that Carney had the opportunity to fully develop his musical abilities. Carney played the alto and baritone saxophone and the bass

▼ *Harry Carney mastered the baritone saxophone, but he was also a gifted clarinet player.*

clarinet in the orchestra, but the baritone saxophone remained his favorite instrument. It had previously occupied a role only as a rhythm section instrument, but Carney developed his own rich sound and clear melodic style and turned it into a solo instrument. He mastered the technique of circular breathing to play long sequences of notes. The unique sound of Carney's baritone saxophone, in turn, contributed to the distinctive sound of Ellington's reed section.

Carney and the Duke
Carney once declared that he had no patience for composing, but he collaborated with Ellington on a number of compositions—*Rockin' in Rhythm'* (1931 with Irving Mills), *Ev'ah day* (1937), and *Blue Reverie* (1937)—and published one composition on his own, *Warm-up Folio for Baritone Saxophone: With Piano Accompaniment* (1943). Carney recorded extensively, notably on the albums *Harry Carney with Strings* (Clef, 1956) and *Moods for Girl and Boy* (Verve, 1956). Carney's collaboration with Duke Ellington was fruitful for both and lasted until Ellington's death in 1974. Their relationship was a close one. Carney drove Ellington to every gig; and when the Duke died, Carney famously said, "This is the worst day of my life. Without Duke I have nothing to live for." Carney remained with the orchestra under Mercer Ellington but died four months later.

KEY DATES	
1910	Born in Boston, Massachusetts, on April 1.
1927	Moves to New York and joins the Duke Ellington Orchestra.
1956	Records his own albums, *Harry Carney With Strings* and *Moods for Girl and Boy*.
1974	Dies in New York City on October 8.

See also: Ellington, Duke

Further reading: Stewart, Rex. *Jazz Masters of the 30s*. New York, NY: Da Capo Press, 1972.
http://www.geocities.com/BourbonStreet/Delta/8586/carney.html (Biography, pictures, and clips).

CARROLL, Diahann
Actor, Singer, Charity Campaigner

From teenage singer to the first black star of her own television series, Diahann Carroll has been a pioneer in the world of entertainment during the civil rights era.

Early start
Born in 1935 into a middle-class family, Carol Diahann Johnson was 10 years old when she won a scholarship to study at New York's High School of Music and Art in 1945. From there she went on to study at New York University while moonlighting as a model and nightclub singer.

Carroll's stage and film debuts came in 1954 with *House of Flowers* and *Carmen Jones* respectively, the latter a modernization of Bizet's opera *Carmen*. She went on to play Cara in the film version of *Porgy and Bess* (1959) and won a Tony Award for her part in the Broadway musical *No Strings* in 1962. Around this time she began a nine-year romance with the actor Sidney Poitier after working with him on *Porgy and Bess*.

Breaking stereotypes
Carroll's big break came in 1968 when she won the title role of *Julia*, becoming the first black actor to star in her own television series. A single mother and independent career woman, Julia was an improvement on the stereotypical roles commonly assigned to African American actors during the 1950s and 1960s.

In 1974 Carroll was nominated for an Oscar for her portrayal of a mother of six children living on welfare in *Claudine*, and there followed a string of TV shows and movies, including a role on *Dynasty* in the late 1980s. About this time Carroll wrote her autobiography. Expanding her interests further in 1997, she licensed her name to a line of clothing, accessories, and eyewear targeted at African American women. She also continued to act, sing, and make music.

A cancer survivor herself, Carroll promotes the early treatment and prevention of breast cancer. In 1992 she was awarded the Black Woman of Achievement Award from the National Association for the Advancement of Colored People (NAACP) and in 1996 was acknowledged by Project Inform for her work in the battle against HIV and AIDS.

▼ *In 2000 Diahann Carroll starred in three television movies, including* **Sally Hemings: An American Scandal.**

KEY DATES	
1935	Born in the Bronx, New York, on July 17.
1954	Broadway debut in *House of Flowers*; film debut in *Carmen Jones*.
1968	Stars in the television sitcom *Julia* until 1971; wins a Golden Globe for the role.
1997	Launches her own line of clothing and eyewear.
1998	Diagnosed and treated successfully for breast cancer.

See also: Poitier, Sidney

Further reading: Carroll, Diahann, and Ross Firestone. *Diahann: An Autobiography.* Boston, MA: Little, Brown & Co.,1986. http://www.lifetimetv.com/shows/ip/portraits/9802/9802_index.html (Biography).

CARSON, Benjamin S.
Neurosurgeon, Speaker, Writer

Benjamin Solomon Carson, Sr., is a pioneer in the field of pediatric neurosurgery, or brain surgery in children, and a positive role model for young Americans. Once a failing student with a violent temper, he turned himself around and in 1984 became director of pediatric neurosurgery at Johns Hopkins Hospital, Baltimore, where he was the youngest physician to head a major division.

Heading for jail or the grave
Carson had a difficult start in life. He was born in Detroit, Michigan, on September 18, 1951, into a poor downtown home. His mother, Sonja, had dropped out of school in third grade and married at age 13. Sonja was a major influence in Benjamin's later successes and those of his older brother, Curtis.

When Benjamin was eight, Sonja discovered that her husband had another wife and five other children. She filed for divorce and began working as a domestic help to support her sons. She was determined that the boys would have a better start in life than she had; but by the time Ben was in fifth grade, he was failing nearly every subject and had earned the nickname "Dummy" from his classmates. He had low self-esteem and a violent temper, and was liable to lash out at other children, sometimes even at his mother. As Carson remembers, "I was most likely to end up in jail, reform school, or the grave."

Horrified at Benjamin's report card and determined that her boys should succeed, Sonja resolved to take drastic steps (*see box*). Forced to learn, the boys found that they actually enjoyed it, and their grades improved. With a newfound hunger for knowledge and a dream of becoming a doctor, Benjamin went on to graduate as an honor student from high school and entered Yale University on an academic scholarship in 1968. His desire to become a doctor was influenced by the family's experiences with hospitals. Because they were on medical assistance, the family had to wait for hours before they were seen. Carson would dream that one day the loudspeaker would be calling his name as an attending doctor.

Gifted hands
After he graduated from Yale, Carson returned to his home state and attended the University of Michigan's School of Medicine. Although he initially wanted to specialize in psychiatry, by the end of his first year he found himself

▲ *During his career as a surgeon Benjamin S. Carson gained a reputation as a pioneer of lifesaving operations on very young children.*

drawn to neurosurgery. When he graduated in 1977, Carson secured a much sought-after surgical internship and later a residency in the neurosurgical department at Johns Hopkins Hospital, Baltimore.

At age 32, Carson was made director of pediatric neurosurgery at Johns Hopkins in 1984. Since then he has achieved world renown for saving the lives of children who had little hope of survival. In 1987, for example, he gained international acclaim as head of a surgical team of 70 that successfully separated conjoined twins who had been joined at the back of the head. Previous operations to

INFLUENCES AND INSPIRATION

Benjamin Carson's mother, Sonja, believed in her sons and encouraged them to believe in themselves. She was convinced he and his brother could be successful regardless of their poor background. Insisting "You weren't born to be a failure. You can do it," she motivated her sons to work hard at school. She also implemented her own education system at home, reducing the time her children watched television, refusing to let them play with friends until their homework was complete, and making them read two books each week from the Detroit Public Library. Although she could not read herself, Sonja made the boys submit written reports to her on each book they read. Although Carson originally disliked the new regime, he soon found that he was learning quickly, and that he enjoyed it. As his confidence improved, so did his grades.

separate twins joined in this way had resulted in the death of one or both of the patients.

Carson's other surgical achievements include his development of the first intrauterine procedure to relieve pressure on the brain of a fetal twin with hydrocephalus, a sometimes fatal buildup of fluid in the brain that causes the head to enlarge and can lead to deterioration of the brain. He also developed a procedure to treat cerebral hemispherectomy, in which a child with uncontrollable seizures can be cured by removal of half of his or her brain. His clinical patient care and research specialities were neurooncology (brain tumors), achondroplasia (human dwarfism), and congenital spinal deformities.

Reaching out

In 1997 Carson took a leave of absence from his medical practice to give motivational talks and lectures to young people around the country. With his wife Candy, with whom he has three sons, he designed a program called "Think Big," which aims to show young people how they can turn their aspirations and dreams into reality. He has written three books: an autobiography, *Gifted Hands* (1990), and two that outline his philosophy of life, *Think Big* (1996) and *Getting the Big Picture* (2000).

In addition to being chief of pediatric neurosurgery, Carson's appointments include professor of neurosurgery, plastic surgery, oncology, and pediatrics, and codirector of the Johns Hopkins Craniofacial Center. He performs about 400 surgeries each year—over twice the number of the average neurosurgeon. He has written some 90 neurosurgical publications and has received 24 honorary degrees and countless awards.

Carson and his wife have also founded the Carson Scholars Fund, a not-for-profit organization that rewards academic achievement with college funding. More recently he helped establish the Benevolent Endowment Network Fund (BEN), an organization that provides grants to assist uninsured or underinsured families with children who are facing specific types of medical care expenses, particularly neurosurgery.

A role model and inspiration to young and old alike, in 2001 Carson was elected by CNN and *Time Magazine* as one of America's top 20 physicians and scientists. Carson attributes his skills and talent as a surgeon to God. He has a strong religious faith, and as a sign of his belief he says a prayer before every operation.

KEY DATES

1951   Born in Detroit, Michigan, on September 18.

1973   Awarded a degree in psychology from Yale University, Connecticut.

1977   Awarded medical doctorate (MD) by the University of Michigan School of Medicine.

1984   Appointed director of pediatric neurosurgery at Johns Hopkins Hospital.

1987   Leads a surgical team that successfully separates conjoined twins.

1990   Publishes autobiography, *Gifted Hands*.

1997   Takes leave of absence to lecture young people on motivation and goal achievement.

2000   Publishes *Getting the Big Picture*.

2001   Named one of the top 20 physicians and scientists in the United States.

Further reading: Carson, Ben, and Cecil Murphey. *Gifted Hands.* Grand Rapids, MI: Zondervan, 1990.
www.achievement.org/autodoc/page/car1bio-1 (Biography and interview).

CARSON, Julia
Politician

Julia Carson was born on July 8, 1938, in Louisville, Kentucky, the daughter of a young single mother. Carson moved to Indianapolis when she was one year old. Life was financially hard for the family—Carson's mother worked as a housekeeper—but education provided a path to a brighter future. Carson attended the Crispus Attucks High School, graduating in 1955. She married shortly afterward but the relationship quickly broke down, leaving her to bring up two small children on her own.

Early political life

In 1965 Carson was hired by Indiana congressman Andrew Jacobs, Jr., to work as a legislative assistant. Encouraged by Jacobs, a Democrat, Carson soon began to pursue a political career of her own. Carson's political life was characterized by a desire to attack poverty and discrimination. Her values were shaped by her anger at the way in which her mother was treated when she was growing up. In 1972 Carson was elected to the Indiana House of Representatives. In 1976 she moved to the Indiana State Senate where she would serve for 14 years. During this time she also ran two businesses, the Cummins Engine Co., and a clothing store, J. Carson.

In 1990 Carson became trustee for the Center Township, a poverty relief agency in Indianapolis. The agency was about $20 million in debt when Carson took over. However, partially by initiating antifraud procedures, she managed to both turn the organization's finances around and improve its service. Her achievements earned her a Woman of the Year award from the *Indianapolis Star* in 1992.

Congresswoman

In 1996 Carson's mentor Jacobs retired from Congress. Carson ran for his office and won, defeating Republican Virginia Blankenbaker and becoming the first woman and the first African American Indiana had sent to Congress. Carson had to undergo emergency double bypass surgery for a heart complaint and was sworn into office from her hospital bed. The illness did not slow her down, however, and she became an energetic congresswoman, achieving reelection in 1998, 2000, 2002, and 2004.

In office Carson served on numerous influential committees and dealt with legislation on topics such as gun control and food safety. She was also a member of

KEY DATES	
1938	Born in Louisville, Kentucky, on July 8.
1955	Graduates from the Crispus Attucks High School.
1965	Begins work as a legislative assistant.
1972	Elected to the Indiana House of Representatives.
1976	Elected to Indiana State Senate.
1996	Elected to Congress.

the Committee on Financial Services, which oversaw the banking and insurance industries. The committee helped shape the Fair and Accurate Credit Transaction Act, passed by Congress in 2003, which gave consumers greater powers to fight identity theft and improved access to credit reports. Carson was also a member of the House Committee on Transportation and Infrastructure, in which role she influenced the Transportation Equity Act of 2005, helping secure $57.5 million to improve Indianapolis's transportation system.

In the spring of 2003 the United States and its allies went to war against Iraq, an oil-rich country under the rule of a dictator, Saddam Hussein. Carson had been a vocal critic of the George W. Bush administration's stance on Iraq. In 2002 she voted against giving the president unilateral authority to declare war on Iraq, arguing that it was Congress's prerogative.

As a woman who had to battle racism her whole life, it was fitting that it was Carson who sponsored the bill to award a Congressional Gold Medal to civil rights pioneer Rosa Parks. Of Carson's own struggle against prejudice, her mentor Jacobs commented: "The only thing some people learn from oppression is hatred and revenge. Others learn compassion and empathy. From the physical pain of material poverty and the mindlessly cruel persecution of nitwit racism, Julia Carson made her choice of hard work, compassion, and a pleasing sense of humor."

See also: Parks, Rosa

Further reading: Rummel, Jack. *African-American Social Leaders and Activists.* New York, NY: Facts on File, 2003.
http://www.juliacarson.org (Carson's official site).

CARTER, Benny
Musician, Arranger, Composer

Benny Carter mastered many instruments, including the alto saxophone, clarinet, piano, trumpet, and trombone, and played both in ensembles and solo. He was a gifted arranger, composer, and also a bandleader.

Developing his talent

Bennett Lester Carter was born in 1907 in New York City. He was encouraged to learn music and received his first piano lessons from his mother. He began playing the trumpet and then learned the alto saxophone. In 1923 his family moved to Harlem, and Carter began to play in bands. In 1925 he entered Wilberforce University in Ohio to study theology but joined a band instead. He played in the Fletcher Henderson Orchestra and later turned his hand to arranging when he became music director of McKinney's Cotton Pickers in Detroit in the early 1930s. About this time Carter composed two pieces, "Blues in My Heart" (1931) and "When Lights Are Low" (1936), both of which became jazz standards.

Jazz standardbearer

Between 1935 and 1938 Carter lived in Europe and helped popularize jazz there; he was staff arranger of the BBC Dance Orchestra (1936–1938) in London and recorded with local musicians in France, Scandinavia, and the Netherlands. Carter returned to the United States in 1938 and settled in Los Angeles in 1942, where, in addition to leading his own orchestra, he arranged and composed for films. His first composition was for *Stormy Weather* (1943). He became one of the first black musicians to break into the closed studio circuit of Hollywood, where he composed and arranged for several films and television series such as *Ironside* (1967–1975) and *It Takes a Thief* (1968–1970).

▲ *This 1981 photograph of Benny Carter shows him in his 70s, when he was still performing.*

As academic courses in jazz became more established, Carter's achievements were increasingly recognized. He was visiting professor at several universities and was awarded honorary doctorates from Princeton and Rutgers universities. In the 1980s and 1990s Carter became almost a living icon in the jazz world; his death in 2003 is considered the end of the last direct link with early jazz.

See also: Henderson, Fletcher

Further reading: Berger, Morroe, Edward Berger, and James Patrick. *Benny Carter: A Life In American Music.* 2 vols. Mettuchen, NJ: Scarecrow Press, 2001.
www.bennycarter.com (Biography).

KEY DATES

1907	Born in New York City on August 8.
1931	Joins McKinney's Cotton Pickers as music director.
1936	Becomes staff arranger for the BBC Dance Orchestra, London.
1943	Composes for his first film, *Stormy Weather.*
2003	Dies in Los Angeles, California, on July 12.

CARTER, Betty
Singer

Betty Carter was born Lillie Mae Jones on May 16, 1930, in Flint, Michigan. As a young girl she learned piano at the Detroit Conservatory of Music, where she made rapid progress. Her musical talent enabled her to play alongside famous musicians such as Charlie Parker by the time she was 15. At age 16 she began to sing professionally, and in 1948 she joined the Lionel Hampton band, adopting the stage name Lorraine Carter.

Music making

"Lorraine Carter" soon evolved into Betty Carter owing to Lionel Hampton giving her the nickname "Betty Bebop." She and the band set up in New York in 1951. Carter soon struck out on her own, and throughout the 1950s she sang with a variety of different performers and bands, including some of the most famous names in jazz, such as Max Roach, Dizzy Gillespie, and Miles Davis. She also ventured into recording, making her first album, *Meet Betty Carter and Ray Bryant,* with pianist Ray Bryant in 1955. Carter made four more albums in the 1950s but was unable to significantly raise her profile; some of the albums were poorly received by critics. With two young sons to support, life was hard.

Fame arrives

Carter finally found fame through her collaboration with legendary pianist and singer Ray Charles. She had worked with Charles in the late 1950s, and in 1961 they released the album *Ray Charles and Betty Carter*. Containing classic

▲ *The dynamic Betty Carter in midperformance in 1985 at Ronnie Scott's, London, England.*

tracks such as "Baby, It's Cold Outside," the album was an instant success.

From 1961 to 1968 Carter put most of her efforts into raising her children, cutting back on live performances and recording only two albums. She returned to music in 1969, working with her own trio, and even started her own recording company in 1971. Her wide vocal range, rhythmic sophistication, and ability to improvise made her a favorite of musicians and critics. In 1988 she signed with the Verve label, for which she produced the Grammy award-winning album, *Look What I Got*. She performed into the 1990s and taught singing until she died from cancer on September 26, 1998.

See also: Charles, Ray; Davis, Miles; Gillespie, Dizzy; Parker, Charlie "Bird"; Roach, Max

Further reading: Merlis, Bob, and Davin Seay. *Heart & Soul—A Celebration of Black Music Style in America, 1930–1975* New York, NY: Billboard Books, 2002.
http://home.att.net/~timcramm/betty.htm (Fan site).

KEY DATES	
1930	Born in Flint, Michigan, on May 16.
1948	Joins the Lionel Hampton band.
1951	Moves to New York.
1955	Records her first album, *Meet Betty Carter and Ray Bryant*.
1961	Gains a wider audience and fame through the release of the album *Ray Charles and Betty Carter*.
1971	Starts her own recording company, Bet-Cor Productions.
1998	Dies in New York on September 26.

CARTER, Cris
Football Player, Broadcast Commentator

Cris Carter was a record-breaking National Football League (NFL) wide receiver in the 1990s. At 6 feet 3 inches (1.9m) tall and 208 pounds (94.3kg), he became famous for his catches and was hailed as "the best hands in football." Superfit and mainly injury-free, he played all 16 games in 13 of his 15 seasons in the sport.

Carter emerged as a football player in the 1980s at Ohio State University. Teammates later recalled that he was the only player on the squad whose catches in practice would draw spontaneous applause.

Professional career
After college Carter turned pro and spent his first three years with the Philadelphia Eagles. In 1990 he moved to the Minnesota Vikings, with whom he remained for the next 12 seasons. In 2001 he switched to the Miami Dolphins, where he played what turned out to be his final season.

▼ *Cris Carter on the sidelines in a game between the Minnesota Vikings and the Jacksonville Jaguars in Bloomington, Minnesota, on December 20, 1998.*

During his distinguished Viking's career Carter broke numerous NFL records. Between 1993 and 1999 he made seven consecutive appearances in the Pro Bowl. He twice caught 122 passes in a season (1994 and 1995) and in 1999 became only the second player, after Jerry Rice, to reach 1,000 career catches.

By the time he retired, Carter ranked second on the NFL's all-time list for total receptions (1,101) and receiving touchdowns (130); only Rice had more. He was third behind Rice and James Lofton in receiving yards (13,833), and fourth in career catches behind Rice, Andre Reed, and Art Monk. He held nearly all Vikings' team records, including those for career receptions (835), career receiving yards (10,238), career touchdowns (95), and career yards from scrimmage (10,258). Of the sport's major prizes, the only one that eluded him was a Super Bowl ring.

Life off the field
Off the field Carter established a charity for underprivileged children and set up the Viking Super Challenge, which aims to combat truancy and drug abuse in schools. He also founded the Cris Carter Academic Honor Roll Program for high school students who excel in both sports and academic study. In 1996 he became an ordained minister. In 2002 Carter became a broadcaster with HBO, for whom he cohosted *Inside the NFL*.

KEY DATES	
1965	Born in Troy, Ohio, on November 25.
1987	Joins Philadelphia Eagles.
1990	Begins a 12-season run with Minnesota Vikings.
2001	Moves to Miami Dolphins.
2002	Retires from football, launches career as a broadcast commentator.

See also: Rice, Jerry

Further reading: Carter, Butch, and Cris Carter. *Born to Believe.* Halifax, Nova Scotia: Full Wits Publishing Inc., 2000. www.allsports.com/nfl/players/Cris-Carter.html (Biography).

CARTER, Eunice
Public Prosecutor

Eunice Carter's outstanding career, first as a public prosecutor in New York and later as an international diplomat, ranks her among the prominent African Americans of her time.

She was born Eunice Roberta Hunton on July 16, 1899, in Atlanta, Georgia. Her parents were highly educated and committed to working for the improvement of the African American community. Carter attended Smith College, Massachusetts, where she received her BA and MA, graduating in 1921. She married Lisle C. Carter, a dentist, in 1924 and had a son, Lisle, Jr., two years later.

Success in New York

In 1932 Carter was the first African American to earn a law degree from Fordham University Law School. She was admitted to the New York Bar in 1934 and in 1935 became the first African American woman to work in the district attorney's office in New York. She was the only African American, and the only woman, on an investigation team

▼ *In the 1930s, as an assistant for New York District Attorney Thomas E. Dewey, Carter helped topple some of the city's leading Mafia bosses.*

KEY DATES

1899 Born in Atlanta, Georgia, on July 16.

1921 Graduates from Smith College.

1932 Receives law degree from Fordham University.

1935 Appointed as public prosecutor.

1938 Awarded honorary degree, doctor of laws (LLD), from Smith College.

1945 Ends public service career.

1947 Becomes a consultant for United Nations Economic and Social Council for the International Council of Women.

1955 Elected chair of the International Conference of Nongovernmental Organizations in Geneva.

1962 Appointed member of U.S. National Committee for UNESCO.

1970 Dies in New York City on January 25.

known as "Twenty Against the Underworld," which uncovered Mafia crime in New York City. In 1937 she became the chief of the Special Sessions Bureau, supervising criminal cases until the end of her public service career in 1945. In 1938 she was awarded an honorary degree, doctor of laws (LLD), from Smith College.

In her later life Carter was involved in the work of nongovernmental organizations both in the United States and internationally. She became the chairperson for the National Council of Negro Women (NCNW), was a consultant to the German government advising on women in public life, and also held several positions in the United Nations. Carter died of cancer on January 25, 1970.

Further reading: Berry, Dawn Bradley. *The 50 Most Influential Women in American Law.* Los Angeles, CA: Contemporary Books, 1996.
www.law.stanford.edu/library/wlhbp/profiles/CarterERH.html (Biography).

CARTER, Robert L.
Civil Rights Lawyer

An outspoken advocate of civil rights, Judge Robert L. Carter was awarded the National Association for the Advancement of Colored People (NAACP) Spingarn Award in 2004. It joined numerous other awards and honors recognizing his 50 years or more battling racial discrimination and promoting social and economic justice.

A promising student

Robert Lee Carter was born in Careyville, Florida, in 1917, but moved with his mother to Newark, New Jersey, as a young boy. He grew up an outstanding student and after moving up two grades graduated from high school at age 16. Carter attended Lincoln University, Pennsylvania, and Howard University School of Law, both on scholarships, before going on to earn his master of laws from Columbia Law School in 1941.

In 1941 Carter was drafted into the Army and served in the Air Corps as a second lieutenant. For three years he suffered the racial prejudice that was prevalent in the military at the time, an experience that led him to campaign for racial justice.

Making legal history

Carter was hired as a legal assistant to Thurgood Marshall at the NAACP Legal Defense and Education Fund (LDF) in 1944. By 1956 he had succeeded Marshall as the NAACP's general counsel and remained in this post until 1968.

During the 1950s and 1960s he argued and won 21 of 22 cases in the U.S. Supreme Court, including some of huge significance. Among them were *Brown v. Board of Education* (1954), in which the Supreme Court ruled segregation in the nation's public schools to be

▲ *In 1970 Robert L. Carter testified before the Senate Select Committe on Equal Education that there were more all-white and all-black schools then than in 1954, largely because of housing discrimination.*

unconstitutional, and *NAACP v. Alabama* (1958), in which the Supreme Court held that the NAACP membership could maintain its anonymity.

Carter joined a private law firm in 1969 and remained there until his 1972 appointment to a federal judgeship on the District Court for the Southern District of New York. During his career Judge Carter has served on numerous committees and has held adjunct faculty positions at the University of Michigan and New York University law schools and at Yale University's graduate school. He was also cofounder of the National Conference of Black Lawyers (NCBL) and has written widely on discrimination.

See also: Civil Rights; Discrimination; Marshall, Thurgood; Supreme Court

Further reading: Carter, Robert L., and John Hope Franklin. *A Matter of Law: A Memoir of Struggle in the Cause of Equal Rights.* New York, NY: New Press, 2005.
http://www.jtbf.org/article_iii_judges/carter_r.htm (Biography).

KEY DATES	
1917	Born in Careyville, Florida, on March 11.
1941	Earns master of laws degree.
1944	Completes army service and begins work for NAACP.
1956	Succeeds Thurgood Marshall as LDF's general counsel.
1972	Appointed judge of the U.S. District Court for the Southern District of New York.

CARTER, Rubin
Boxer

▲ **Rubin Carter, in London, England, for his fight with Harry Scott in 1965, polishes his head after a visit to a barber. Carter lost the fight on points.**

Rubin Carter was a prominent boxer whose 1967 conviction for a triple murder became a famous and controversial case commemorated in a song by Bob Dylan.

The fourth of seven children, Rubin Carter was born in 1937. He was sent to a juvenile reformatory at the age of 14 for assault and robbery. In 1954 he escaped from custody and joined the Army, but his superiors judged him unfit for military service and discharged him after only two years. On his return to the United States he served the remainder of his sentence, but within two months of his release in 1957 he committed another violent robbery for which he received a four-year term.

Boxing

Freed in 1961, Carter became a professional boxer. An aggressive middleweight with a big punch, he knocked out many of his opponents quickly, earning him the nickname "Hurricane." A year later he was in the world top ten. In December 1964 he fought reigning world champion Joey Giardello for the title but lost on a unanimous judges' decision. Carter accepted defeat graciously, but after that disappointment he faded from the limelight.

Miscarriage of justice

In the early hours of June 17, 1966, two men entered the Lafayette Bar and Grill in Paterson, New Jersey, and shot four people, three of them fatally. A few months later Carter and his friend John Artis were charged with the murders. The case against them depended on the evidence of two petty criminals, Alfred Bello and Dexter Bradley, who claimed to have seen the defendants armed outside the bar on that night. In 1967 Carter and Artis were found guilty by an all-white jury and sentenced to life in prison.

Many observers feared that there had been a miscarriage of justice. One of the most prominent critics of the trial was the musician Bob Dylan, whose 1976 song "Hurricane" asserted Carter's innocence. Bello and Bradley subsequently retracted their original evidence, and the New Jersey Supreme Court ordered a retrial, this time before a multiracial jury. The new proceedings reached the same verdict: Carter and Artis went back to jail.

After vigorous campaigning by supporters a district court judge ruled in 1985 that Carter and Artis had not received a fair trial and ordered the convictions set aside. Both men were freed in 1988, and Carter went to live in Canada, where he now makes his living as a motivational speaker. Artis became a social worker, and works with troubled youths in Virginia.

Rubin Carter's involvement or otherwise in the murders at the Lafayette Bar and Grill may never be known; it remains a controversial subject. *The Hurricane*, a 1999 film starring Denzel Washington as Carter, muddied the waters further by distorting many of the facts and incidentally libeled former middleweight champion Giardello, who was paid a substantial sum by the producers in an out-of-court settlement.

KEY DATES	
1937	Born in Paterson, New Jersey, on May 6.
1964	Fights for world middleweight boxing title but loses to defending champion.
1967	Jailed for life for triple murder.
1985	Conviction set aside.
1988	Released from prison.
1999	*The Hurricane*, a film based on Carter's life, is released.

See also: Washington, Denzel

Further reading: Carter, Rubin. *The Sixteenth Round: From Number 1 Contender to #45472.* New York: Viking Press, 1974. lib.law.washington.edu/ref/hurricane.htm (Biography).

CARVER, George Washington
Agricultural Chemist, Agronomist, Researcher

Born into slavery during the Civil War in about 1864, near Diamond Grove, Missouri, George Washington Carver, Jr., rose above widespread racism and a difficult childhood to lead a memorable life as a scientist, inventor, educator, artist, and poet. A slight, mild-mannered, and eccentric individual in his personality and appearance, Carver was led throughout his life by a simple desire to serve humanity.

George and his mother Mary are thought to have been abducted by Confederate slave raiders from the plantation of his owner, Moses Carver, near Diamond Grove when he was a baby. Although Moses was able to find and reclaim George after the end of the Civil War in 1865, George's mother had disappeared.

The "plant doctor"
Moses and his wife Susan decided to raise George and his brother Jim as their own children. While his stronger brother helped Moses with the farm work, the frail and sickly George spent most of his time with Susan, learning to read, draw, and cook (*see box on p. 100*). This was also the time when young George became interested in nature. He earned the nickname "plant doctor" as he helped neighbors and friends care for ailing plants.

By the time George was 10 or 12 years old, Moses and Susan realized they could no longer satisfy his thirst for knowledge. With no school available for black children in the area, George left the farm in search of an education. He was able to attend a school for black children in Neosho, Missouri, for a time, but the youngster mainly educated himself by reading and through his own experiences. In order to support himself, he did odd jobs as a housekeeper, hotel cook, gardener, and laundryman.

While working as a farm laborer in his late twenties, Carver was able to attend high school in Minneapolis, Kansas. Racial barriers made it difficult to find a college, but Carver finally joined Simpson College, Indianola, Iowa, as its first black student. He studied piano and art. Eager to specialize in science, he transferred to Iowa Agricultural College (now Iowa State University) in 1891, where he gained a BS in agricultural science in 1894 and an MS in 1896. He was also the first African American to serve on the Iowa College faculty, teaching classes in soil conservation and chemurgy (the development of industrial applications for farm products).

▲ *George Carver in 1942, the year before he died. For his contributions to agriculture he is remembered as the "miracle worker."*

Revolutionary research
In 1896 Carver left Iowa for Alabama and the Tuskegee Normal and Industrial Institute to take up a post as director of agricultural research. Despite lucrative offers of employment in the following years, Carver devoted the rest of his life to research at Tuskegee, a school headed by black educator Booker T. Washington. Although Carver sought initially to improve the lives of poor black farmers or sharecroppers, his research eventually helped revolutionize the whole southern agricultural economy.

Part of the revolution depended on experiments on and promotion of crop rotation: alternating nitrogen-fixing (soil-enriching) crops such as peanuts, peas, soybeans, and sweet potato with soil-depleting cotton and tobacco crops. At the time Carver embarked on his research in the early

Moses and Susan Carver had no children of their own, so they decided to treat George and his brother Jim as if they were their own. Susan nursed the sickly baby George back to health, although he remained a frail child who often suffered from illnesses. Later Susan taught him to read, write, and do simple arithmetic. George studied her old spelling book until he "almost knew it by heart." Because of his poor health George did not do hard work on the farm but helped Susan with household tasks, learning to cook, mend clothes, and do laundry. He also helped in the family garden and spent many hours exploring the local fields and woods, learning about nature and caring for plants. "I literally lived in the woods. I wanted to know every strange stone, flower, insect, bird, or beast," Carver said. He also learned to transplant and cultivate native plants.

1900s, cotton and tobacco were practically the only crops grown in the agriculture-dependent South. Soils were depleted, and the agricultural economy was still suffering from the aftermath of the Civil War, in particular the nonavailability of slave labor.

Part of the battle to win farmers over to Carver's ideas involved creating a market for the new crops, and he also embarked on experiments to develop industrial applications for peanuts, sweet potatoes, and soybeans. Some of the more than 325 marketable products he derived from peanuts included peanut butter, shampoo, cheese, milk, dyes, soap, linoleum, and cosmetics, while the 100 or more derivatives from sweet potatoes included flour, molasses, rubber, and ink.

Carver went public with the results of his experiments in 1914, a time when the boll weevil, a kind of beetle, was destroying cotton fields across the South. As more southern farmers began to rotate their crops and turned to peanuts, sweet potatoes, and their derivative products, the region began to recover. Later developments by Carver included replacing textile dyes formerly imported from Europe. During his lifetime he produced more than 500 different shades of dye.

Serving humankind

Carver was not interested in fame or fortune, and late in his career he declined an invitation to work for inventor Thomas A. Edison at a salary of more than $100,000. Despite the countless products produced through his research, Carver only ever received three patents.

In 1941 Carver donated his life savings to establish the Carver Research Foundation at Tuskegee to continue his work. Among the awards and honors he received were an honorary membership of Britain's Royal Society of Arts in 1914, the Spingarn Medal in 1923, an annual award given by the National Association for the Advancement of Colored People (NAACP), and the Roosevelt Medal for restoring southern agriculture in 1939.

It has been claimed that the value of Carver's achievements was exaggerated, but he himself remained modest to the end. Carver died of anemia in Tuskegee, Alabama, in 1943. On July 14, 1943, President Franklin D. Roosevelt honored Carver by designating a park near Diamond Grove, Carver's childhood home, as a national monument. It was the first such monument to an African American in the United States.

See also: Slavery; Washington, Booker T.

Further reading: Carver, George Washington, and Gary R. Kremer. *George Washington Carver: In His Own Words.* Columbia, MO: University of Missouri Press, 1991.
www.princeton.edu/~mcbrown/display/carver.html
(Biography).

KEY DATES

1864   Born near Diamond Grove, Missouri (some sources suggest Carver's birth date may have been as early as 1861).

1894   Receives BS in agricultural science from Iowa Agricultural College, followed by an MS in 1896.

1896   Becomes director of agricultural research at Tuskegee Normal and Industrial Institute.

1914   Makes public his research into derivative products of peanuts and sweet potatoes.

1923   Awarded Spingarn Medal for contributions to the advancement of African Americans.

1941   Donates life savings to establishment of Carver Research Foundation at Tuskegee.

1943   Dies in Tuskegee, Alabama, on January 5.

CARY, Mary Ann Shadd
Educator, Teacher, Lawyer

As well as being a well-known philanthropist and abolitionist, Mary Ann Shadd Cary worked as a teacher and a lawyer, and was the first African American woman to own a newspaper. She was also the first black woman to address major African American conventions in the United States and the second African American woman to receive a law degree in the country.

A born teacher

Mary Ann Shadd was born in Wilmington, Delaware, on October 9, 1823. Her parents Harriet and Abraham Shadd were free, but the family lived in a slave state, which made it difficult for Mary to get a proper education. Shadd's father (*see box on p.102*) was a subscription agent for the antislavery newspaper the *Liberator*, owned by the white abolitionist William Lloyd Garrison. Both her parents were established leaders in the black community. Shadd was the oldest of 13 children, and at age 10 her parents took her to West Chester, Pennsylvania, where she was educated in a Quaker school. Completing her education at 16, Shadd returned to Wilmington, Delaware, opened up her own school, and taught both black and white children. While teaching and still young, Shadd wrote articles on slavery and freedom, some of which were published in the *North Star*, a well-known black advocacy paper in the United States. She then moved out of Wilmington and taught at schools in New York and Norristown, Pennsylvania.

Fugitive slaves

While living in Wilmington, Shadd was made aware of the plight of fugitive slaves by her parents, who were heavily involved in the Underground Railroad, which helped slaves free themselves by using a secret network of escape routes running throughout the United States, providing them with a safe passage to Canada, Mexico, and the Caribbean. The movement relied on the cooperation of likeminded people, black and white, against slavery. Shadd's parents are thought to have assisted around a thousand slaves, some of whom they sheltered at their house.

In 1850 Congress passed the Fugitive Law, which gave slave owners the power to hunt down escaped slaves anywhere in the United States. To counter the success of the Underground Railroad, fines and prison sentences were imposed on individuals who helped runaways. Shadd was so angry with the new law that she moved to Canada with

▲ *Mary Ann Shadd Cary spent much of her life fighting against slavery by helping fugitive slaves escape to freedom.*

her brother Isaac, determined to do what she could to undermine it. In the same year Canada passed laws that protected fugitive slaves and allowed blacks, Catholics, and Protestants to establish their own schools. From 1850 to the outbreak of the Civil War (1861–1865) there was an exodus of blacks from the United States into Canada. Shadd planned to use Canada as the base from which she could oversee the easy movement and settlement of fugitive slaves from the United States. With the help of African Americans living in Toronto she founded a weekly newspaper called the *Provincial Free Man*, designed to provide news and assistance to the 4,000 blacks living in Canada and to assist the new arrivals. Its themes included equality, integration, and self-education. The paper was first printed in Windsor from 1853 to 1854; it then moved

INFLUENCES AND INSPIRATION

One of the greatest influences on the life of Mary Ann Shadd Cary was her own father, Abraham Shadd. A relatively wealthy shoemaker, Shadd was heavily involved in the antislavery movement; his house was a "station" on the Underground Railroad, and he helped many slaves attain their freedom. In 1833 Shadd helped found the American Anti-Slavery Society and also became president of the National Convention for the Improvement of Free People of Color in the United States.

In 1853 Shadd followed his daughter to Canada, where he continued to be politically active. He was elected to Raleigh Town Council in 1859, becoming the first black to be elected to political office in Canada. He died in 1882.

to Toronto in 1854 to 1855. In 1856 Shadd married Thomas F. Cary, a Toronto resident, and moved to Chatham, Canada. They had two children, Sarah and Linton. After 1855 Cary ran her paper from Chatham; however, it was discontinued on September 20, 1857. Cary eventually moved to Windsor, Canada, near Detroit, Michigan. Cary would often travel into the United States to support the fugitive slave movement. In particular she fought the propaganda spread in black communities that claimed life for blacks in Canada was harder than it was in the United States.

Cary made many public appearances both in Canada and the United States. She was an outstanding public speaker, delivering speeches with a distinct and elegant style that people remembered and responded to.

Tensions rise

In 1858 the white antislavery crusader John Brown visited Chatham; he likely met Cary before his assault on Harper's Ferry in western Virginia in 1859. During that siege Brown, his two sons, and several other armed abolitionists barricaded themselves in the village armory, but they were eventually seized by local militia and marines. Brown was later hanged and became a martyr for abolitionists in the North. The event worried the South and increased the tensions between slaveowners there and politicians in the North, contributing to the outbreak of the Civil War.

At the beginning of the war Cary was living in Michigan, working as a teacher. She accepted a commission from Governor Levi P. Morton of Indiana to become a recruiting army officer, whose task it was to recruit blacks to join the Union Army.

Work in Washington

Following President Lincoln's Emancipation Proclamation in 1863 Cary settled in Washington, D.C., where for 17 years she worked as a principal in three large public schools in the district under the supervision of Howard University. In 1869 she enrolled in the Howard University School of Law, taking evening courses, and graduated in 1883. She continued to write articles for magazines and newspapers, working with the former slave Frederick Douglass on the *National Era*, a weekly abolitionist newspaper. Because she was a woman, Cary had to wait three years to graduate. Following her graduation, she practiced law.

In the 1880s Cary campaigned for women's rights. In 1880 she organized the Colored Women's Progressive Franchise, dedicated to protecting and promoting women's rights. In 1881 Cary joined the National Woman's Suffrage Association (NWSA) and worked together with the activists Susan B. Anthony and Elizabeth Cady Stanton to ensure that women would be allowed to vote. Cary died at the age of 70 in Washington, D.C., on June 5, 1893.

KEY DATES	
1823	Born in Wilmington, Delaware, on October 9.
1833	Attends Quaker school in West Chester, Pennsylvania.
1839	Sets up her own school in Wilmington.
1851	Moves to Canada.
1853	Founds her own weekly newspaper.
1856	Marries Thomas F. Cary.
1883	Gets law degree.
1893	Dies in Washington, D.C., on June 5.

See also: Douglass, Frederick; Emancipation and Reconstruction; Segregation and Integration; Slavery

Further reading: Bearden, Jim, and Linda Jean Butler. *Shadd: The Life and Times of Mary Shadd Cary.* Toronto: N.C. Press, 1977.
www.lkwdpl.org/wihohio/cary-mar.htm (Biography).

CASSELL, Albert
Architect

Albert Cassell was a leading African American architect during the first half of the 20th century and a contemporary of Julian Abele. Cassell is best known for the buildings he contributed to Howard University, Washington, D.C., the most prestigious black university in the United States. His Founders Library (dedicated in 1939) became a beacon of African American achievement and liberty during a period of racial segregation and discrimination.

Professor and architect

Albert Irving Cassell was born in Towson, Maryland, on June 25, 1895. His father, Albert, was a truck driver, while his mother, Charlotte, took in laundry to supplement the family income. Cassell studied architecture at Cornell University in Ithaca, New York, although his studies were interrupted by the United States's participation in World War I from 1917 to 1918. During the war Cassell served in France as a second lieutenant in the Army. He graduated from Cornell in 1919 and began his career as an architect working with William Hazel on a project for Tuskegee Institute in Alabama that same year.

In the early 1920s there was only a small number of African American architects practicing in the United States, most of whom worked exclusively for black clients, such as church communities and educational institutes like Howard University. Cassell was no exception. In 1920 he became assistant professor in the architecture department of Howard University and in 1924 the university's chief architect. He was responsible for planning the massive expansion that Howard underwent during the 1920s and 1930s.

Cassell's buildings for Howard University included the Medical School (dedicated in 1928), the Chemistry Building (1936), and the Frederick Douglass Memorial Hall (1936). However, the centerpiece of Cassell's plan—and his architectural masterpiece—was the Founders Library, built high up on the campus hill where the Main Building had stood for 70 years before it was demolished to make way for the new library. Cassell designed the library in the neoclassical style—the style in which Washington, D.C.'s historic state buildings had been built in the 18th century, and which symbolized the republican ideals of freedom and equality. The Founders Library, named for the 17 founders of Howard University, cost $1,106,000, of which $1 million was provided by Congress.

KEY DATES

1895   Born in Towson, Maryland, on June 25.

1919   Graduates from Cornell University, Ithaca, New York.

1920   Becomes assistant professor of architecture at Howard University, Washington, D.C.

1939   Dedication of the Founders Library, Howard University.

1941   Completion of the James Creek Alley Housing Development, Washington, D.C.

1969   Dies.

A visionary planner

Cassell left Howard University in 1938 after his architectural plans for the campus were complete. He spent much of the remainder of his career designing and building housing projects for Washington's working-class African Americans, many of whom lived in the overcrowded conditions of the city's "alley" dwellings. Cassell's government-funded James Creek Alley Housing Development, built in around 1941, was the first public housing scheme in Washington's Southwest neighborhood and was a pioneer for the emerging "garden apartment" movement of the period, which set tenement blocks in communal grounds. Cassell's largest housing project was Mayfair Mansions, a $5 million apartment complex in Washington, D.C., which was built between 1942 and 1946.

Cassell was responsible for many other buildings in Washington and Maryland, including the neoclassical Prince Hall Masonic Temple on U Street, Washington, D.C., built between 1922 and 1930, and Morgan State University in Baltimore, Maryland. Cassell died in 1969.

See also: Abele, Julian

Further reading: Wilson, Dreck Spurlock (ed.). *African-American Architects: A Biographical Dictionary, 1865–1945.* New York, NY: Routledge, 2003.
http://www.howard.edu/library/Development/Cassell/Founders.htm#Albert%20I.%20Cassell (Article providing a useful context for understanding Cassell's achievements).

CATLETT, Elizabeth
Artist, Sculptor

Elizabeth Catlett is a renowned artist best known for bold, politically influenced sculptures and prints created in the 1960s and 1970s. The New York art critic Michael Brenson said that Catlett's sculptures "communicate a deeply human image of African Americans, while appealing to values and virtues that encourage a sense of common humanity."

Road to success

Born in Washington, D.C., on April 5, 1915, Catlett was one of three children. Her father, a teacher at Tuskegee Institute, Alabama, died before she was born; her mother worked as a truant officer in schools to support her family. Catlett studied at Mott Elementary School and Dunbar High School.

Interested in art from an early age, Catlett went to Howard University School of Art. Although she had originally taken an examination and won a scholarship to go to the Carnegie Institute of Technology in Pittsburgh, she was refused admittance to the all-white institution when they discovered her race.

Catlett studied design, printmaking, and drawing at Howard and was friends with fellow students James Wells (1902–1993) and James Porter. In a 1981 interview Catlett stated that Porter convinced her to change her major to painting since there was no sculpture division at Howard at the time. She graduated from the school with a BS in 1935. Three years later Catlett became the first student to get an MFA in sculpture from the University of Iowa, where she studied with the artist Grant Wood (1891–1942).

In 1941 Catlett studied ceramics at the Art Institute of Chicago, where she met and married African American artist Charles White (1918–1979). They lived in Chicago and in New York, where Catlett studied sculpture with the Russian sculptor Ossip Zadkine (1890–1967) and lithography, a type of printing, at the Art Students' League.

In 1946 Catlett was able to study in Mexico after she won a Julius Rosenwald Fellowship. She worked at the Taller de Grafica Popular (People's Graphic Arts Workshop), a group of printmakers who used their work to promote social and political change. They worked on a series of linoleum cuts of black heroes and created posters, leaflets, and other material to tackle illiteracy in Mexico. Catlett remained with them until 1966.

After divorcing White, Catlett married the Mexican artist Francisco Mora in 1947 and settled permanently in Mexico. In 1959 she became the first woman to teach at the School of Fine Arts of the National Autonomous University of Mexico, where she was head of sculpture until her retirement in 1976.

Expression

Catlett used her art as a vehicle through which to promote social awareness and change. Her experiences as an African, American, and Mexican freed her from nationalism and ethnic boundaries and gave her work a wider approach and appeal. Catlett's art is figurative but with an abstract appearance. Among her most famous works are the linocut *Sharecropper* (about 1952) and the abstract marble sculpture *Nude Torso* (1999). She has created many outdoor sculptures, such as the life-size statue of musician Louis Armstrong that stands in the New Orleans park named after him.

Catlett has won several awards, and her work appears in many art collections. She says, "I have always wanted my art to service my people—to reflect us, to relate to us, to stimulate us, to make us aware of our potential."

See also: Armstrong, Louis; Porter, James; White, Charles

Further reading: Herzog, Melanie. *Elizabeth Catlett: An American Artist in Mexico.* Seattle, WA: University of Washington Press, 2000.
http://www.clevelandart.org/exhibcef/catlett/html/4578495.html (Biography with examples of her work).

KEY DATES	
1915	Born in Washington, D.C., on April 15.
1935	Graduates from Howard University School of Art.
1940	Receives MFA from University of Iowa.
1946	Wins Julius Rosenwald Fellowshop and is able to study in Mexico.
1947	Joins Taller de Grafica Popular.
1959	Becomes the first woman to head the sculpture department of the National School of Fine Arts at the National Autonomous University of Mexico.

CHAMBERLAIN, Wilt
Basketball Player

If a basketball expert is challenged to pick the greatest player of all time, Wilt Chamberlain is likely to be one of the names near the top of the list. Chamberlain has had few equals in basketball history. The 7 foot 1 inch (2.1m) forward scored over 30,000 points in National Basketball Association (NBA) games. Using great technique, including dunks and finger-spinning, Chamberlain scored baskets with alarming frequency—he scored over 100 points in a single game and regularly over 50 points. Seven times he was named All-NBA First Team. He was also a figure of some controversy, his dominance on the court attracting negative response from the crowd. When his team lost, Chamberlain would be the one to take the blame.

Finding his feet
Born Wilton Norman Chamberlain on August 21, 1936, in Philadelphia, Wilt came from a large family of 11 children, and some believe his competitive instinct may have arisen from his home environment. At school he showed an unusual level of skill in sports, particularly in track and basketball. In many ways he preferred track, but he excelled at basketball. Although numerous school teams attempted to recruit him, he became a local star on the Overbrook (Pennsylvania) High School team between 1951 and 1955. Chamberlain took the team to new heights, losing only three games in three seasons and finishing with a team record of 58 wins and only three losses. Chamberlain also acquired some of the nicknames that would stay with him throughout his career, including "Wilt the Stilt" (he stood 6 feet tall when he was only 10) and "the Big Dipper." He was regularly scoring 50 or more points in a game, and in one game against Roxborough he scored 90 points, 60 of them in 10 minutes.

As his high school career came to a close, Chamberlain was approached by over 100 colleges attempting to recruit him for their basketball teams—he chose the University of Kansas, home to the Kansas Jayhawks, because it had a long tradition of basketball. By 1955, the first year in which he was named an All-American, the NBA professional game was beckoning. Wilt had experienced the quality of the NBA since he had already played against NBA players in some summer season games. He was earmarked to play for the NBA Philadelphia Warriors on graduation. Meanwhile he displayed his talents at Kansas, taking them to a National Collegiate Athletic Association (NCAA) championship game against top-ranked North Carolina in 1957, which Kansas lost by one point in triple overtime.

The big league
Following his university graduation in 1958, Chamberlain did not go directly to the Warriors but instead fulfilled a childhood dream by spending a year with the Harlem Globetrotters. In 1959, however, he joined the Warriors and got 43 points and 28 rebounds in his first game. He had a similar average for his whole first season and was awarded the NBA Rookie of the Year award.

It was in the 1960s that Chamberlain performed some of his most legendary feats. In 1961–1962 his average was 50.4 points per game, scoring at least one point each minute on court. He also became the first player to achieve

▼ *Wilt Chamberlain in 1959 when he was playing for his childhood heroes the Harlem Globetrotters.*

INFLUENCES AND INSPIRATION

In 1950 Chuck Cooper became the first African American to play in the NBA. In the 1950s and 1960s Chamberlain was one of a number of African American players who followed Cooper's lead. Contemporaries of Chamberlain included Bill Russell, Oscar Robinson, and Elgin Baylor, all great players. While growing up, one of Chamberlain's inspirations was the Harlem Globetrotters, an almost all African American basketball team. In 1958 Chamberlain turned dream into reality when he joined them for a year. He remembered the experience of playing for the Globetrotters as his most enjoyable in basketball. Chamberlain was also shaped by the many coaches under whom he played, particularly Alex Hannum with the 76ers, who showed Chamberlain how to be more of a team player and more than purely a scoring machine.

---

over 4,000 points in a year. On March 2, 1967, Chamberlain played in a late-season game in which he set a record that remains unbroken, scoring 100 points to give Philadelphia a 169–147 win over the New York Knicks.

Between 1963 and 1964 the Philadelphia Warriors became the San Francisco Warriors, which Chamberlain left in 1964 to join the Philadelphia 76ers. There he developed more of a team game, scoring less but, alongside such players as Hal Greer and Chet Walker, guiding the 76ers to a championship defeat of San Francisco in 1967. Chamberlain also won three consecutive Most Valuable Player (MVP) awards. In 1968 the 76ers made less progress, and Chamberlain was traded to the Los Angeles Lakers.

Retirement and coaching

Chamberlain finished his career with the Lakers, playing with them from 1968 to 1973. He often averaged about 20 points per game, and in 1972 he was again named MVP. In 1973 the Lakers lost the final to the Knicks, and Chamberlain decided it was time to retire, taking with him a remarkable career total of 31,419 points and 23,924 rebounds. Only later basketball legends Kareem Abdul-Jabbar and Michael Jordan were able to compete with Chamberlain's records.

Retirement from basketball did not mean retirement from sports. Chamberlain became a professional volleyball player, and also took part in some track events, running several marathons. He also acted as a coach to the San Diego Conquistadors between 1973 and 1974.

Raising the profile of the game

Chamberlain and other African American players such as Bill Russell, a defensive center with the Boston Celtics, were considered such exciting players to watch that growth in the popularity of basketball in the 1960s and 1970s is largely attributed to their influence. In particular, games that featured Chamberlain and Russell playing against each other generated enormous interest. Chamberlain was inducted into the Basketball Hall of Fame in 1979. Despite being approached by more basketball teams, Chamberlain stuck to his retirement plans. Although he is remembered as one of the greatest basketball players ever, his 1991 autobiography, *A View from Above*, was very controversial. In it he boasts about his extreme womanizing. Chamberlain died of a heart attack in Los Angeles on October 12, 1999.

KEY DATES	
1936	Born in Philadelphia, Pennsylvania, on August 21.
1951	Begins playing for Overbrook High School team.
1955	Begins playing for Kansas Jayhawks..
1958	Joins the Harlem Globetrotters for one year.
1959	Joins the Philadelphia Warriors.
1964	Joins the Philadelphia 76ers.
1968	Traded to the Lakers.
1973	Retires from professional basketball.
1979	Inducted into Basketball Hall of Fame.
1999	Dies in Los Angeles, California, on October 12.

See also: Abdul-Jabbar, Kareem; Baylor, Elgin; Jordan, Michael; Russell, Bill

Further reading: Chamberlain, Wilt. *A View from Above*. New York, NY: Signet, 1992.
www.sportingnews.com/archives/wilt/index.html (Biography, stats, and pictures).

CHAPMAN, Tracy
Musician

▲ *Tracy Chapman performs at the Albert Hall in London, England, in March 2003.*

Sparking a folk music revival with the extraordinary success of her debut album, singer-songwriter Tracy Chapman is celebrated for her compassionate, socially conscious lyrics and distinctive voice.

Chapman was born on March 30, 1964, and raised in Cleveland, Ohio. Her parents divorced when she was four, and her mother's struggle to provide for her family developed Chapman's awareness of the plight of black women living in poverty and influenced her song-writing. Chapman's mother played guitar and fostered her daughter's musical interests, introducing her to a diverse range of music. In the first grade Chapman was given a ukulele and soon afterward learned to play the organ and the clarinet. Aged 14, Chapman acquired her first guitar and began composing songs. Her musical influences included folk singers Joni Mitchell and Bob Dylan.

An unlikely star
Chapman achieved a minority placement scholarship to Wooster School, Danbury, Connecticut, and later won a scholarship to Tufts University, Medford, Massachusetts. There Chapman majored in anthropology and developed an interest in African music and culture. As a student she composed songs and performed in local coffeehouses and folk clubs. Chapman recorded a set of demos at the college radio station and was signed by Elektra Records in 1987. Her debut album, *Tracy Chapman* (1988), was widely acclaimed, and Chapman went on tour opening for the band 10,000 Maniacs. A few months later she performed at the internationally televised concert held to celebrate the 70th birthday of South Africa's imprisoned black leader Nelson Mandela; her first single, "Fast Car," was rapturously received and became a worldwide hit. Following the concert, *Tracy Chapman* sold over 10 million copies, went multiplatinum, and won Chapman three Grammy awards, including Best New Artist.

Themes of love, honesty, freedom, justice, and the environment recur throughout Chapman's albums *Crossroads* (1989), *Matters of the Heart* (1992), *New Beginning* (1995), *Telling Stories* (2000), and *Let It Rain* (2002). During her career Chapman has performed at many benefit concerts, including Amnesty International Human Rights Tour and the Freedomfest in London, England, in 1988 and at Bob Dylan's 30th Anniversary concert in 1992.

KEY DATES

1964	Born in Cleveland, Ohio, on March 30.
1987	Signs with Elektra Records.
1988	Releases debut album, *Tracy Chapman*.
1989	Wins three Grammys for *Tracy Chapman*.
1996	Fourth album, *New Beginning*, enters the album chart Top 10.
2005	Releases seventh album, *Where You Live*.

Further reading: Slonimsky, N., Laura Kuhn, et al. *Baker's Biographical Dictionary of Musicians.* New York, NY: Schirmer Books, 2001.
http://www.about-tracy-chapman.net (Biography).

CHAPPELLE, Emmett W.
Astrochemist, Biochemist

Emmett W. Chappelle was born in Phoenix, Arizona, on October 25, 1925. He graduated from the University of California in 1950 and received his MS from the University of Washington, Seattle, in 1954. He began his professional career as a graduate instructor teaching biochemistry at Meharry Medical College in Nashville, Tennessee, but in 1954 got a research associate position in the department of chemistry at Stanford University. He was subsequently made a staff scientist in biochemistry at Stanford's Institute of Advanced Studies.

KEY DATES

1925 Born in Phoenix, Arizona, on October 25.

1963 Begins working for Hazleton Laboratories, first as a biochemist, then as an exobiologist and astrochemist.

1977 Appointed to the National Aeronautics and Space Administration.

2001 Retires from NASA.

Space race

In the 1950s there was great scientific interest in the Soviet and American space exploration missions. Chappelle's own interest in bio- and astrochemistry was further developed by the work he carried out for Hazelton Laboratories in Falls Church, Virginia, from 1963 to 1973. Chappelle then worked as a biochemist for a division of the Research Center for Space Exploration. In 1977 he was appointed to the National Aeronautics and Space Administration's (NASA) Goddard Space Flight Center as a remote sensing scientist, initially to work on projects associated with the manned space missions. His research, carried out with his coscientist Grace Picciolo, led to the development of new methods to detect bacteria in water, which were then used in the diagnosis of human urinary tract infections.

▼ **Emmett W. Chappelle in 1961 studying the process by which green plants convert carbon monoxide to harmless carbon dioxide.**

In his own research Chappelle exploited the advances being made at the time in combining fiber optics with smaller lasers capable of being transported into space. The advances permitted NASA scientists to develop remote-sensing methods, among whose many applications were measuring large-scale changes in Earth's terrain and its oceans and seas.

Chappelle also carried out research on such topics as the effects of acid rain on red spruce forests. He and other NASA scientists used techniques developed in his own research to study aspects of stress and growth retardation in plants and marine algae on a continental scale. In 2001 Chappelle retired from NASA.

Worldwide recognition

Chappelle is widely recognized in the scientific community as one of the most distinguished 20th-century American scientists. Throughout his career he has been prominent in the American Chemical Society, the American Society of Microbiology, and the American Society of Black Chemists. He has also mentored many minority science students.

Further reading: Sammons, Vivian O. *Blacks in Science and Medicine.* New York, NY: Hemisphere Publishers Corp., 1990. www.aaregistry.com/african_american_history/1969/ One_of_Arizonas_finest_Emmett_Chappelle (Biography).

CHARLES, Ray
Singer

One of the most influential figures in American popular music, Ray Charles was one of the first singers to perform soul, which combined elements of gospel, rhythm and blues (R&B), and rock music. He is sometimes called "the Genius," a name coined by Frank Sinatra.

Early life
Ray Charles Robinson was born in Albany, Georgia, on September 23, 1930. He spent his early years in Greenville, Florida. The Robinson family lived in extreme poverty; when Charles was seven, he lost his eyesight, most likely as a result of untreated glaucoma. From that year until 1945 he attended the School for the Deaf and the Blind in St. Augustine. He mastered braille and took formal piano lessons; he also learned to play the alto saxophone, trumpet, clarinet, and organ. He was a very good musician and was able to memorize vast amounts of music—as many as 2,000 bars at a time.

Beginnings
After Charles's mother died of cancer when he was 15, he left school and moved to Jacksonville, where he spent three years playing the piano in local clubs. Success did not come easily, however: "Times and me got leaner," Charles later recalled, "but anything beats getting a cane and a cup and picking out a street corner."

Charles gave up his surname to avoid confusion with the boxer Sugar Ray Robinson. He moved to Seattle, Washington, where he formed the McSon Trio, which was based on the Nat King Cole jazz group. The band moved to Los Angeles, where they recorded their first single, "Confession Blues." In the early 1950s the band released several singles, including "Baby Let Me Hold Your Hand."

Road to success
Charles's first real success came when he arranged Guitar Slim's hit record "Things That I Used to Do" (1953). The single became a million-copy seller; but more than that, Guitar Slim's unrestrained vocals and riffing horns influenced Charles's style on future records, as was seen in his 1955 hit record "I Got a Woman." Often described as the first soul record, the track, which is heavily influenced by gospel, features Charles singing in an abandoned style. The success of the single propelled Charles to stardom.

▲ *Ray Charles in 1960, at the period of his greatest success both artistically and commercially.*

Over the next five years Charles had 20 more hits on the R&B charts. He became famous for gospel-style numbers, many of which featured sung question-and-answer-style dialogue with his female backing group, the Raeletts. One such recording, "What'd I Say" (1959), is still regarded by many critics as his finest work. Although the record was banned by several American radio stations, which objected to the suggestive interplay between Charles and his backing singers, "What'd I Say" sold a million copies and established Charles for the first time in the lucrative white music market. It also earned him a move from Atlantic Records to ABC. His new label gave him greater artistic freedom and let him retain the copyright on his recordings. Charles was also given his own label, Tangerine Records.

Peak years
Charles entered the most successful period of his career, producing his first No. 1 hit, "Georgia on My Mind," composed by Hoagy Carmichael (1899–1981), in 1960

INFLUENCES AND INSPIRATION

Charles was not the first musician to combine gospel-style vocals with a blues–rock beat—Thomas A. Dorsey, Solomon Burke, and Little Richard were among those who had done it earlier. Yet it was Charles who became most famous for it, although he also bore the brunt of criticism from people who believed that it was sacrilegious.

At the height of his career Charles produced a synthesis of several styles, applying secular lyrics to gospel songs, and giving the accompanying music a jazz background.

The artists who most clearly influenced Charles's early work were Louis Jordan, Nat King Cole, and Charles Brown. There are numerous echoes of these musicians' sounds in his early recordings. Charles was also influenced by the musicians with whom he toured and worked, notably Lowell Fulson, Guitar Slim, and Ruth Brown.

Charles's influence on the development of contemporary popular music has also been great. *Time* magazine went so far as to assert that "There is no modern singer who has not learned something from Charles."

Among the musicians who have publicly acknowledged their debt to Ray Charles are Stevie Wonder, Aretha Franklin, the Beatles, Van Morrison, and Norah Jones.

KEY DATES

1930	Born in Albany, Georgia, on September 23.
1955	Releases his first hit single, "I Got a Woman."
1962	Releases the hit album *Modern Sounds in Country and Western Music*.
1981	Shocks fans by touring in South Africa, where an apartheid government rules.
1987	Wins the Grammy Award for Lifetime Achievement.
2004	Dies in Beverly Hills, California, on June 10.

and his second, "Hit the Road, Jack," the following year. Both records made him an international name.

Charles was never content to plow the same furrow. He was versatile and developed musically, often influenced by the musicians with whom he played (*see box*). An important figure in the jazz scene in the 1950s, Charles performed notably on albums such as *Soul Brothers* (1958; with Milt Jackson of the Modern Jazz Quartet) and *Genius + Soul = Jazz* (1961).

The album *Modern Sounds in Country and Western Music* (1962) was a revolutionary departure in which Charles reworked established hits as ballads for a big band: One track from the album, "I Can't Stop Loving You," became a No. 1 hit single.

Although Charles had further hits, including "Busted" (1963) and "Crying Time" (1966), and continued to play to sellout audiences all over the world, his creative powers were weakened by his battle with heroin addiction, and some critics argue that his music became less innovative and more sentimental. After several arrests for drug possession Charles kicked the habit in the late 1960s. In 1972 he returned to something like his old form with a version of "America the Beautiful," which was so affecting that many of Charles's fans argued that it should be adopted as the national anthem.

Politics

In 1981 many of Charles's admirers were shocked when he toured in South Africa, which was ruled by a minority white government that enforced apartheid, a system of laws that completely separated whites and blacks. Charles further alienated his liberal supporters by performing at President Ronald Reagan's second inaugural ball in 1985. Charles's manager later commented that for the fee that Charles earned, "He would have sung 'America the Beautiful' at a Ku Klux Klan rally."

Charles won a total of 13 Grammys, including a 1987 Award for Lifetime Achievement. He recorded more than 60 albums. Charles lived to have his life made into an Oscar-winning film, *Ray*, in 2004. He died of liver failure in June that year. His final album, *Genius Loves Company*, was an album of duets with singers such as Norah Jones and Elton John. It was released after his death.

See also: Cole, Nat King; Dorsey, Thomas A.; Franklin, Aretha; Little Richard; Wonder, Stevie

Further reading: Charles, Ray, and David Ritz. *Brother Ray: Ray Charles' Own Story.* New York, NY: Da Capo Press, 1992
http://www.raycharles.com (Charles's official site).

CHEADLE, Don
Actor

An acclaimed actor, Don Cheadle has a laid-back charm and style that makes him popular with audiences around the world. He appeared in many successful films in the early 21st century, including *Ocean's 11* (2001) and *Hotel Rwanda* (2004).

Donald Cheadle was born in Kansas City, Missouri, on November 29, 1964. His father was a psychologist and his mother a bank manager. Cheadle's family moved to Nebraska while he was still young. From an early age he realized that he had a gift and could entertain people. He was also interested in jazz and was so good at both acting and music that when he left high school, he was offered scholarships from music and acting schools. He chose to pursue an acting career and attended the California Institute of the Arts in Valencia.

Gaining a reputation

Cheadle's first film role followed shortly after his graduation, when he had a small part in the comedy *Moving Violations* (1985). He then went on to guest star in several top TV series, including *Hill Street Blues* (1987) and *Night Court* (1988); in 1992 he landed a regular role in *The Golden Palace*, although the show only ran for one season. From 1993 to 1995 Cheadle played the role of the earnest district attorney John Littleton on the successful

▼ *Don Cheadle (right) in his role as hotelier Paul Rusesabagina in the critically acclaimed 2004 film* **Hotel Rwanda.**

series *Picket Fences* (1992–1996), about life in a small American town when a series of bizarre crimes take place.

He continued to appear in films and began to receive attention after he got the main role in the Vietnam War film *Hamburger Hill* (1987). Other roles followed, but he made his real screen breakthrough playing Mouse, the best friend of a private investigator played by Denzel Washington, in the adaptation of Walter Mosley's *Devil in a Blue Dress* in 1995. Despite rumors that he would receive an Oscar nomination for the role, he got other awards instead. Cheadle went on to star in two successful movies in 1997, *Boogie Nights* and John Singleton's *Rosewood*.

Honors and awards

In 1998 Cheadle won a Golden Globe award and an Emmy nomination for his portrayal of the entertainer Sammy Davis, Jr., in *The Rat Pack*. That year he began working with the director Steven Soderburgh, first in *Out of Sight* and then in *Traffic* (2000). They also collaborated in a remake of the Rat Pack classic *Ocean's 11*, and the sequel *Ocean's 12* (2004). In both films Cheadle played an English crook.

Having successfully played a variety of character parts, Cheadle finally began to earn the acclaim critics believed he deserved. In 2005 he received an Oscar nomination for his role in *Hotel Rwanda* as hotelier Paul Rusesabagina, who saved more than 1,200 refugees during the Rwandan genocide. Cheadle also branched out into producing and in 2005 directed *Tishomingo Blues*, which Steven Soderburgh executive-produced.

KEY DATES	
1964	Born in Kansas City, Missouri, on November 29.
1995	Appears in *Devil in a Blue Dress.*
1998	Appears in *Out of Sight*, directed by Steven Soderburgh.
2005	Receives Academy Award nomination for best actor in *Hotel Rwanda.*

See also: Davis, Sammy, Jr.; Washington, Denzel

Further reading: www.usatoday.com/life/people/2005-01-03-cheadle_x.htm (Interview with Cheadle).

CHENAULT, Kenneth
Business Leader

One of the most powerful people on Wall Street, Kenneth Irvine Chenault is chairman and chief executive officer (CEO) of the $20 billion charge card company American Express (AmEx). Succeeding outgoing CEO Harvey Golub in 2001, Chenault, a veteran executive, rose to the top through a combination of hard work, determination, and insight. He is one of only three African American CEOs of a Fortune 500 company in the United States.

Married to Kathryn Cassell, a law graduate, Chenault has two sons. In addition to his work with American Express he sits on the boards of several companies and not-for-profit organizations.

Education

Chenault, who grew up in Hempstead, Long Island—a middle-class, mainly white community—was initially something of an underachiever. Although he received A's in favorite subjects such as history, he failed to apply himself elsewhere. Despite this, he received an innovative and inspirational education in both junior high and high school. By the time Chenault graduated from Waldorf High School, he was an honor student, class president, and captain of the basketball, soccer, and track teams.

Although he initially chose to take up a sports scholarship at Springfield College, Massachusetts, Chenault soon felt the need for a greater academic challenge. On the recommendation of former principal Peter Curran (*see box*) Chenault went on to earn a degree in history from Bowdoin College, Maine, later enrolling at Harvard Law School. There he earned his law degree, graduating in 1976, and went on to work for Wall Street law firm Rogers & Wells before returning to Boston and joining a management consultancy, Bain & Co., run by some of his former classmates. He was quickly promoted but left in 1981 to start working for AmEx in its Travel Related Services (TRS) strategic planning department, which operates the domestic credit card and travel agency business and provides about 75 percent of the entire company's revenues.

Rising star

From the moment he joined AmEx, Chenault began making vital contributions to the company's success. His record of accomplishments include being named president of AmEx's Consumer Card Group in 1989, running its struggling merchandise services for two years, during which time he grew its revenues from $150 million to $500 million, and overseeing increased circulation in the company's charge card divisions.

During this period Chenault rose through the ranks of TRS, becoming president of the department in the United States in 1993. Two years later he became vice chairman, and in 1997 was named by his predecessor, Harvey Golub as president, chief operating officer (COO), and Golub's top choice as successor.

Golub's own rise to the chairmanship had been a rocky one, his predecessor James D. Robinson having been ousted after an attempt at repackaging AmEx as a "financial supermarket" caused the near-collapse of the TRS department and threatened the survival of the company itself. During the process of restructuring AmEx in the wake of the event, Golub came to rely increasingly on Chenault's marketing and leadership skills. During his time as president of TRS Chenault reinvented the department, broadening the locations in which domestic charge cards could be used. He was also largely behind a

▲ **Kenneth Chenault, pictured here when head of American Express, is one of the most successful African American businessmen in the United States.**

INFLUENCES AND INSPIRATION

Although Chenault was a late bloomer, his principal at Waldorf High School, Peter Curran, was a great influence on him. He shared Chenault's love of history, valued leadership, and saw the unfulfilled potential in the youngster.

While Chenault was at Bowdoin College, he spent hours at the Afro-American Center debating the issues of the time with classmates. Unlike many black activists, he was very much of the opinion that the African American cause could be best served by rising to a position of influence within the establishment rather than attacking it from the outside.

Fiercely competitive and a lifelong athlete, Chenault is acutely aware of the parallels between sports and business. He explains his leadership style as "The coach has to understand the capabilities of the different members of the team, to inspire people, to instill hope. The coach is accountable for the performance of the team."

Chenault is full of praise for his predecessor, Harvey Golub, an inspirational leader from whom he has learned much, and who has been important in his career.

drive to improve employee satisfaction across the company and helped develop AmEx's cultural and organizational attributes.

During the latter part of the 1990s Golub gradually shared more and more of his duties with Chenault. He then stepped down as CEO earlier than expected at the end of 2000 and, with the board having accepted his recommendation of Chenault as his successor, handed over the chairmanship to Chenault at the company's annual general meeting in April 2001.

Impossible problem solver

Although Chenault inherited a company in excellent shape, AmEx faced a period of decreased economic activity. Chenault had to make immediate and dramatic changes in the company. He was forced to lay off thousands of employees both before and after the devastating attacks on New York City on September 11, 2001, which themselves damaged the American Express headquarters.

In the wake of 9/11, American Express faced $1 billion in lost credit, a travel sector contraction of some 40 percent, and a loss of confidence both within the company and across its consumer base. However, with Chenault at the helm AmEx not only survived, it actually gained a relative advantage. In particular, Chenault looked to create company growth that was sustainable and realistic while at the same time reinforcing AmEx's core values and identity. In this respect Chenault's leadership style—widely seen to be a mix of integrity, concern for people, and an ability to motivate and inspire—has been crucial. Despite some hard decisions and many firings, therefore, Chenault remains popular with his employees. His prompt action and strong leadership are widely seen to have stabilized the company. By 2003 Chenault was not only one of New York City's most successful and influential executives but also one of its highest paid, reputed to have earned well over $18 million the previous year.

As well as heading AmEx and holding high positions in other companies and organizations, Chenault lectured at colleges and universities in the United States. Much of the advice he offers reflects his own leadership style, but he emphasizes that for successful companies, progress relies heavily on their ability to adapt and openness to change.

KEY DATES

1951   Born in Long Island, New York, on June 2.

1973   Awarded degree in history by Bowdoin College, Brunswick, Maine.

1976   Graduates with his law degree from Harvard Law School.

1981   Joins American Express as director of strategic planning.

1993   Promoted to president of American Express' Travel Related Services (TRS) department.

1997   Named president and chief operating officer of AmEx.

2001   Becomes chairman and CEO of American Express.

Further reading: Kranz, Rachel. *African-American Business Leaders and Entrepreneurs (A to Z of African Americans).* New York, NY: Facts on File, 2004.
www.findarticles.com/p/articles/mi_m1077/is_n9_v52/ai_ 19565994 (Article on Chenault from *Ebony*, July, 1997).

CHERRY, Don
Musician

Don Cherry was a jazz cornetist who was influenced by musical traditions from around the world. He is hailed as one of the fathers of the musical genre known as "world music."

Donald Eugene Cherry was born in Oklahoma City on November 18, 1936, but was raised in Los Angeles. He began playing trumpet in junior high school and by his late teens was working as a professional musician.

Ornette Coleman

In 1956 Cherry met the saxophonist Ornette Coleman and soon joined the Ornette Coleman Quartet. The quartet released its first album, *Something Else!!!*, in 1958. Their music was seen as revolutionary, causing controversy among traditional jazz fans.

By 1960 the Coleman Quartet had released a number of important recordings, including *Improvising Artists* and *The Shape of Jazz to Come*. At the time Cherry began working with the cornet, or pocket trumpet—a miniature

▼ *Don Cherry with characteristically bulging cheeks at the recording session for his album* **Complete Communion** *(1965).*

KEY DATES

1936   Born in Oklahoma City, Oklahoma, on November 18.

1956   Meets the saxophonist Ornette Coleman and joins his quartet.

1958   Releases *Something Else!!!* as part of the Ornette Coleman Quartet.

1965   Records two of his most highly regarded albums, *Complete Communion* and *Symphony for Improvisers*.

1995   Dies in Malaga, Spain, on October 19.

version of the full-size model. The instrument allowed Cherry to establish his own distinctive playing style as he explored the varied tone qualities of the instrument.

Jazz greats

After leaving Coleman's band in 1961, Cherry went on to work with a wide variety of musicians in the United States and Europe, including John Coltrane, Sonny Rollins, and Albert Ayler.

Following a tour of Europe in 1964, Cherry spent time in Paris, France, where he put together his own band. He returned with them to New York in 1965 to launch himself as a bandleader with the recording of two of his most highly regarded albums, *Complete Communion* and *Symphony for Improvisers*.

In 1970 Cherry taught at Dartmouth College, England, and recorded with the Jazz Composer's Orchestra in 1973. He then lived in Sweden for four years, using it as a base for travels in Europe and the Middle East. His interest in different forms of Asian, African, and Middle Eastern music became a source of inspiration to him, and he began to use traditional instruments in his pieces.

Cherry's experimental style came to be referred to as "world music." In 1978 he formed a trio named Codona that combined aspects of Brazilian and Indian music with a variety of folk styles. At the same time, he joined the band Old and New Dreams, made up of former Ornette Coleman players who mainly played Coleman's material.

Cherry performed into the early 1990s. He died of liver failure in Malaga, Spain, on October 19, 1995.

See also: Ayler, Albert; Coleman, Ornette; Coltrane, John

Further reading: Carr, Roy. *A Century of Jazz.* New York, NY: Da Capo Press, 1997.
www.wnur.org/jazz/artists/cherry.don/ (Biography).

CHESNUTT, Charles W.

Writer

Charles Waddell Chesnutt was the first major African American novelist. As well as being a writer, Chesnutt also worked as a teacher, trained as a lawyer, and ran a successful stenographic firm.

Chesnutt was born on June 20, 1858, in Cleveland, Ohio, to parents of mixed racial background. When he was eight, Chesnutt's family moved to Fayetteville, North Carolina. Alongside his formal schooling, Chesnutt taught himself many subjects, including stenography. As an adult Chesnutt worked as a teacher in the Carolinas before becoming assistant principal of the State Colored Normal School in North Carolina in 1877. Eager to develop his literary talents, he wrote short stories in his spare time.

Although Chesnutt was fair-skinned and could have passed as a white man, he was very aware of his ancestry. Eager to get away from the racism of the South, he moved north, eventually settling in his birthplace of Cleveland, where he studied law. In 1887 he passed his Ohio bar exam and set up a legal shorthand, or stenographic, firm.

Writing career

By this point Chesnutt had had several short stories published. The first to make a real impact, however, was "The Goophered Grapevine," a story of magic and slavery that appeared in the August 1887 edition of the *Atlantic Monthly*. It was the first time an African American had been published in a prestigious magazine. The story brought Chesnutt to the nation's attention. It was followed by two

▲ *Charles Chesnutt chronicled the lives of poor African Americans living in the South.*

collections of short stories, *The Conjure Woman* and *The Wife of His Youth and Other Tales of the Color Line*, published in 1899, that concentrated on the lives of slaves.

In 1900 Chesnutt published his first novel, *The House behind the Cedars,* which told the story of a girl of mixed race living in the postwar South. On the back of his earlier publishing successes he closed his office and concentrated on writing full time. However, his next novel, *The Marrow of Tradition* (1901), was not as successful as his first, and he reopened his stenographic office. His last novel, *The Colonel's Dream*, appeared in 1905.

Disheartened by poor sales, Chesnutt abandoned his literary career to concentrate on campaigning for better treatment of African Americans. In 1928 he was awarded the National Association for the Advancement of Colored People's (NAACP) Spingarn Medal for his pioneering depictions of the lives of African Americans. He died on November 15, 1932.

KEY DATES	
1858	Born in Cleveland, Ohio, on June 20.
1877	Begins work at State Colored Normal School.
1887	Sets up stenographic office; "The Goophered Grapevine" appears in the *Atlantic Monthly*.
1899	Publishes two collections of short stories.
1900	Publishes *The House behind the Cedars*.
1905	Abandons literary career.
1928	Awarded NAACP Spingarn Medal.
1932	Dies in Cleveland, Ohio, on November 15.

Further reading: Chesnutt, Helen. *Charles Waddell Chesnutt, Pioneer of the Color Line.* Chapel Hill, NC: University of North Carolina Press, 1952.
http://www.berea.edu/faculty/browners/chesnutt (Digital archive dedicated to Chesnutt's work).

CHESTER, Thomas
Educator, Journalist, Lawyer

Campaigner, educator, journalist, and lawyer, Thomas Morris Chester was a man who set many precedents for African Americans.

Born in Harrisburg, Pennsylvania, in 1834, the son of a local restaurateur and former slave, Chester was one of the first African Americans to attend college. He studied at Avery College, Pittsburgh, which was a focus of the pre-Civil War "back to Africa" movement, which advocated returning freed slaves to Liberia, a colony on the west coast of Africa that had been established for that purpose by the American Colonization Society in 1821.

In 1854 Chester left the United States to continue his education at the Alexandria High School in Liberia's capital, Monrovia. Despite a brief return to Vermont to graduate from the prestigious Thetford Academy, he stayed on in Liberia to found the *Star of Liberia* newspaper. His lifelong involvement in the education of black Americans began as a school director in Liberia.

Civil War

When his father died in 1859, Chester returned to the United States. During the Civil War (1861–1865) Chester spent two years in the North, lecturing on abolition, the importance of black pride and self-respect, and the return of African Americans to Africa, in particular to Liberia.

In 1864 he was employed by the *Philadelphia Press* as a Civil War correspondent. Although Chester refused to enlist in the Army because he did not agree with its policy that African Americans could not rise above the position of sergeant, he assisted in the war effort by recruiting black troops. He helped form the Massachusetts 54th and 55th Regiments, which were celebrated in the 1989 film *Glory*. Despite his criticism of the Army, Chester was made a captain, the first African American to hold the rank.

After the war Chester became a diplomat, journeying to Europe, and eventually settling in London. He studied law at the Middle Temple, and in 1870 he became the first black lawyer in England. In 1875 he returned to the United States to practice law in Louisiana. He later became the first African American lawyer to appear before the supreme courts of Pennsylvania and the District of Columbia.

Chester died in Harrisburg, Pennsylvania, in 1892. He is buried in Lincoln Cemetery, Pensbrook.

▼ ***Thomas Chester in about 1870, when he was working as a lawyer in England.***

KEY DATES	
1834	Born in Harrisburg, Pennsylvania, on January 17.
1854	Leaves United States to attend Alexandria High School, Monrovia, Liberia.
1859	Returns to United States; travels in the North lecturing on such subjects as abolition and civil rights.
1870	Becomes England's first black barrister.
1875	Returns to United States to practice law.
1892	Dies in Harrisburg on September 20.

Further reading: Blackett, R.J.M. (ed.) *Thomas Morris Chester: Black Civil War Correspondent.* New York, NY: DaCapo Press, 1991.
www.aaregistry.com/african_american_history/660/Lawyer_and_politician_Thomas_Chester (Biography).

CHILDRESS, Alice
Playwright, Actor, Director

Playwright, actor, and director Alice Childress was a pioneer in the development of African American theater. In plays such as *Trouble in Mind* (1954) and *Wedding Band: A Love/Hate Story in Black and White* (1966) she brought realistic, fully rounded black characters onto the mainstream stage, challenging the often stereotyped portrayal of African Americans that had dominated American theater up to that point. Childress's masterly skill as a dramatic writer, combined with her humor, compassion, and acute, unsparing observation of contemporary U.S. race relations, made her one of the great American playwrights of the 20th century.

The Harlem actor

Alice Herndon Childress was born in Charleston, South Carolina, on October 16, 1916. Her parents separated when she was still a child, and she went to live with her maternal grandmother in Harlem, then the center of a flourishing black arts movement now known as the Harlem Renaissance. From an early age Childress wanted to be an actor, but her grandmother's death forced her to drop out of high school and make her own living. After 1935 she also had a daughter, Jean, to support.

In June 1940 writer Abram Hill and actor Frederick O'Neal founded the American Negro Theater (ANT) with 18 other black writers and actors, including Childress, who worked as an actor, coach, and director. At the time most black roles in the theater—both on and off Broadway— were in plays written by white dramatists and were often highly stereotypical or sentimentalized. Parts for black

▲ *Alice Childress wrote plays that dealt with the realities of black lives.*

females, in particular, were rare and were usually of the domineering "Mammy" or prostitute types. Nevertheless, through the 1940s Childress was able to establish a reputation as one of the leading black actors of the time. In 1944 she won a Tony Award nomination for her role in the ANT's successful all-black Broadway production of *Anna Lucasta* by the Polish American Philip Yordan. The play had originally been written about a Polish American family; but after it had been rejected by white companies, the ANT had revised it to make it suitable for a black cast. The play was an immediate success and after five weeks moved to Broadway

Frustrated by the lack of satisfying black female roles, Childress began writing plays herself. Her first play, *Florence*, was produced in 1949 by the ANT. It was about a black woman who at first resists but finally supports her daughter's decision to become an actress. The mother's change of heart occurs when she meets a white actor at a railroad station who offers her daughter a job as a maid because, as she points out, there are not enough theater jobs even for white women. Childress directed and starred in the play.

KEY DATES	
1916	Born in Charleston, South Carolina, on October 16.
1925	Moves to New York City to live with her grandmother.
1940	Helps set up the American Negro Theater.
1949	Produces her first play, *Florence*.
1956	Wins the first Obie Award given to a woman for her play *Trouble in Mind*.
1973	Publishes children's novel *A Hero Ain't Nothin' but a Sandwich*.
1994	Dies in New York City on August 14.

INFLUENCES AND INSPIRATION

The success of black female playwrights like Childress and Lorraine Hansberry during the 1950s has tended to obscure the achievements of earlier playwrights and the influence that they had on them and on other writers. Childress's work owes a debt to Angelina Weld Grimké's play *Rachel* (produced 1916; published 1920), the first full-length play to be written, produced, and acted by African Americans. Although Grimké lived as a white woman, her paternal grandmother was a black slave, and she wrote her play in response to activist W. E. B. DuBois's call for black theater for and about black people.

Like Childress, Grimké (1880–1958) used her play to address serious issues, in this case the murder of black men by white mobs and, in particular, its effects on the widows and orphans of the victims. The title character, Rachel, is a middle-class black girl growing up around 1900 who discovers that both her father and half-brother have been the victims of lynching. Horrified by the violent, murderous racism of her society, Rachel vows not to have any children of her own. Although the play suffered from wooden, sentimental dialogue and an overly propagandistic message, its powerful theme and realistic characters had a lasting effect on later African American dramatic writing.

"I will not keep quiet…"

Over the following decades Childress continued to write plays dealing with the reality of black life and addressing contemporary issues. Her works often focused on poor black Americans struggling to survive in urban ghettos and examined the tragic consequences of racism. "I concentrate on portraying have-nots in a have society," Childress once said, "those seldom singled out by mass media, except as source material for derogatory humor and/or condescending clinical, social analysis." However, her primary concern was never with social protest but with the creation of fully rounded, convincing black characters.

Childress also wrote historical plays, such as *Wedding Band* (1966), the story of a doomed mixed-race love affair set during World War I (1914–1918); plays with music, such as *Just a Little Simple* (1950); and biographical plays such as *The Freedom Drum* (1968), about the young Martin Luther King, Jr. She also wrote plays for children, notably *When the Rattlesnake Sounds* (1975) and *Let's Hear It for the Queen* (1976). In all of her work Childress was passionately concerned about portraying African American lives as accurately and as honestly as she could. In 1987 she declared: "I will not keep quiet, I will not stop telling the truth."

One of Childress's most successful plays was *Trouble in Mind* (1954), which won her an Obie Award in 1956 for best original Off-Broadway production, the first ever awarded to a woman. The play is a satirical attack on the predominantly white world of the New York theater and tells how a black actor, Wiletta Mayer, is fired from a production when she objects to the unconvincing way in which her part is written. The play might have transferred to Broadway had not Childress herself stoutly refused to make changes that would have weakened its racial themes.

This refusal to compromise in telling the truth about black lives is also evident in Childress's novels, particularly those she wrote for children and young adults. In her best-known fictional work, *A Hero Ain't Nothin' but a Sandwich* (1973), she tells the story of 13-year-old Benjie, who struggles not only with the difficulties of ghetto life but also with his heroin addiction. The novel's fierce honesty made it extremely controversial, and it was banned from some school libraries. In 1978, however, the book was made into a movie starring Cicely Tyson and Paul Winfield, with a screenplay by Childress.

Childress's achievements were widely recognized during her lifetime. She received a Paul Robeson Award for Outstanding Contribution to the Arts and won a Rockefeller grant as well as a Harvard appointment to the Radcliffe Institute for Independent Study (now the Mary Ingraham Bunting Institute). Childress died of cancer on August 14, 1994.

See also: DuBois, W. E. B.; Hansberry, Lorraine; Harlem Renaissance; Tyson, Cicely; Winfield, Paul

Further reading: Brown-Guillory, Elizabeth, Margaret Alexander Walker, and Gloria T. Hull. *Their Place on the Stage: Black Women Playwrights in America*. Westport, CT: Praeger Publishing, 1990.
http://www.scils.rutgers.edu/~cybers/childress2.html (Biography and bibliography).

CHINN, May Edward
Physician

May Edward Chinn was the first African American woman to graduate from Bellevue Medical College, New York. She went on to become a cancer specialist despite the difficulties and obstacles facing women in medicine in the early 20th century.

Chinn's remarkable story begins with her birth on April 15, 1896, in Great Barrington, Massachusetts. Her father had escaped from slavery in Virginia when he was 11 years old, and her mother was a Native American working as a housekeeper for the influential Tiffany family in Long Island. At age five Chinn was sent to boarding school, but after a severe illness she returned home to her mother. The Tiffany family encouraged Chinn's interest in education, languages, and music, and in 1917 she passed the entrance examination for Teachers' College at Columbia University, New York.

Music to science

Chinn intended to major in music at the college but at the recommendation of one of her teachers was redirected into the sciences. She excelled at her studies, forging an interest in medicine and working as a lab technician in clinical pathology in her senior year. Following her graduation in 1921, she entered Bellevue Hospital Medical College, New York. In 1926 Chinn became the first African American woman to graduate from the college. She joined Harlem Hospital, where she was the

▼ **In 1980 Columbia University awarded May Edward Chinn an honorary doctorate of science.**

KEY DATES	
1896	Born in Great Barrington, Massachusetts, on April 15.
1921	Graduates from Columbia University.
1926	Graduates from Bellevue Medical College; begins work at Harlem Hospital but later opens a private practice.
1944	Begins working at the Strang Cancer Clinic.
1976	Retires from private practice.
1980	Dies in New York City on December 1.

first African American woman intern and the first to attend accidents alongside paramedics. At the time no African American, let alone a woman, could find full-status work in a major U.S. hospital. The situation prompted Chinn to open a private practice with other African American medical experts in 1926.

Chinn developed a specialty in cancer treatment despite many white physicians withholding their research from her. Between 1928 and 1933 she helped investigate more effective tests for cervical cancer. In 1944 she began working at the Strang Cancer Clinic at Memorial Hospital, staying there in staff positions until 1974, when she retired from the hospital. In 1957 Chinn received a citation from the New York City Cancer Committee of the American Cancer Society. In 1976 she retired from private practice.

Acts of care

Even in retirement Chinn was not idle. She established an organization for promoting African American women in medical sciences, and her extensive work in urban health issues gained her a place on the advisory committee on urban affairs to the surgeon-general. She received honorary degrees from New York University and Columbia University. Chinn died, aged 84, on December 1, 1980, in New York City.

Further reading: Butts, Ellen, and Joyce R. Schwartz. *May Chinn: The Best Medicine.* New York, NY: W.H. Freeman & Co., 1995.
http://www.nlm.nih.gov/changingthefaceofmedicine/physicians/biography_61.html (Biography and photo gallery).

CHISHOLM, Shirley
Politician, Educator

Politician and educator Shirley Anita St. Hill Chisholm was the first African American woman elected to the U.S. Congress. She won a seat as a representative from her home state of New York in 1968. Four years later she ran for the Democratic Party presidential nomination. Through legislative work she helped many underrepresented communities, especially women, people of color, and the poor. Reverend Jesse Jackson called Chisholm a "woman of great courage" who used her voice as an advocate for her constituents.

High achiever
Chisholm was born in Brooklyn, New York, on November 30, 1924, during the 1920s celebration of black art, literature, and culture called the Harlem Renaissance. Like many African Americans at the time, her parents, Ruby and

▼ *Shirley Chisholm in 1972, when she announced her candidacy for the Democratic presidential nomination.*

Charles St. Hill, struggled to provide for their children, spending most of their time away from home at work.

Chisholm's mother sent her and her two siblings to live on their grandmother's farm in Barbados. Chisholm excelled in school and took seriously her father's advice to make something of herself. One of Chisholm's teachers, Louis Warsoff, who taught political science, recognized her ability and encouraged her to go into politics.

Chisholm attended Brooklyn College and decided to become a teacher, majoring in sociology and minoring in Spanish. She joined the Harriet Tubman Society and developed an interest in black history. During her senior year Chisholm met a Guyanese newspaper editor, Wesley McD. Holder, who became her campaign manager. She graduated from college in 1946, married Conrad Chisholm in 1949, and obtained an MA in education from Columbia University. After serving as director of the Hamilton-Madison Child Care Center in New York City from 1953 to 1959, Chisholm became an education consultant for the city's Division of Day Care—supervising 10 centers, 78 teachers, and a budget of more than $300,000.

Unbought and unbossed
Chisholm was drawn into politics in the 1960s as African Americans across the country made a bid for equal rights during the civil rights movement. Working in Bedford-Stuyvesant with her husband, Chisholm formed the Unity Democratic Club and helped register black and Hispanic voters. She gained a loyal following from a neighborhood initiative to replace local uncaring officials. In 1964 Chisholm was drawn into the larger political arena when she ran for the state legislature and won. Using the slogan "Vote for Chisholm for Congress—Unbought and Unbossed," Chisholm was elected to Congress in 1968 after fighting a hard campaign against James Farmer, leader of the Congress on Racial Equality (CORE), a national civil rights organization.

As one of only nine black congressional members, in 1969 Chisholm became a founding member of the Congressional Black Caucus, an organization that campaigns for African American issues. Realizing that she needed far-reaching support to promote the issues of women, people of color, and the poor, Chisholm used her vote strategically to negotiate with powerful politicians. In her first year she helped elect Louisiana Democrat Hale

INFLUENCES AND INSPIRATION

Shirley Chisholm was an inspiration for African American women aspiring to political leadership. She challenged the status quo, running for Congress and the Democratic presidential nomination. Representative Barbara Jordan from Texas followed in Chisholm's footsteps as the first black congresswoman from the South, elected in 1972.

Chisholm was a role model for California representative Barbara Lee (elected 1998) and inspired her to enter politics. Like Chisholm, a pivotal moment in Lee's career came in 2002, after she voted against a U.S. war, in Lee's case Afghanistan.

Other dynamic, outspoken African American women in office who have been influenced by Chisholm and followed in her footsteps include representative Maxine Waters (elected 1991) of California, Florida congresswoman Corrine Brown (elected 1993), and congresswoman Sheila Jackson Lee (elected 1995) of Texas.

Boggs who was white, as majority leader over the African American Michigan Democrat John Conyers. Boggs rewarded her with an appointment to the Education and Labor Committee. Chisholm also visited Alabama governor George Wallace (1919–1998) in the hospital after he had been shot in a failed assasination attempt by Arthur Bremer in 1972. Chisholm's compassion was surprising since Wallace had been her rival in the 1972 presidential race and was an ardent segregationist. In return, however, Wallace helped Chisholm secure votes from other congressional leaders to get a bill passed that extended the minimum wage for domestic workers.

In 1970 Chisholm published her first book, *Unbought and Unbossed*, a memoir in which she describes her experience as one of the few black representatives in Congress and reveals details about her political opinions. Chisholm became the subject of a 2004 film documentary by Shola Lynch, *Chisholm '72 Unbought and Unbossed*, that aimed to encourage minority voters in the United States by highlighting Chisholm's achievements.

During her 12 years in office Chisholm campaigned for civil rights, in particular those of women and minorities, and attacked Congress for sometimes being too much like a club. In the 1970s she spoke out against the Vietnam War (1964–1973). In 1972 Chisholm became the first African American to run for the Democratic Party presidential nomination. Although the nomination went to South Dakota Senator George McGovern, Chisholm was awarded an impressive 152 votes by the delegates compared to McGovern's 1,865.

Winding down

Before her retirement from Congress in 1983 Chisholm mainly fought for labor and education issues. She returned to education after leaving Capitol Hill, becoming the Purington Chair at Mount Holyoke College, Massachusetts, teaching political science and women's studies. She also lectured around the United States. In 1984 she supported Reverend Jesse Jackson's campaign for the Democratic presidential nomination. In 1993 she refused an offer from President Bill Clinton (1993–2001) to become the U.S. ambassador to Jamaica. During her life Chisholm earned numerous awards and honorary degrees. The Clairol Corporation named her "Woman of the Year" in 1973 for outstanding work in public affairs. In 1993 she was inducted into the National Women's Hall of Fame.

KEY DATES

1924   Born in New York City on November 30.

1952   Receives MA in education from Columbia University.

1959   Education consultant with the New York City Division of Day Care.

1968   First African American woman elected to Congress as a representative from New York.

1972   First African American to run for the Democratic presidential nomination.

1983   Becomes Purington Chair, Mount Holyoke College.

2005   Dies in Ormond Beach, Florida, on January 1.

See also: Civil Rights; Farmer, James; Harlem Renaissance; Jackson, Jesse; Jordan, Barbara; Political Representation

---

Further reading: Scheader, Catherine. *Shirley Chisholm, Teacher and Congresswoman.* Hillside, NJ: Enslow Publishers, 1990. http://bioguide.congress.gov/scripts/biodisplay.pl?index=C000371 (Congress biography).

CHRISTIAN, Charlie
Musician

One of the greatest jazz guitarists of the 1930s and 1940s, Charlie Christian pioneered the guitar's role as a solo instrument within the "swing" sound. His influence on subsequent black and white guitarists from B. B. King to Jimi Hendrix and Eric Clapton was immense.

Solo guitar

Charles Henry Christian was born on July 29, 1916, in Bonham, Texas, a small town to the northeast of Dallas. From his earliest years Christian was surrounded by music and musicians: His father was a talented trumpet player and his oldest brother, Edward, a jazz pianist. After his father went blind, the family moved to Oklahoma City, hub of the vibrant Midwest jazz scene.

While still a teenager, Christian showed remarkable talent on the guitar, impressing local and Midwest audiences alike with his masterly and lengthy improvisations. Previously guitarists had played only a background role in jazz orchestras, providing the music with rhythm and color. Christian, by contrast, proved that the guitar could hold its own as a solo instrument, like the

▼ **Charlie Christian was the most brilliant electric guitar soloist of his time.**

KEY DATES

1916 Born in Bonham, Texas, on July 29.

1937 Buys his first electric guitar.

1939 Plays with the Benny Goodman Sextet for the first time in Beverly Hills, California.

1942 Dies in New York City on March 2.

trumpet or saxophone. In 1937 he began to use an electric guitar, developing his distinctive one-line solo style featuring sustained and "bent" notes.

A national celebrity

In 1939 Christian came to the attention of the jazz producer John Hammond, who introduced him to the renowned white orchestra leader Benny Goodman (1909–1986), the so-called "King of Swing." Initially hesitant about including a guitarist in one of his bands, Goodman was won over when Christian played with the Benny Goodman Sextet at a club in Beverly Hills, California, in August that year. Goodman's bands were among the first to include both white and black players; performing alongside Christian in the sextet were players such as the white pianist Johnny Guarnieri (1917–) and the black vibraphone player Lionel Hampton (1908–2002).

Over the next two years Christian made numerous recordings with Goodman, including such classics as "Shivers" (1939), "Royal Garden Blues" (1940), and "Air Mail Special" (1941). He also played alongside figures such as Charlie Parker and Thelonious Monk, and influenced the bebop style that emerged during the 1940s.

Christian died of tuberculosis in New York City in 1942. He was just 25 years old, but his achievements as an electric guitarist have influenced all guitarists since.

See also: Hendrix, Jimi; King, B. B.; Monk, Thelonious; Parker, Charlie

Further reading: Broadbent, Peter. *Charlie Christian: Solo Flight.* Blaydon-on-Tyne: Ashley Mark Publishing Co., 2003. http://www.charlie-christian.com (Official site with testimonials and samples of Christian's work).

CHUBBY Checker
Singer

One of the outstanding rock-'n'-roll singers of the 1960s, Ernest Evans is best known for his 1960 song "The Twist," the accompanying dance of which became a national craze. Evans's nickname, Chubby Checker, was given to him as a joking reference to another black rock-'n'-roll singer of the time, Fats Domino.

Doing the Twist

Evans was born in Spring Gulley, South Carolina, on October 3, 1941, but was raised in Philadelphia, Pennsylvania, where he attended South Philadelphia High School. After school he worked in a poultry store, where he entertained customers with his impressions of popular singers of the day such as Chuck Berry and Elvis Presley. The store owner was impressed enough to put Evans in contact with the rock-'n'-roll radio host and promoter Dick Clark, with whom the singer recorded his first single, "The Class," in 1959.

Checker's first real hit, however, came with his recording of Hank Ballard's "The Twist," which reached No. 1 on the charts in 1960 and then again in 1962—the only record ever to have achieved the distinction of being No. 1 twice more than a year apart. The fast-paced, happy-go-lucky song launched a national dance craze—dubbed "Twistmania" by the media—and was followed by a string of Top 10 hits, including "The Fly" (1961), "Let's Twist Again" (1961), for which Checker won a Grammy Award for Best Rock Performance, and "Slow Twistin'" (1962).

In 1966, after 32 chart hits, Checker's run of success came to an end as the rock craze with which he was so closely associated itself declined in popularity. Some observers have claimed that this change of fortunes was in part due to his marriage in 1964 to Catherina Lodders, the Dutch winner of the 1962 Miss World beauty contest. At the time of their wedding mixed-race marriages were often disapproved of by both black and white communities, and Checker suffered prejudice as a result.

A music professional

Checker's career as a singer, however, was far from over. He and his band—renamed the Wildcats in the 1980s—toured extensively and continued to record new material. In 1982 Checker released the disco-inspired album *The Change Has Come* and in 1988 returned to the Top 40 when he appeared on a rap version of "The Twist" by the Fat Boys.

▲ *Chubby Checker in 1962, the year "The Twist" reached No. 1 on the charts for the second time.*

Despite his continuing presence and popularity on the music scene, Checker and his music will forever be associated with the exhilarating rock-'n'-roll era of the 1960s.

KEY DATES	
1941	Born in Spring Gulley, South Carolina, October 3.
1960	"The Twist" reaches No. 1 on the charts.
1962	"The Twist" reaches No. 1 for the second time.
1964	Marries Dutch former Miss World Catherina Lodders.
1982	Releases the album *The Change Has Come*.

See also: Ballard, Hank; Berry, Chuck; Domino, Fats

Further reading: Stuessy, Joe, and Scott David Lipscomb. *Rock and Roll: Its History and Stylistic Development.* Englewood Cliffs, NJ: Prentice Hall, 1998.
http://Chubbychecker.com (Site devoted to Chubby Checker).

CINQUÉ, Joseph
Slave, Mutineer

Joseph Cinqué was born Sengbe Pieh in the West African village of Mani in 1813. The son of a rice farmer, Cinqué later became the center of a controversial legal case in the United States that involved parties from Africa, Europe, and North America, and rallied the U.S. antislavery movement. The case was fought all the way to the Supreme Court, where former president John Quincy Adams defended Cinqué and other Africans involved in the case. The *Amistad* case, as it came to be known, influenced the course of U.S. history. It was also the subject of the 1997 film *Amistad*, directed by Steven Spielberg.

Sold into slavery

Cinqué, a farmer, was married with a son and two daughters when in late January 1839 he was captured on the way to work by four men from an enemy tribe. He was taken to a "slave factory" where he was sold to a Spanish slave trader and eventually transported across the Atlantic to Havana, Cuba. At a slave auction Cinqué and 49 African slaves were sold to José Ruiz to work on his sugar plantation at Puerto Principe, another Cuban port 300 miles (483km) from Havana. In late June 1839 the slaves and four African children belonging to another plantation owner, Pedro Montez, were put aboard an American-built schooner originally named *Friendship* but renamed *Amistad* when it was bought and registered by a Spaniard. Although Spain had prohibited the importation of new slaves since 1820, the two Spanish planters managed to obtain official permits to transport the slaves.

Mutiny

Although the journey from Havana to Puerto Principe was expected to take two to three days, storms slowed the progress of the *Amistad*. During the voyage the crew became abusive to the slaves, some telling them that they would be killed and eaten on the ship's arrival at Puerto Principe. On hearing this, Cinqué resolved to take over the ship. On July 1 Cinqué used a loose spike he had taken from the deck of the *Amistad* to remove the shackles that bound him and his fellow slaves. Armed with sugarcane knives they found in the cargo hold, the mutineers seized the ship and killed the captain and cook. Cinqué spared the lives of Ruiz and Montez, and ordered the Spaniards to sail in the direction of the rising sun, or east toward Africa. Strong winds, however, drove the ship northeast to the

United States. For two months the *Amistad* drifted, and Cinqué held command, forcing the others to conserve food and water, allotting a full ration only to the four children and taking the smallest portion for himself. On August 1839 the ship stopped near the eastern tip of Long Island for food and water. Before long a Navy ship encountered the *Amistad*, and its commander ordered his men to seize the Africans.

Imprisonment

In Connecticut the slaves were charged with murder and piracy. Although the murder charges were eventually dismissed, the slaves remained in prison while the planters, the Spanish government, and the captain of the ship all laid claim to them. Acting through the administration of President Van Buren in Washington, D.C., the Spanish government sought to return the Africans to Cuba, where they would likely have been put to death. President Van Buren had no strong views on the slavery question, but he wanted to extradite the slaves to Cuba because his reelection in 1840 depended on the support of

▼ *In 1839 the* **New York Sun** *commissioned a portrait of Cinqué while he awaited trial in New Haven. It was published in its August 31 edition.*

INFLUENCES AND INSPIRATION

The *Amistad* case had an important influence on the course of U.S. history. Although the Supreme Court's decision to return the slaves on board the *Amistad* to Africa was not an attack on slavery, it brought the abolitionists together and prevented the movement from breaking up. The case so embittered feelings between the antislavery North and the slaveholding South that it is seen as one of the events that led to the outbreak of the Civil War (1861–1865). The missionary work that began with the freedom of those on board the *Amistad* led to the establishment in 1846 of the American Missionary Association, then the largest abolitionist society in the United States. After the war the association established more than 500 schools and colleges in the South for the education of newly liberated African Americans.

the proslavery southern Democrats. Abolitionists, on the other hand, were convinced of Cinqué's innocence and that of the other Africans. They saw the case as an opportunity to rally the dispersed ranks of the abolition movement by humanizing slavery. Abolitionists who opposed extradition hired a defense team for the slaves. The lawyers argued in a federal court that the slaves were kidnap victims rather than property, since they had been brought to Cuba in direct violation of Spain's slave laws. During the proceedings Ruiz renamed Sengbe Pieh José Cinqué (later Anglicized to Joseph Cinqué) in an effort to prove that Sengbe had not been recently imported and that Ruiz himself was therefore not guilty of violating Spanish law. In the trial Cinqué made a favorable impression on the court, at one point rising and shouting in English: "Give us free! Give us free!" The court ruled in favor of the defense, concluding that the slaves on the *Amistad* had been kidnapped and sold into slavery in violation of Spanish law, and should be freed and taken back to Africa. Many people disagreed with the verdict, including Van Buren, who ordered an appeal.

Freedom

The abolitionists defending the African captives recognized the need for a renowned public figure to plead their case before the Supreme Court. They persuaded former president John Quincy Adams to lead the defense. On February 24, 1841, Adams addressed the court for four and a half hours. On March 9, 1841, the Supreme Court issued its final verdict: The defendants were to be freed. Joseph Cinqué was one of 35 former slaves who returned to Africa with the help of sympathetic missionary societies. The others died either in prison or on the journey back to Africa. When Cinqué returned home, he discovered that his family had disappeared and his entire village had been destroyed by war. It is suspected that his family was sold into slavery. Cinqué died in Sierra Leone in 1879.

See also: Slavery; Supreme Court

Further reading: Owens, William A., *Black Mutiny: The Revolt on the Schooner* Amistad. Baltimore, MD: Black Classic Press, 1997.
www.law.umkc.edu/faculty/projects/ftrials/amistad/
AMISTD.HTM (Account of the *Amistad* trial).

KEY DATES

1813   Born in the West African village of Mani.

January–June 1839   Captured and sold into slavery; eventually taken to Cuba, where he is sold to José Ruiz.

July 1839   Leads a mutiny aboard the *Amistad*.

August 1839   The *Amistad* is captured by crew of USS *Washington* off Long Island, New York; Africans taken to Connecticut to await trial in a New Haven jail.

January 8, 1840   The *Amistad* civil trial begins.

January 15, 1840   District Court judge rules that the Africans are to be freed.

September 1840   Circuit Court judge upholds District Court decision; government appeals to the Supreme Court.

February–March 1841   Supreme Court orders Africans to be freed.

March–November 1841   Cinqué and other Africans remain in the United States for education.

November 1841   Cinqué and other survivors from the *Amistad* leave with American missionaries for Africa.

January 1842   Arrives in Sierra Leone; Cinqué and many of the *Amistad* Africans abandon missionaries.

1879   Cinqué dies in Sierra Leone at an American mission.

CIVIL RIGHTS

The wording of the Declaration of Independence—"We hold these truths to be self-evident: that all men are created equal...."—seems powerful in its simplicity. But Thomas Jefferson, the author of those words, was a slave owner. And although the concept of equal rights has been around since 1776, the real achievement of equal treatment under the law came much later.

The meaning of civil rights
The first 10 amendments to the Constitution are together known as the Bill of Rights. Although technically "amendments" or "changes" to the Constitution, the Bill of Rights was passed within four years of the adoption of the Constitution itself in 1789. However, the Bill of Rights did not establish civil rights; it concerns itself solely with civil liberties.

A civil liberty is, essentially, a right to be left alone by the government. A civil right, on the other hand, is something a citizen is entitled to expect from the government. Civil liberties include freedom of speech, freedom of religion, freedom from unreasonable searches and seizures, and freedom from cruel and unusual punishment. The government protects civil liberties simply by not limiting what people can say and not imposing sentences such as torture.

As defined by political scientists Theodore Lowi and Benjamin Ginsberg, however, a civil right is "a legal or moral claim that citizens are entitled to make

KEY DATES	
1791	Bill of Rights ratified: It protects civil liberties but not civil rights.
1865	Ratification of first of three civil rights amendments (Thirteenth, Fourteenth, Fifteenth): marks first provision for civil rights in the Constitution.
1896	*Plessy v. Feguson* decision: The Supreme Court strikes a blow against civil rights by endorsing "separate but equal" facilities.
1954	*Brown v. Board Education* decision: The Supreme Court overturns *Plessy* decision and strikes down racially segregated schools.
1955	Montgomery bus boycott begins.
1963	Martin Luther King, Jr., leads march on Washington, D.C.
1964	Civil Rights Act passed by Congress.
1965	Voting Rights Act passed by Congress.

upon government." Instead of being a right to be left alone, a civil right is an obligation that the government should intervene on an individual's behalf.

A modern example of a civil right is the right to be free from discrimination, especially on the grounds of race. If a voter is turned away from the polls because of his or her race, or a customer is refused service at a restaurant because of skin color, those individuals' civil rights have been violated. It is the obligation of the federal government to come to their defense.

Neither the Constitution nor the Bill of Rights make any mention of the right to be free from discrimination; nor do they say anything about race, ethnicity, or gender.

The 1800s
Although the Constitution did not contain the words "slave" or "slavery" several sections plainly

sanction slavery. Not all African Americans were slaves: There were free blacks in the North and even some in the South. But the vast majority of African Americans in the South were slaves, and even free blacks in the North were treated as second-class citizens.

In the decades leading up to the Civil War (1861–1865), there was a very active antislavery movement in the North. Although abolitionists could agree on the desirability of ending slavery, however, there was little agreement on whether African Americans should have full social equality with whites. Some people, like fiery publisher William Lloyd Garrison, argued for full integration of American society; others, like up-and-coming Republican politician Abraham Lincoln, favored some form of racial separation or inequality. At times Lincoln endorsed the idea of resettling freed slaves in Africa; the African nation of Liberia had been established by an abolitionist faction in the 1820s for that very purpose.

Tensions between the North and the South over slavery were the major cause of the Civil War. After the Union victory at Antietam in 1862, President Lincoln issued the Emancipation Proclamation, which pledged to free slaves held in the Southern states. The move was symbolic: The slaves Lincoln "freed" were precisely those not under his control. But at the same time Lincoln authorized a more practical measure: The Union began to recruit and arm large numbers of free black soldiers, including many former slaves. The Union would have been hard-pressed to win the war without their participation.

The Union victory in the war was quickly followed by the passage of the so-called Civil Rights Amendments to the Constitution. The Thirteenth Amendment outlawed slavery and the Fifteenth Amendment guaranteed the right to vote to all males, regardless of skin color. (Women would not receive a similar guarantee until the Nineteenth Amendment was ratified in 1920.) The Fourteenth Amendment required federal and state governments to ensure that all citizens received the "equal protection of the law." These amendments were the first explicit reference to civil rights in the Constitution.

The promise on paper of equal treatment often meant little in practice. In 1883 the Supreme Court declared that the Fourteenth Amendment did not prevent "private" discrimination: Employers, landlords, and business

owners were under no obligation to treat everyone equally.

An even more devastating retreat from equality came with the end of Northern military rule in the South in 1876. During the period called Reconstruction, Northern authorities ensured that freed slaves in the South could vote, run for office, attend school, and open businesses. When the troops left, Southern state governments again fell under the dominance of former slave holders and other wealthy white voters.

The post-Reconstruction state governments passed laws known as black codes and Jim Crow laws that stripped away the legal equality of African Americans in the South: Blacks were prevented from voting and segregated from white society. The state of Alabama made it a crime for black and white citizens to play billiards together and for white nurses to be assigned to hospital wards with black patients. In Georgia no blacks were permitted in public parks reserved for whites and no African American could be buried

The office of the Detroit, Michigan, branch of the National Association for the Advancement of Colored People (NAACP) in the 1940s. The organization was founded in 1909.

in cemetery space reserved for whites. Mississippi made it a crime simply to speak publicly in favor of racial equality.

This strict segregation received the approval of the Supreme Court in the *Plessy v. Ferguson* case in 1896. While it was true that the Fourteenth Amendment required that all citizens receive the "equal protection of the law," a majority of the Court argued "separate but equal" treatment was constitutional. Separate schools, parks, and railroad cars were rarely equal in quality or comfort, but they were legal.

1900–1940

In 1900 the African American population was still heavily concentrated in the South. Facing poverty and segregation, many Southern blacks moved to the cities of the North, the Midwest, and the West, where factory jobs paid better than working on Southern farms and the right to vote was usually protected. But even there, African Americans almost always faced discrimination and some form of segregation.

African Americans outside the South were more able to organize into effective groups. The National Association for the Advancement of Colored People (NAACP), founded in 1909, and the National Urban League, founded in 1911, advanced the cause of civil rights in the northern states. The NAACP's Legal Defense Fund used the courts to try to enforce existing civil rights laws and to point out the inequalities of segregation. The NAACP had greater difficulty organizing African Americans in the South; there blacks often relied on religious leaders and church congregations to provide a sense of community organization.

The Great Depression of the 1930s proved critical, in an indirect way, for the pursuit of civil rights. In the midst of the Depression President Franklin D. Roosevelt fought for blacks to be included in jobs programs around the country and sought to ban race-based discrimination among companies working for the federal government. Shortly before the 1936 election, FDR appointed the renowned African American educator Mary McLeod Bethune as his special adviser for minority affairs. In response to these practical and symbolic gestures, African American voters flocked to Roosevelt's Democratic Party.

But the Democrats were also the party of conservative white Southerners, and had been since Reconstruction. FDR's fellow Democrats in the South still prevented most Southern blacks from voting, and they effectively blocked many of Roosevelt's limited proposals for protecting civil rights, including antilynching laws that would have made racially motivated killings in the South federal crimes.

The 1940s

A final key factor in setting the stage for the dramatic progress in civil rights came with World War II (1939–1945). African Americans served in large numbers, but in segregated units and usually in noncombat roles. The great success of the all-black "Tuskegee Airmen" fighter squadron and the "Red Ball Express" transport unit put the lie to the claim that black soldiers were inferior to whites. Black soldiers and veterans, such as Lieutenant Jackie Robinson, were less willing to accept second-class status, either in the military or back home in civilian life.

Partly in recognition of the African American contribution in wartime, President Harry S. Truman ordered an end to segregation in the military in 1948. That same year, Jackie Robinson became the first African American player in baseball's major leagues for generations. Although Congress (especially the Senate) was still reluctant to pass new civil rights legislation, the wall of segregation was indeed crumbling.

The 1950s

In the late 1800s the Supreme Court had been a major opponent of civil rights. But in the late 1940s and early 1950s, the Court began to chip away at the *Plessy* decision in a series of cases. The antisegregation side of the case was frequently argued by the

Arkansas Governor Orval Faubus protests the desegregation of schools in the Little Rock school district in 1958.

NAACP Legal Defense Fund, then led by the brilliant attorney and jurist Thurgood Marshall.

Finally, in 1954, the Court struck a major blow for civil rights in the *Brown v. Board of Education* case, which declared that "separate but equal" segregated schools were unconstitutional. From the Brown decision on, the Supreme Court steadily undermined the legal basis for racial discrimination.

But the real challenge to racial discrimination in the 1950s and 1960s came not in formal courts of law; it came from the words and actions of courageous African American leaders such as Martin Luther King, Jr., and from the participation of millions of black

Rosa Parks in 1956 re-creates the moment when she refused to give up her bus seat, sparking the Montgomery bus strike of 1955.

and white Americans who took part in the civil rights movement.

The mass civil rights movement is often dated to 1955, with the success of the Montgomery Bus Boycott and the birth of the Southern Christian Leadership Conference (SCLC; *see box*). What

the civil rights movement sought was in one sense just what the Fourteenth Amendment seemed to promise: the equal protection of the law. To King and other civil rights leaders, this meant an end

TURNING POINT

A crucial victory in the history of the civil rights movement began with an event that was routine in the life of African Americans in Montgomery, the capital city of Alabama.

Rosa Parks, a well-educated black woman who was employed as a seamstress, boarded a Montgomery city bus in the normal way for African Americans: She boarded by the front door, paid her fare, exited the front door, reboarded by the rear door, and took her seat in one of the rows in back of the bus, in the colored section. Like all black riders, she had suffered this indignity hundreds of times.

On December 1, 1955, she suffered a further indignity: The bus was very crowded that day, and black passengers in the first row of the colored section were ordered to move back to make

room for white passengers. That day, Rosa Parks refused to move. She defied the orders of the bus driver, and she was arrested by the Montgomery city police.

Parks was an active member of the local NAACP. Instead of accepting her punishment, she agreed to make her case the center of a new attack on segregation. A boycott of the privately-owned bus service was organized by local college professor Jo Ann Robinson and a local Baptist minister, Martin Luther King, Jr.

The group led by King, Robinson, and Parks hoped that a boycott would put economic pressure on the bus company and the city as a whole, and attract national attention to the injustice of the segregated buses. King paid a personal

price: He was charged with violating a law banning organized boycotts and was fined $500.

Even in the face of enormous pressure from elected white officials and the racist White Citizen's Council, the boycott held. For over a year black riders shunned the city buses and relied instead on a system of private taxis that shuttled black residents around the city.

In December 1956, a year after the boycott began, the Supreme Court ordered all bus systems to be desegregated. Building on the victory, King took the core of his Montgomery group and used it to found the Southern Christian Leadership Conference, which would be at the heart of the civil rights movement for the next decade.

to Jim Crow laws and other official endorsements of segregation. Equality also meant something more than the absence of legal segregation; it meant an end to the pervasive inequalities in American society, a society that had for too long treated African Americans as inferior.

The early 1960s

The use of civil disobedience quickly became a hallmark of the civil rights movement. It involves deliberately breaking a law to show publicly how unjust that law is. For example, African Americans deliberately sat in white-only areas of restaurants and waiting rooms.

Although the demonstrators were often arrested and sometimes beaten, their purpose was to display the unfairness and the brutality of segregation to the country as a whole. King was arrested several times while engaging in civil disobedience, and he used the opportunity to write his famous "Letter from a Birmingham Jail" to make his case to the American people.

While civil disobedience was an appropriate tactic for individuals and small groups, the movement also organized protest marches in which tens or hundreds of thousands of marchers showed the extent of popular support for civil rights. The 1963 March on Washington (*see box*) and the 1965 march on Selma, Alabama, were two of the most important.

The emphasis on civil disobedience and peaceful mass marches and rallies was in keeping with the strategy of nonviolence favored by King and most of the other mainstream civil rights leaders. Their opponents, however, did not share a similar

On August 28, 1963, a massive demonstration organized by Martin Luther King, Jr., and other black leaders, converged on Washington, D.C., King gave his most famous speech at the demonstration, speaking to a quarter-million civil rights supporters gathered in front of the Lincoln Memorial.

Although at the time many of the opponents of civil rights (including FBI director J. Edgar Hoover) labeled King a communist and a subversive, his speech deliberately placed the cause of civil rights within the mainstream of American history. Speaking on behalf of an oppressed minority, King deliberately phrased his appeal in terms that could move the hearts and minds of all American people.

"I say to you today, my friends, so even though we face the difficulties of today and tomorrow, I still have a dream.

It is a dream deeply rooted in the American dream.

I have a dream that one day this nation will rise up and live out the true meaning of its creed: 'We hold these truths to be self-evident: that all men are created equal.'

I have a dream that one day on the red hills of Georgia the sons of former slaves and the sons of former slave owners will be able to sit down together at the table of brotherhood.

I have a dream that one day even the state of Mississippi, a state sweltering with the heat of injustice, sweltering with the heat of oppression, will be transformed into an oasis of freedom and justice.

I have a dream that my four little children will one day live in a nation where they will not be judged by the color of their skin but by the content of their character."

commitment to avoiding violence. Marchers and protesters were beaten or intimidated, often by law enforcement officials. Bull Connor, the notoriously racist police chief of Birmingham, Alabama, used police dogs and water cannons to attack marchers in his city. Many officials who wore the uniform of a police officer or sheriff's deputy during the day wore the white hood and robes of the KKK at night. Civil rights activists in Mississippi and Alabama were murdered by such moonlighting police.

The violence directed at the peaceful civil rights movement had the effect that King desired: The sympathy of the American people, and the mood in Washington, D.C., swung decisively in favor of civil rights. President Lyndon B. Johnson, himself a white Southerner, successfully pushed Congress to pass the two most significant civil rights laws in American history.

The Civil Rights Act of 1964 outlawed racial discrimination in hiring, in housing, and in public accommodations such as hotels and restaurants. The Voting Rights Act of 1965 introduced federal supervision of elections and voter registration, preventing state governments from disenfranchising black voters. After 100 years the promises of the Fourteenth and Fifteenth amendments were finally redeemed.

The late 1960s and 1970s

The struggle for civil rights continued after 1965, but the civil rights movement of the 1950s and 1960s began to disintegrate. One major cause was the Vietnam War (1964–1973) to which ground troops were committed in 1965. Young and poor African Americans were drafted into the army in large numbers, and many civil rights leaders (King included) publicly criticized Johnson, who in turn felt betrayed by those he had tried to help. The war steadily eroded Johnson's popularity among the American people and the commitment to nonviolence among civil rights leaders.

The social and political upheaval associated with the war also emboldened a more confrontational group of black leaders. King's former rival, Malcolm X, had been assassinated in 1965, but other, more militant voices arose to take his place. Huey Newton, Eldridge Cleaver, and Bobby Seale started the Black Panther Party, and along with Stokely Carmichael (Kwame Toure) and Maulana Karenga this new generation embraced the ideal of black power.

Instead of hoping for a color-blind society, the new black leaders of the late 1960s saw America's racial divide as a permanent condition. The proper response was not peaceful coexistence and integration but the construction of a strong and largely separate black community

within the United States. King's assassination in the spring of 1968 triggered violent riots across the country, and from that point on any hope for the continuation of a unified civil rights movement based on the principles of nonviolence was gone.

Many white Americans had a different reaction to Vietnam. In 1968 presidential candidate Richard M. Nixon campaigned on a promise of restoring "law and order" on behalf of a "silent majority" of Americans tired of social change. Nixon's election brought an end to the alliance between the civil rights movement and the White House. No longer would the president be publicly sympathetic to the expansion of civil rights.

However, the Nixon administration did expand the affirmative action programs begun under Johnson, which aimed to provide short-term preferences for African Americans for federal jobs and contracts. Many private employers and universities established similar practices. The Supreme Court later barred the use of formal "quotas" that reserved a set number of jobs or openings for minorities, and the overall legality of affirmative action remained unclear.

Civil rights today

In one important sense, the civil rights movement was a victim of its own success. Segregation required by law or protected by law (de jure segregation) was destroyed, and would be legally and politically unthinkable to revive. To some degree, therefore, organizations such as the NAACP and SCLC declined because they had accomplished their mission.

However, if the hope of the civil rights movement was to bring social and economic as well as legal equality, then much remains to be done. And while de jure segregation is dead and buried, de facto segregation—or segregation in practice—remains.

Most African Americans live in neighborhoods that are overwhelmingly black, and most African American children attend schools that are scarcely more integrated now than in the days of the Brown decision. But while the extent of progress may be debatable, progress is undeniable. African Americans are in positions of power, wealth, and prominence all across society, with greater influence in politics, business, and culture than ever before.

See also: Affirmative Action; Bethune, Mary McLeod; Carmichael, Stokely; Cleaver, Eldridge; Emancipation and Reconstruction; Karenga, Maulana; King, Martin Luther, Jr; Malcolm X; Marshall, Thurgood; Military; National Oganizations; Newton, Huey; Parks, Rosa; Robinson Jackie; Seale, Bobby

Further reading: Woodward, C. Vann. *The Strange Career of Jim Crow*. New York, NY: Oxford University Press, 2001. Branch, Taylor. *Parting the Waters*. New York, NY: Simon & Schuster, 1989. Bowen, William, and Derek Bok. *The Shape of the River*. Princeton, NJ: Princeton University Press, 2004. http://www.census.gov/statab/www/sa04baa.pdf (Database of recent economic, educational, and social statistics showing differences by race and ethnicity). http://www.pbs.org/beyondbrown/history/fullhistory.html (*Brown v. Board of Education* case). http://www.splcenter.org/index.jsp (Southern Poverty Law Center site).

CLARK, Kenneth B.
Social Scientist, Psychologist, Educator

A groundbreaking psychologist and social scientist, Kenneth Bancroft Clark is best known for his role as an expert witness in the landmark 1954 Supreme Court case *Brown v. Board of Education*, which ended racial segregation in public schools in the United States.

Clark was born on July 24, 1914, in the U.S.-controlled Panama Canal Zone, where his father worked as a cargo superintendent. His mother's determination to give her children a good education led her to leave her husband and settle in Harlem, New York City. As a young boy Clark flourished academically, eventually winning a place to study psychology at Howard University in Washington, D.C., from which he graduated in 1935. In 1940 he earned a PhD from Colombia University in New York City.

Clark's main concern as a psychologist was the destructive effect of racism on young black people. In order to study the issue, he and his wife, psychologist Mamie Phipps Clark (1917–1983), founded the Northside Testing and Consultation Center, later the Northside Center for Child Development, in Harlem. One of their most famous experiments involved asking young black children to chose the "bad" doll out of two dolls—one black and one white. Most of the children chose the black doll— evidence, the Clarks argued, that racism caused black children to have low self-esteem.

A landmark case

In the early 1950s Clark was chosen as an expert witness by the National Association for the Advancement of Colored People (NAACP) in a series of legal challenges to the racial segregation of public schools. Clark prepared a paper on the effects of segregation for the final Supreme Court hearing in 1954; the paper was cited by the court as having had a powerful influence on its decision to overturn segregation.

In 1962 Clark established Harlem Youth Opportunities Unlimited (HARYOU), which aimed to make radical improvements in the educational achievements of black children. However, the organization collapsed before it could implement any of Clark's ideas. Disillusioned, Clark went on to write one of his most influential books, *Dark Ghetto: Dilemmas of Social Power* (1965), in which he attacked racism, in particular its effects on black children.

At the core of Clark's ideas was the belief that education must be about learning to respect other people. Clark argued that for as long as educational systems fail to grasp this, both the individual and society will suffer.

▼ **Kenneth Clark at around the time he submitted a key report in the 1954 Supreme Court ruling against segregation in public schools.**

KEY DATES

1914   Born in the Panama Canal Zone on July 24.

1946   With his wife, Mamie Clark, cofounds the Northside Testing and Consultation Center.

1954   Submits report to the Supreme Court that helps overturn racial segregation in public schools.

1965   Publishes his influential book *Dark Ghetto: Dilemmas of Social Power*.

2005   Dies in Hastings-on-Hudson, New York, on May 1.

See also: Supreme Court; Segregation and Integration

Further reading: Clark, Kenneth B. *Dark Ghetto: Dilemmas of Social Power*. Middletown, CT: Wesleyan University Press, 1989. http://c250.columbia.edu/c250_celebrates/remarkable_columbians/kenneth_mamie_clark.html (Columbia page on the Clarks).

CLARK, Septima P.
Educator, Civil Rights Activist

Septima Poinsette Clark fought hard to overcome racism and discrimination in American society, particularly through her work in the educational system. Sometimes referred to as the "grandmother of the civil rights movement," Clark dedicated her life to improving the lives of fellow African Americans.

Born in Charleston, South Carolina, in 1898, Septima Poinsette was the second child of Peter Porcher Poinsette, a former slave, and Victoria Anderson, a freeborn African American. She graduated in teaching from Avery Institute, Charleston, in 1916 and became a teacher on John's Island, where she taught children and adults. Illiteracy and poverty were rife there, and schooling was crammed into the short period between harvests. The school itself was a crumbling, cramped building that was unsuitable for teaching its 130 students. Meanwhile John's Island also had a new facility that catered to just three white students who were taught by a white woman earning three times Clark's salary.

In 1919 Clark returned to teach at Avery Institute. She fought hard to get posts for black teachers in the Charleston school system through her work with the National Association for the Advancement of Colored People (NAACP). In 1920 she married Nerie Clark, with whom she had two children; but after her husband died in 1925, she worked in the public schools of North and South Carolina and Ohio. Clark went to Columbia, South Carolina, to teach in public schools and worked with the NAACP in their bid to equalize wages between white and black teachers. She was also studying during this time and earned BA and MA degrees in 1942 and 1945 respectively.

When her mother became ill, Clark returned to Charleston, where she carried on teaching and worked with the Young Women's Christian Association and NAACP. Her refusal to give up her membership in the NAACP led to her being banned from teaching in South Carolina public schools; the South Carolina legislature prohibited state employees from being members of civil rights groups. Unable to teach in South Carolina, Clark took a job in Tennessee.

Highlander Folk School and citizenship schools

Clark's relationship with the integrated Highlander Folk School near Chattanooga, Tennessee, led to her involvement in the citizenship movement. The Highlander

KEY DATES

1898   Born in Charleston, South Carolina, on May 3.

1919   Teaches at Avery Institute, Charleston, and becomes involved with the NAACP.

1961   Joins the Southern Christian Leadership Council.

1982   Receives the Order of the Palmetto.

1987   Dies on John's Island, South Carolina, on December 15.

Folk School was a place where white and black liberals could meet and discuss matters such as voting rights. In order to register to vote, American citizens had to be able to read and understand parts of the Constitution. With Highlander's help Clark established adult literacy programs and citizenship schools, which furnished blacks with the skills that enabled them to register to vote. The Highlander Folk School was closed by the educational authorities in 1959. In 1961 Clark joined the Southern Christian Leadership Conference (SCLC), which continued Highlander's citizenship program; a year later it cofounded the Voter Education Project. Clark worked with Andrew Young and Dororthy Cotton Clark to reestablish the Highlander Folk School in southern Georgia.

Clark returned to Charleston in 1970. There she lectured on women's rights, organized daycare centers, and helped raise funds for scholarships. Clark was later elected to the same Charleston County School Board that had fired her for NAACP membership. In her later years she received several awards, including a Living Legacy Award from President Jimmy Carter in 1979 and the Order of the Palmetto, South Carolina's highest civilian award, in 1982. On December 15, 1987, Clark died on John's Island.

See also: Young, Andrew Jackson, Jr.

Further reading: Clark, Septima Poinsette. *Ready from Within: Septima Clark and the Civil Rights Movement* (edited by Cynthia Stokes Brown). Navarro, CA: Wild Trees Press, 1986. http://search.eb.com/women/articles/Clark_Septima_ Poinsette.html (Detailed biography).

CLARKE, John Henrik
Historian, Scholar

Renowned historian and scholar John Henrik Clarke became internationally recognized for his unique blend of activism and scholarship. As a nationalist and pan-Africanist Clarke was committed to the liberation and uplifting of African people. As a self-taught scholar, he helped pioneer the development of African heritage and black studies programs nationwide.

Early inspiration

John Henry Clark was born into a poor family in Alabama on January 1, 1915. He later added an "e" to his last name and changed Henry to Henrik after the Norwegian playwright Henrik Ibsen. Clarke's early interest in history came from his great-grandmother, who told stories of his family's ordeal during slavery. As a young Sunday school teacher in Columbus, Georgia, Clarke was dismayed to find that there were no images of African people in the Bible. While working at a high school, Clarke stumbled on a book entitled *The New Negro* by Alain Locke, who played a key role in the Harlem Renaissance, the flowering of black writing in Harlem, New York, in the 1920s. Clarke read Locke's essay "The Negro Digs Up His Past." This encounter with the ancient history of African people was the first step in a lifelong journey of historical discovery.

A journey of discovery

Clarke moved to New York, intending to use Harlem as the laboratory for his studies for the true history of African people. His search, however, took him to libraries, museums, attics, archives, and collections in Africa, Asia, the Caribbean, Latin American, and Europe, and resulted in numerous publications.

Clarke was associate editor of *Freedomways Magazine* from 1962 to 1982. He edited more than 30 books, including *Malcolm X: The Man and His Times* (1969), *Harlem USA* (1971), and *Marcus Garvey and the Vision of Africa* (1973). Of his more than 200 short stories the most famous is "The Boy Who Painted Christ Black" (1940), which has been translated into more than a dozen languages and was turned into an Emmy Award-winning television program in 1966.

Clarke taught at several universities around the world, but his longest tenures were at Hunter College and Cornell University, New York, where he pushed for the establishment of black studies departments. He was praised for his detailed and inspiring lectures, concern for students, and positive influence on several generations of African American leaders and scholars. Clarke retired in 1985 and died in New York City on July 16, 1998.

▼ *John Henrik Clarke gives a talk in 1994; he continued to be in demand after his retirement.*

See also: Garvey, Marcus; Harlem Renaissance; Locke, Alain; Malcolm X

Further reading: Clarke, John Henrik. *My Life in Search of Africa*. Chicago, IL: Third World Press, 1999. http://www.2souls.com/main/Knowledge%20Warehouse/prhclark/John%20Henrik%20Clarke.htm (Site in honor of Clarke).

KEY DATES	
1915	Born in Union Springs, Alabama, on January 1.
1933	Moves to Harlem, New York City.
1940	Publishes "The Boy Who Painted Christ Black."
1985	Cornell University names 9,000-volume, 60-seat library branch in Clarke's honor.
1994	Receives the Phelps–Stokes Fund's Aggrey Medal in "recognition of his unique contribution to our knowledge and understanding of African civilization."
1998	Dies in New York City on July 16.

SET INDEX

Volume numbers are in **bold** type.

A

Aaliyah **1**:4; **3**:56
Aaron, Hank **1**:5–6
Abbott, Cleveland Leigh **3**:11
Abbott, Robert Sengstacke **1**:7, 79; **3**:21; **9**:22
Abdul-Jabbar, Kareem **1**:8; **7**:14
Abele, Julian **1**:9
Abernathy, Ralph **1**:10–11; **6**:15
abolitionism *see* antislavery movements
Abolition Society **8**:34
Adams, John Hurst, quoted on Louis Farrakhan **4**:35
Adams-Ender, Clara **6**:38
Adderley, Cannonball **1**:12; **7**:18
affirmative action **1**:13–14; **9**:19
   "father of" *see* Fletcher, Arthur Ward Connerly against **3**:32
African Blood Brotherhood (ABB) **2**:32
"African Calculator" *see* Fuller, Thomas
African Free School **5**:83
African Methodist Episcopal (AME) Church **1**:27, 28; **3**:15, 75
   Henry McNeal Turner and **9**:125
   Reverdy Ransom and **8**:72
"Africa One" **4**:21
Afro-American Association (AAA) **9**:14
Afro-American League **4**:59
Afrocentricity **7**:34; **9**:95; **10**:58, 123
AIDS
   Essex Hemphill and **5**:62
Ailey, Alvin **1**:15
   Alvin Ailey American Dance Theater (AAADT) **1**:15; **6**:7
Aldridge, Ira **1**:16
Alexander, Archibald **1**:17
Alexander, Raymond Pace **1**:18, 19
Alexander, Sadie Tanner Mossell **1**:18, 19–20
Ali, Muhammad (Cassius Clay) **1**:21–22, 64; **3**:34; **4**:33; **5**:88
   and Archie Moore **7**:79
   and Floyd Patterson **8**:19
   and Joe Frazier **4**:71
   and Leon Spinks **9**:65
   and Sonny Liston **6**:124
   Don King and **6**:82–83
   influence on George Foreman **4**:54
   influence on Marcus Allen **1**:26
   influence on Sugar Ray Leonard **6**:115
Ali, Nobel Drew **1**:23
All African People's Revolutionary Party **2**:86
Allen, Debbie **1**:24
Allen, Marcus **1**:25–26
Allen, Richard **1**:27–28; **3**:15; **4**:58; **6**:39; **8**:35, 82; **9**:48
Allen, Sara Bass **1**:28
Allen, Woody **9**:39

All Girl Orchestra **1**:41
Alston, Charles H. **6**:106, 107
American Anti-Slavery Society **3**:39, 108, 109; **8**:35
American Civil Rights Initiative (ACRI) **3**:32
American Colonization Society **1**:134
American Express (AmEx)
   Kenneth Chenault and **2**:112–113
Amer-I-Can Foundation **2**:53
American Freedom Coalition **1**:11
American Medical Association (AMA) **1**:112
American Missionary Society **2**:125
American Negro Academy **3**:49, 50; **9**:6
American Negro Theater (ANT) **1**:98; **2**:117
American Promise **8**:50
American Revolution **7**:64
   James Armistead and **1**:39
Amin, Jamil Abdullah al- *see* Brown, H. Rap
Amistad case **2**:124–125
Amos, Harold **1**:29
Amos, Wally **1**:30
Anatomy of a Murder (film) **4**:11, 12
Anderson, Eddie "Rochester" **1**:31
Anderson, Ivie **1**:32
Anderson, Marian **1**:33–34; **3**:83; **6**:55; **7**:46; **8**:53; **9**:18
Anderson, Michael P. **1**:35
Anderson, Myers **9**:101, 102
"André 3000" *see* Benjamin, André
anemia, sickle-cell **2**:21
Angelou, Maya **1**:36–37
Anita L. DeFrantz v. United States Olympic Committee (1980) **3**:79
ANP *see* Associated Negro Press
Anthony, Susan B. **2**:102; **3**:109
antilynching bills **3**:100
Anti-Lynching Crusaders **3**:100
antislavery movements **8**:34–35; **9**:48
Anti-Slavery Society *see* American Anti-Slavery Society
Appiah, Anthony **1**:38; **4**:99
Architect's Renewal Committee of Harlem **2**:6
Armistead, James **1**:39
Armstrong, Henry **1**:40
Armstrong, Lil **1**:41, 42; **7**:134
Armstrong, Louis **1**:41, 42–43; **7**:134
   and Bessie Smith **9**:54
   Beauford Delaney and **3**:80
   influence on Billie Holiday **5**:87
Armstrong, Robb **1**:44
Armstrong, Samuel Chapman **10**:35, 36
Arrested Development **7**:51
Aristocrat Records
   and Muddy Waters **10**:45
   see also Chess Records
Asante, Molefi Kete **1**:45; **7**:34
   quoted on Henry Dumas **3**:119
Ashanti **1**:46
Ashe, Arthur **1**:47–48; **3**:26
Ashford, Evelyn **1**:49

Ashley, Maurice **1**:50
Ashworth, Aaron **1**:51
Ashworth Law **1**:51
Askin, Luther B. **1**:52
Associated Negro Press (ANP) **1**:79
Association of Black Culture Centers (ABCC) **5**:96
Association of Southern Women for the Prevention of Lynching **3**:100
Astaire, Fred **7**:51
Attaway, William **1**:53
Attucks, Crispus **1**:54
Ayler, Albert **1**:55

B

back to Africa movement **2**:116; **3**:81
   Marcus Garvey and **4**:96; **8**: 35, 37
   Martin Robinson Delaney and **3**:81
Badu, Erykah **1**:56
Bailey, Buster **2**:54
Bailey, Pearl **1**:57–58
Baisden, Michael **1**:59
Baker, Ella **1**:60; **3**:133
Baker, Josephine **1**:61–62
Baker, LaVern **1**:63
Baker, Ronald G. **1**:64
Baldwin, James **1**:65–66; **9**:54
Ballard, Florence **8**:118
Ballard, Hank **1**:67
Bambara, Toni Cade **1**:68
Band of Gypsies **5**:67
Banks, Ernie **1**:69
Banks, Tyra **1**:70
Banneker, Benjamin **1**:71–72
Bannister, Edward Mitchell **1**:73
Baraka, Amiri **1**:74–75; **2**:63; **10**:105
Barkley, Charles **1**:76–77
Barnes, Denise "Dee" **3**:114
Barnett, Claude A. **1**:78–79
Barry, Marion S., Jr. **1**:80; **6**:73
"Bars Flight" (poem) **9**:100
Barthé, Richmond **1**:81
Bartholomew, Dave **3**:103
Basie, Count **1**:82–83; **6**:105
   and Joe Williams **10**:96
Basquiat, Jean-Michel **1**:84–85
Bass, Charlotta **1**:86
Bass, Joseph Blackburn **1**:86
Bassett, Angela **1**:87; **7**:54
Bates, Daisy Lee **1**:88
Batiste, Alvin **7**:18
Batiste, Harold **7**:18
Battle, Kathleen **1**:89
battle royals **6**:23
Baylor, Elgin **1**:90
Beamon, Bob **1**:91–92; **6**:118
Bean Eaters, The (book) **2**:38, 39
Bearden, Bessye **5**:37
Bearden, Romare **1**:93–94; **5**: 37; **10**:105
Beat Generation **1**:74
Beatles, the **2**:110
Beattie, John **3**:116
Beavers, Louise **1**:95
bebop **3**:19; **4**:46, 110; **7**:76; **8**:11; 98

Bechet, Sidney **1**:96; **5**:85
Beck, Jeff **5**:67
Beckwourth, Jim **1**:97
Beckwourth Pass **1**:97
Bedford, Nathan **4**:19
Bedford-Stuyvesant Restoration Corporation **9**:104
Belafonte, Harry **1**:66, 98–99; **3**:54
   Sidney Poitier and **8**:32
Bell, Clarence "Pudgy" **3**:25
Bell, James "Cool Papa" **1**:69, 100–101
Bell, James Madison **1**:102
Belle, Albert **1**:103
Bellinger, Louis **1**:104
Bellson, Louie **1**:57
Benevolent Endowment Network Fund (BEN) **2**:91
Benjamin, André **1**:105; **8**:20, 56
Benjamin L. Hooks Institute for Social Change **5**:94
Bennett, Gwendolyn **1**:106; **3**:67
Bennett, Lerone, Jr. **1**:107
Benny, Jack **3**:71
Benson, George **1**:108; **2**:79
Benton, Robert **9**:39
Berbick, Trevor **1**:22
Berry, Chuck **1**:109–110; **7**:12
Berry, Halle **1**:111; **3**:53, 54
Berry, Leonidas H. **1**:112
Berry, Mary Frances **1**:113
Berry Plan **1**:112
Bethune, Mary McLeod **1**:114–115; **2**:4, 42, 128; **5**:59–60; **6**:64, 69; **7**:118–119; **8**:43
Bethune, Thomas *see* Blind Tom
Betty Boop cartoons **2**:80
Betty X *see* Shabazz, Betty
Beyoncé **1**:116
Bibb, Henry Walton **1**:117
Bigard, Barney **1**:118
"Big Boi" *see* Patton, Antwan
"Big E, The" *see* Hayes, Elvin
Biggie Smalls *see* Notorious B.I.G.
Biggers, John **1**:119
Bill of Rights **2**:126
Binga, Jesse **3**:21
Biography of the Negro in Africa and America, A (book) **10**:122
Birth of a Nation, The (film) **1**:86; **9**:82, 117; **10**:36
Birth of the Cool (album) **3**:69; **7**:114
"Bird" *see* Parker, Charlie
Bishop, Sanford D., Jr. **1**:120
Black, Keith L. **1**:127
black arts movement **1**:75; **3**:7; **8**:67, 78
Black Arts Repertory Theater/School **1**:75
Black Arts/West **2**:63
"Black Baron of Colorado" *see* Ford, Barney
Blackbirds (revue) **1**:70; **8**:102
Black Boy (book) **10**:124, 125
Black Cabinet **1**:115; **10**:53
Black Caucus *see* Congressional Black Caucus
black codes **2**:127
Black Dispatch (newspaper) **3**:126
"Black Edison" *see* Woods, Granville T.

Black Enterprise (magazine) **4**:126
Black Entertainment Television (BET) **6**:33, 34, 35
black identity and popular culture **1**:121–127
"Black Mary" *see* Fields, Mary
"Black Moses" *see* Hayes, Isaac
Black Muslims **1**:21
Black Panther Party (BPP) **2**:46, 86, 131; **6**:69; **8**:39; **9**:14–15
　and Bobby Seale **9**:14–15
　and Eldridge Cleaver **3**:4–5
　and H. Rap Brown **2**:46–47
　and Huey Newton **7**:126–127; **9**:14
　and Kathleen Neal Cleaver **3**:6; **9**:14
　and Stokely Carmichael **2**:85–86
"Black Patti" *see* Jones, Madame Sissieretta
"Black Pearl" *see* Baker, Josephine
"Black Picasso" *see* Basquiat, Jean-Michel
black power movement **4**:26, 131; **8**:38, 39
　Stokely Carmichael and **2**:85–86
Black Stephen *see* Esteban
Black Swan **5**:4; **8**:8; **10**:44
black theology movement **3**:31
blackface minstrelsy **1**: 121–122
Blackwell, David Harold **1**:128
Blackwell, Ed **3**:22; **7**:18
Blackwell, Elizabeth **3**:20
Blackwell, Unita **1**:129; **3**:133; **5**:23
Blake, Eubie **1**:61, 130; **9**:40
Blake, James **1**:48
Blakey, Art **1**:131; **2**:44; **7**:114
Blalock, Alfred **9**:107, 108
blaxploitation **1**: 124; **5**: 9; **8**: 134; **10**: 10, 11
Blige, Mary J. **5**:36
Blind Tom **1**:132
Blood for Britain project **3**:116
"blue baby syndrome" **9**:107–108
blues **7**:113; **8**:8
　Ethel Waters and, **10**:44
　John Lee Williamson and **10**:103
　Junior Wells and **10**:54
　Morgan Freeman and **4**:79
　Muddy Waters and **10**:45
　W. C. Handy and **5**:28–29
　Memphis Blues **5**:28, 29
　Piedmont **5**:126
Bluford, Guion S. **1**:133
Blyden, Edward W. **1**:134; **8**:36
Boas, Franz **5**:113
Boggs, Hale **2**:120–121
Bo Diddley *see* Diddley, Bo
Bond, Horace Mann **2**:4
Bond, J. Max, Jr. **2**:6
Bond, Julian **2**:5
Bonds, Barry **2**:7–8
Bonds, Bobby **2**:7, 8
Bonner, Marita **2**:9
Bontemps, Arna **2**:10; **10**:29
Boondocks, The (comic strip) **7**:48
Boone, Herman "Ike" **2**:11
bop *see* music and African Americans
Borges, Luis **10**:105
Boston, Ralph **1**:91, 92; **2**:12
Boston Massacre **1**:54
Boswell, Connee **4**:46
Bouchet, Edward **2**:13

Bowie, Lester **7**:18
Bowser, Mary Elizabeth **2**:14
Boykin, Keith **2**:15
Boykin, Otis **2**:16
"Boy Who Painted Christ Black, The" (story) **2**:134
Boyz N the Hood (film) **4**:117; **5**:115; **9**:38–39
Bradley, Benjamin **2**:17
Bradley, Thomas **2**:18; **9**:52
Bragg, George Freeman, Jr. **2**:19
Brandy (Brandy Rayana Norwood) **2**:20
Branson, Herman Russell **2**:21
Branson, Lloyd **3**:80
Brashear, Carl M. **2**:22–23
Braugher, Andre **2**:24
Braun, Carol Moseley **2**:25
Brawley, Benjamin **2**:26; **5**:95
Brawley, Tawana **9**:27
Brent, John E. **2**:27
Brent, Linda *see* Jacobs, Harriet
Brewster, T. L. **3**:35
Brice, Carol **2**:28
Bricktop **2**:29
Bridges, Sheila **2**:30
Bridgewater, Pamela E. **2**:31
Briggs, Cyril **2**:32
Brisco-Hooks, Valerie **2**:33
Broadside Press **8**:67
Broadside Quartet **8**:129
Broadus, Calvin *see* Snoop Dogg
Brock, Lou **2**:34
Brom & Bett v. Ashley (1781) **4**:76
Brooke, Edward **2**:35–36; **3**:99
Brooke Amendment **2**:36
Brooks, Avery **2**:37
Brooks, Gwendolyn **2**:38–39
Brooks, Tyrone **2**:40
Brotherhood of Sleeping Car Porters **3**:98; **8**:69
"Brother" (poem) **3**:85
Brown, Alonzo **5**:36
Brown, Bobby **2**:41; **6**:90
Brown, Charles **2**:110
Brown, Charlotte Hawkins **2**:42
Brown, Clara **2**:43; **4**:52
Brown, Clifford **2**:44; **8**:98
Brown, Corrine **2**:121
Brown, Dorothy L. **2**:45
Brown, Ed **2**:47
Brown, H. Rap **2**:46–47
Brown, Hallie Quinn **2**:48
Brown, James **2**:49–50; **7**:51; **9**:27
Brown, Janice Rogers **9**:85
Brown, Jesse L. **2**:51
Brown, Jim **2**:52–53
Brown, John **1**:102; **2**:102; **3**:75, 77, 109; **6**:97; **8**:30, 36; **9**:121
Brown, Lawrence **2**:54; **4**:11–12
Brown, Nicole **9**:36
Brown, Ron **2**:55
Brown, Ruth **2**:110
Brown, Sterling A. **2**:56
Brown, William Wells **2**:57
Brown v. Board of Education (1954) **1**:88; **2**:4, 97, 129, 132; **5**:84; **6**:15; **7**:97, 118, 119; **8**:37; **9**:17, 18, 84, 85
　Linda Brown and **9**:83
　Thurgood Marshall and **7**:20, 21
　see also civil rights
Bruce, Blanche K. **2**:58; **3**:97
Bryant, Kobe **2**:59

Bubbles, John **2**:60
　see also Washington, Buck
Buchanan, Buck **2**:61
Buck and Bubbles *see* Bubbles, John; Washington, Buck
Bud Billiken Parade **6**:64
Buffalo Soldiers **7**:64; **10**:89
Bullard, Eugene Jacques **2**:62
Bullins, Ed **2**:63
Bumbry, Grace **2**:64; **5**:65
Bunche, Ralph **2**:65–66
Burgess, John Melville **2**:67
Burke, Kareem "Biggs" **6**:8
Burleigh, Harry T. **2**:68; **4**:25
Burrell, Leroy **2**:69
Burrell, Thomas J. **2**:70
Burroughs, Margaret **2**:71
Burroughs, Nannie Helen **2**:42, 72
Burton, Annie L. **2**:73
Burton, LeVar **2**:74
Bush, George W. **8**:45, 50, 89
Busta Rhymes **2**:75
Butler, Octavia E. **2**:76
Byrd, Bobby **2**:49

C

Cabin in the Sky (film) **1**:31; **10**:44
Calhoun, Lee **2**:77
California Civil Rights Initiative (CCRI) **3**:32
Caliver, Ambrose **2**:78
Callier, Terry **2**:79
Calloway, Cab **1**:57; **2**:80
Campanella, Roy **2**:81
Campbell, Milt **2**:82
Cara, Irene **2**:83
Carew, Rod **2**:84
Carlos, John **8**:38; **9**:59
Carmen Jones (film) **1**:57, 99; **2**:89; **3**:54
Carmichael, Stokely (Kwame Toure) **2**:85–86, 131; **3**:31
Carnegie, M. Elizabeth **2**:87; **6**:38
Carney, Harry **2**:88
Carney, William H. **7**:64, 65
Carroll, Diahann **2**:89
Carson, Benjamin S. **2**:90–91
Carson, Julia **2**:92
Carson, Sonja **2**:90, 91
Carson Scholars Fund **2**:91
Carter, Benny **2**:93
Carter, Betty **2**:94
Carter, Cris **2**:95
Carter, Eunice **2**:96
Carter, Jimmy **5**:84; **6**:37
Carter, Robert L. **2**:97
Carter, Rubin "Hurricane" **2**:98
Carter, Shawn Carey *see* Jay-Z
Carver, George Washington **2**:99–100; **5**:47
Carver, Moses and Susan **2**:99, 100
Cary, Mary Ann Shadd **2**:101–102
Cassell, Albert **2**:103
Castle, Vernon and Irene **5**:29
Catholicism **8**:81, 83; **9**:115
Catlett, Elizabeth **2**:104; **10**:74
Cellucci, Paul **2**:36
Census, racial classification **10**:119
Challenge of Change, The (book) **2**:36
Challenger (space shuttle) **1**:133; **7**:56
Chamberlain, Wilt **2**:105–106; **7**:14
Chandler, Chas **5**:66
Chapman, Tracy **2**:107
Chappelle, Emmett W. **2**:108

Charles, Ray **2**:109–110
　Betty Carter and **2**:94
　Quincy Jones and **6**:52
　quoted on Nat King Cole **3**:19
Charmer, the *see* Farrakhan, Louis
Chavis, Benjamin Franklin *see* Muhammad, Benjamin Franklin
Cheadle, Don **2**:111
Checker, Chubby *see* Chubby Checker
Chenault, Kenneth **2**:112–113
Cherry, Don **1**:55; **2**:114; **3**:22
Chesnutt, Charles W. **2**:115
Chess Records **3**:91; **4**:67,120; **10**:45
　Phil and Leonard Chess and **1**:109–110; **3**:91
　see also Aristocrat Records
Chester, Thomas **2**:116
Chicago
　Great Migration and **4**:127
　race riots (1919) **4**:130
Chicago Defender (newspaper) **1**:7, 79; **4**:129; **5**:107; **9**:21, 22
Chicago Eight **9**:15
Child, Lydia Maria **5**:134
Children's Defense Fund (CDF) **3**:132
Childress, Alice **2**:117–118
Chinn, May Edward **2**:119
Chisholm, Shirley **2**:120–121; **8**:42, 44, 45
Christian, Charlie **2**:122
Christian Mission for the Deaf (CMD) **4**:60
Chubby Checker **2**:123
Cinqué **2**:124–125
civil liberties **2**:126
civil rights **2**:126–131; **9**:18–19
　A. Philip Randolph and **8**:68–69
　Bayard Rustin and **8**:125–126
　E. D. Nixon and **7**:128
　Malcolm X and **7**:9–10
　Martin Luther King, Jr., and **6**:84–85
　Ralph Abernathy and **1**:10–11
　Rosa Parks and **8**:15
　see also affirmative action; color bar and professional sports; emancipation and reconstruction; military; national organizations; political movements; political representation; religion; segregation and integration
Civil Rights Act (1866) **3**:96
Civil Rights Act (1875) **4**:13; **9**:16
Civil Rights Act (1957) **8**:43
Civil Rights Act (1960) **8**:43
Civil Rights Act (1964) **1**:13; **2**:130; **3**:96, 99; **8**:38, 43; **9**:19
Civil War **7**:64, 65; **9**:49
　Cathay Williams and **10**:89
　events leading to **2**:125; **9**:8, 9, 83
　Massachusetts 54th regiment **6**:98
　military and **7**:64
　slavery **4**:17; **9**:48
　spies *see* Bowser, Mary Elizabeth
　Susie King Taylor and **9**:96
　Thomas Chester and **2**:116
　see also emancipation and reconstruction
Clark, Kenneth B. **2**:132
Clark, Septima P. **2**:133

Clarke, John Henrik **1**:36; **2**:134
Clay, Cassius *see* Ali, Muhammad
Cleaver, Eldridge **2**:131; **3**:4–5, 6
Cleaver, Kathleen Neal **3**:5, 6; **9**:14
Clifton, Lucille **3**:7
Clinton, George **3**:8–9, 113, 114; **5**:67; **10**:101
Coachman, Alice **3**:*10*–11
Cobb, Jewel Plummer **3**:12
Cobb, William Montague **3**:13
Cochran, Johnnie **3**:14; **9**:27, 36
Cohen, Hettie **1**:74
Cohn, Roy B. **6**:93
Coker, Daniel **3**:15
Cole, Johnnetta B. **3**:16
Cole, Natalie **3**:17, 19
Cole, Nat King **2**:110; **3**:18–19, 69
Cole, Rebecca J. **3**:20
Coleman, Bessie **3**:21
Coleman, Ornette **2**:114; **3**:22, 40; **7**:18
Collins, Marva **3**:*23*
color bar and professional sports **3**:24–26; **8**:106–107; **10**:77
Colored American (newspaper) **3**:39, 49
Colored Women's League **2**:48
Colored Women's Progressive Franchise **2**:102
Color Purple, The (book and film) **10**:21, 22, 112
Coltrane, John **3**:27–28, 69
Combs, Sean "Puffy" (Diddy; Puff Daddy; P Diddy) **3**:29–30; **5**:36; **6**:91; **9**:24, 31
and Notorious B.I.G. **7**:132
ComfortCake Company, LLC **5**:77
Commission on Interracial Cooperation **5**:95; **7**:99
Committee of Racial Equality (CORE) **3**:98; **4**:34
Commodores, the **8**:93–94
Community Self-Determination Bill **5**:118
Cone, James **3**:31
Congressional Black Caucus **2**:120; **8**:44
Congress of Racial Equality (CORE) **4**:34; **7**:110, 119
Roy Innis and **5**:118
Connection Machine **4**:21
Connerly, Ward **3**:32
Connick, Harry, Jr. **7**:18
Constitution, civil rights and **2**:126, 127
Contract Buyers League (CBL) **10**:55
Convention of Color **4**:58
Conyers, John, Jr. **3**:33; **8**:44
Cook, Will Marion **1**:96
Cooke, Sam **3**:34–35; **4**:66
Coolidge, Calvin **1**:114
"coon songs" **6**:56
Cooper, Anna J. **3**:36
Cooper, Charles "Tarzan" **3**:25
Cooper, Chuck **2**:106
Cooper, J. California **3**:37
Coppin, Frances "Fanny" Jackson **3**:38
CORE *see* Congress of Racial Equality
Corea, Chick **3**:69
Cornish, Samuel **3**:39; **8**:124
Cortez, Jayne **3**:22, 40
Cosby, Bill **3**:41–42, 99; **7**:105; **8**:58; **10**:96
Cose, Ellis **3**:43

Cotton Club **4**:11–12; **5**:33; **7**:114
Count Basie *see* Basie, Count
Countee Cullen *see* Cullen, Countee
Cox, Elbert F. **3**:44
Crain, S. R. **3**:35
"Creole Goddess" *see* Baker, Josephine
Creole Jazz Band **7**:134
Crew, Spencer R. **3**:45
Crisis (magazine) **3**:118; **4**:39; **10**:87
Crockett, George, Jr. **3**:46
Crosthwait, David, Jr. **3**:47
Crouch, Stanley **3**:48
Crummell, Alexander **3**:49–50; **4**:93
crunk **6**:122
Cuffe, Paul **3**:*51*; **4**:58; **8**:35–36
Cullen, Countee **3**:52; **4**:39; **5**:33
Cumming v. Richmond Board of Education (1899) **9**:83, 84
Curran, Peter **2**:113
Curt Flood Act (1998) **4**:49

D

"Daddy Grace" *see* Grace, Charles Emmanuel
D'Amato, Cus **8**:19; **10**:4
Dandridge, Dorothy **1**:99, 111; **3**:53–54; **9**:82
Dash, Damon "Dame" **3**:55–56; **6**:8
Dash, Julie **3**:57–58
Daughters of the American Revolution (DAR) **1**:33–34
Daughters of the Conference **1**:28
Daughters of the Dust (film) **3**:57–58
Davidson, Olivia **3**:59
David Walker's Appeal to the Colored Citizens of the World (document) **10**:25
Davis, Angela **3**:60–61
Davis, Benjamin J. **3**:62
Davis, Benjamin O. **3**:63, 64; **7**:64, 65
Davis, Benjamin O., Jr. **3**:63; **7**:65
Davis, Ernie **3**:65
Davis, Rev. Gary **3**:66
Davis, Jefferson **2**:14; **4**:16
Davis, John Preston **3**:67
Davis, Lorenzo "Piper" **7**:33
Davis, Miles **3**:19, 28, 68–69; **7**:114; **8**:12
Cannonball Adderley and **1**:12
and Wynton Marsalis **7**:18
Davis, Ossie **3**:70; **8**:101
Davis, Sammy, Jr. **3**:71–72; **8**:102
Davis, William Allison **3**:73
Davis-Ellis Intelligence Test **3**:73
Dawson, Mary **4**:28
Dawson, William **3**:74
Dawson, William Levi **4**:130
Day, William Howard **3**:75
Dean, Mark **3**:76
Death Row Records *see* Knight, Suge
DeBaptiste, George **3**:77
Dee, Ruby **3**:70, 78
Deele **3**:134
Def Jam Records **9**:31, 32
DeFrantz, Anita L. **3**:79
De La Beckwith, Byron **4**:30, 31
Delany, Beauford **3**:80
Delany, Martin Robinson **3**:75, 81
Delta Sigma Theta Sorority **5**:59
Demby, Edward T. **3**:82
DePriest, James **3**:83
DePriest, Jessie Williams **3**:84

DePriest, Oscar **3**:84
Derricotte, Toi **3**:85
Destiny's Child **1**:116
Detroit, Great Migration and **4**:127
Dett, R. Nathaniel **3**:86
Devers, Gail **3**:87
Devil in a Blue Dress (film) **2**:111; **7**:94; **10**:39
Diallo, Amadou **9**:27
Dickerson, Earl B. **3**:88
Dickerson, Eric **3**:89
Dickey, Eric Jerome **3**:90
Diddley, Bo **3**:91–92; **4**:100
Diddy *see* Combs, Sean
Diddy, P. *see* Combs, Sean
Die Nigger Die! (book) **2**:46
Dillard, Harrison **3**:93
Dinkins, David **3**:94; **9**:27
Dirty Dozen, The (film) **2**:53
discrimination **3**:95–100
see also segregation and integration
Dobbs, Mattiwilda **3**:101
Doby, Larry **3**:102; **7**:109
"Dock of the Bay" (song) **8**:75, 76
Domino, Fats (Antoine) **3**:*103*–104
Donegan, Dorothy **3**:105
Do the Right Thing (film) **6**:111
Dorantes, Andrés de **4**:24
Dorsey, Thomas A. **3**:*106*; **7**:114
and Mahalia Jackson **5**:126
Douglas, Aaron **3**:*107*
Douglass, Frederick **1**:52; **2**:57, 102; **3**:81, 108–109; **9**:35; **9**:48
and the military **7**:64, 65
Douglass, Sarah Mapps **3**:110
Dove, Rita **3**:*111*
Dozier, Lamont **3**:*112*
Dr. Dre (André Young) **3**:*113*–114, 131; **5**:115
"Dré" *see* Benjamin, André
Dred Scott v. Sandford (1857) **6**:104; **9**:9
Dreiser, Theodore **10**:125
Drew, Charles **3**:*115*–116
Dr. Funkstein *see* Clinton, George
DuBois, W. E. B. **2**:4, 66; **3**:50, 59, 98, 117–118; **4**:76; **5**:32; **8**:37
Harry Herbert Pace and **8**:8
quoted on Joel Augustus Rogers **8**:115
William Monroe Trotter and **9**:117
DuBois, Yolande **3**:52
Dubuffet, Jean **1**:85
Duke Ellington *see* Ellington, Duke
Duke, George **3**:69
Dumas, Henry **3**:119; **8**:77
Dunbar, Paul Laurence **2**:39; **3**:120, 121
Dunbar-Nelson, Alice **3**:120, 121
Duncan, Oscar **3**:97
Duncan, Tim **3**:122
Duncanson, Robert Scott **3**:123
Dungy, Tony **3**:124
Dunham-Bush Inc. **3**:47
Dunham, Katherine **3**:125
Dunjee, Roscoe **3**:126
Durnham, James **3**:127
Du Sable, Jean Baptiste Pointe **3**:128
Dvořák, Antonin **2**:68; **6**:129
Dyer, Leonidas **3**:100
Dyson, Michael Eric **3**:118, 129

E

Earley, Charity Adams **3**:130
Eason, James **4**:97
Eastern Colored League (ECL) **1**:100
Eazy-E (Eric Wright) **3**:113, 131
Ebony (magazine) **1**:107; **6**:25, 26; **9**:50, 109
Ebony Museum of Negro History, Chicago **2**:71
Edelman, Marian Wright **3**:132–133
Edison, Thomas **6**:104
and Granville T. Woods **10**:117
Edmonds, Kenneth "Babyface" **3**:134; **10**:101
education **3**:99–100; **9**:47
Edwards, Herman **4**:4
Eisenhower, Dwight D. **10**:86
Elder, Clarence L. **4**:5
Elder, Lee **3**:26; **4**:6; **9**:18
Elders, Joycelyn **4**:7–8
Eldridge, Elleanor **4**:9
Eldridge, Roy **4**:10
Ellicott brothers **1**:71–72
Ellington, Barney Bigard **4**:12
Ellington, Duke **3**:69; **4**:11–12
and Billy Strayhorn **4**:11, 12; **9**:79
and Ivie Anderson **1**:32
and Johnny Hodges **5**:85
Duke Ellington Orchestra **1**:118; **2**:54, 88; **4**:11; **5**:85; **9**:75; **10**:91
Elliott, Robert Brown **4**:13
Ellison, Ralph **1**:93; **4**:14–15
emancipation **4**:16, 17
and the Emancipation Proclamation (1862) **2**:127; **3**:96; **4**:16–17, 19; **8**:36; **9**:49
reconstruction **2**:127; **3**:96; **4**:16, 17–19; **7**:64; **8**:36, 42
Emeagwali, Philip **4**:20–21
Eminem **3**:114; **4**:42
"Empress of the Blues" *see* Smith, Bessie
Equal Justice Initiative **9**:72
Equiano, Olaudah **4**:22
Erving, Julius **4**:23
Esteban (Estevanico; Black Stephen; Stephen the Moor) **4**:24
Ethiopia **4**:51
ethnopharmacology **8**:6
Europe, James Reese **4**:25; **5**:29
Evans, Gil **3**:69
Evans, Lee **4**:26; **9**:59
Evans, Mari **4**:27
Evanti, Lillian **4**:28
Evers, J. Charles **4**:30
Evers, Medgar **4**:29–30, 31; **5**:97
Evers-Williams, Myrlie **4**:30, 31; **7**:16
Ewing, Patrick **4**:32
Executive Orders
and affirmative action **1**:13
Executive Order 8802 **3**:98
Executive Order 9981 **7**:65
"Exhibit of American Negroes" **7**:107
Exodusters **9**:37

F

Fair and Accurate Credit Transaction Act (2003) **2**:92
Fair Employment Practices Commission (FEPC) **3**:98

Fair Employment Practices Committee (FEPC) **1**:115
Falana, Lola **1**:58
Falashas **4**:51
Famous Amos **1**:30
Famous Flames **2**:49
Farad, Wali *see* Fard, Wallace D.
Farad, W. D. *see* Fard, Wallace D.
Fard, Wali *see* Fard, Wallace D.
Fard, Wallace D. **4**:33; **7**:101, 102
Farley, Jessie **3**:35
Farmer, James **4**:34
Farrakhan, Louis **4**:35–36; **8**:39; **9**:23
Farrakhan, Mother Khadijah **4**:35
"Father of the Blues" *see* Handy, W. C.
Father Divine **4**:37
"Father of Gospel" *see* Dorsey, Thomas A.
"Father of Negro History" *see* Woodson, Carter G.
"Father of the Negro Press" *see* Barnett, Claude A.
Fats Domino *see* Domino, Fats
Fats Waller *see* Waller, Fats
Faubus, Orval **1**:88; **2**:128; **3**:98
Fauset, Crystal **4**:*38*
Fauset, Jessie Redman **4**:39; **5**:33
Federal Communications Commission (FCC)
Benjamin L. Hooks and **5**:93, 94
Federal Writer's Project **4**:14
Fellowship of Reconciliation (FOR) **4**:34
Fetchit, Stepin **3**:71; **4**:40
Fields, Mary (Stagecoach Mary; Black Mary) **4**:41
Fifteenth Amendment **2**:127; **3**:77, 96, 98; **4**:17; **8**:34, 36, 40; **9**:16
50 Cent (Curtis Jackson) **4**:42
Fire!! (journal) **1**:106; **3**:67; **5**:33, 113; **9**:112
"First Lady of Jazz" *see* Fitzgerald, Ella
Fishburne, Laurence **4**:43
Fisher, Rudolph **4**:44
Fisk Jubilee Singers **7**:113
Fitzgerald, Ella **4**:45–46; **7**:114
Five Percenters **4**:36
Five Spot Jazz Club **3**:22
Fletcher, Arthur **4**:47
Flipper, Henry Ossian **4**:48; **7**:65
Flip Wilson Show, The **10**:107
Flood, Curt **4**:49
Flood v. Kuhn (1970) **4**:49
Flowers, Bertha **1**:36, 37
Flowers, Vonetta **4**:50
Ford, Arnold (Rabbi Ford) **4**:51
Ford, Barney **4**:52
Foreman, George **4**:53–54, 71; **7**:82
Forman, James **4**:55
Forten, Charlotte **4**:56–57
Forten, James **4**:58
Fortune, Emanuel **4**:59
Fortune, T. Thomas **4**:59
Foster, Adelaide **8**:94
Foster, Andrew J. **4**:60
Foster, Andrew "Rube" **1**:100; **3**:24; **4**:61–62
Foster, William (Willie; Bill) Hendrik **4**:62
Fourteenth Amendment **2**:127, 129–130; **3**:96, 97; **4**:17; **8**:36, 40; **9**:16, 17
Foxx, Jamie **4**:63

Foxx, Redd **3**:71; **4**:64; **7**:105
Frankfurter, Felix **5**:99
Franklin, Aretha **2**:110; **3**:35; **4**:65–66, 68; **5**:127
Franklin, Carl **4**:68
Franklin, C. L. **4**:65–66, 68
Franklin, John Hope **4**:69
Franklin, Martha Minerva **7**:8
Frazier, E. Franklin **4**:70
Frazier, Joe **1**:21, 22; **4**:54, 71; **5**:88
Frazier, Walt **4**:72
Frederick Douglass's Paper (newspaper) **3**:109
Free African Society **1**:28; **6**:39
free blacks **9**:48
Freedmen's Bureau **3**:75, 97; **4**:17; **5**:83–84; **9**:49
Freedom Riders **2**:85
Freedom Singers **5**:23
Freedom's Journal **3**:39; **8**:124
Freelon, Allan **4**:73
Freelon, Nnenna **4**:*74*, 75
Freelon, Philip **4**:75
Freelon Group **4**:75
Freeman, Elizabeth **4**:76
Freeman, John **4**:77
Freeman, Morgan **3**:23; **4**:78–79; **5**:34
Freeman, Ron **4**:26
Freeman's Village **4**:18
French and Indian War **9**:100
From Slavery to Freedom (book) **4**:69
Frye, Hardy **2**:86
Fudge, Ann **4**:80
Fugees, the **5**:76; **6**:9
Fugitive Act (1793) **3**:96
Fugitive Slave Law (Fugitive Slave Act 1850) **1**:117; **2**:101; **3**:77, 96; **4**:77; **6**:97; **8**:36
Fulani, Lenora **4**:81
Fuller, Charles **4**:82
Fuller, Meta Warrick **4**:83
Fuller, S. B. **6**:21
Fuller, Solomon Carter **4**:84
Fuller, Thomas **4**:85
Fulson, Lowell **2**:110
Funkadelic **3**:9, 114
Funk Brothers **4**:120
Furious Five **4**:123–124
Furman v. George (1972) **6**:43
fusion music **3**:69

G
Gabriel (Gabriel Prosser) **3**:96; **4**:*86*; **5**:83; **8**:35; **9**:129; **10**:18
Gabriel Prosser *see* Gabriel
Gaines, Clarence "Big House" **4**:87
Gaines, Ernest J. **4**:*88*
Gaither, Jake **4**:89
Gamble, Kenny **4**:*90*; **5**:*104*
Gandhi, Mohandas K. **6**:85
Gardner, John **6**:16
Garner, Erroll **4**:*91*
Garner, Margaret **4**:*92*
Garnet, Henry Highland **3**:75; **4**:*93*; **9**:48
Garrison, William Lloyd **1**:52; **3**:109; **8**:35; **9**:48, 119
Garvey, Amy Ashwood **4**:94, 96, 97
Garvey, Amy Jacques **4**:*95*, 97
Garvey, Marcus **3**:98; **4**:*96–97*; **5**:*32*; **9**:18
and Amy Ashwood Garvey **4**:94, 96, 97
and Amy Jacques Garvey **4**:95, 97

and the UNIA **4**:51, 96; **7**:118; **8**:37
Audley Moore and **7**:80
clash with Cyril Briggs **2**:32
influence on Noble Drew Ali **1**:23
Gaston, A. G. **4**:*98*
Gates, Henry Louis, Jr. **1**:38; **4**:*99*; **10**:108
Gaye, Marvin **3**:19, 35; **4**:*100–101*; **8**:119
gay rights *see* Boykin, Keith
George, Zelma Watson **4**:102
Georgia, Georgia (film) **1**:37
Gervin, George **4**:103
Getz, Stan **9**:30
G-funk *see* Clinton, George
Gibbs, Mifflin W. **4**:104
Gibson, Althea **3**:26; **4**:105–4,166; **5**:*28*
Gibson, Bob **4**:107
Gibson, Josh **1**:100; **4**:108
Giddings, Paula **4**:109
Gillespie, Dizzy **3**:69; **4**:110; **6**:52; **7**:85, 114; **8**:12, 98
Gilliam, Dorothy **4**:111
Giovanni, Nikki **4**:112
Gladden, Washington **9**:98
Gleaves, Richard H. **3**:97
Glory (film) **2**:116; **10**:39
Glover, Savion **4**:113
"Godfather of Soul" *see* Brown, James
God's Son *see* Nas
Goldberg, Whoopi **4**:114; **7**:54
Goldman, Ronald **9**:36
Gone With the Wind (film) **7**:43, 58
Goode, Sarah E. **4**:115
Goode, W. Wilson **4**:*116*
Gooding, Cuba, Jr. **4**:117; **9**:38
Goodman, Benny **2**:122; **7**:114
Goodman, Robert **5**:124
Gordon, Dexter **4**:118
Gordy, Berry, Jr. **4**:119–120; **5**:120; **7**:115; **9**:32
and Diana Ross **8**:118
and Marvin Gaye **4**:100, 101
and Stevie Wonder **10**:114–115
and the Supremes **8**:118
gospel music **7**:114
Aretha Franklin and **4**:65
Mahalia Jackson and **5**:126–127
Sam Cooke and **3**:34–35
Thomas A. Dorsey and **3**:106
Gossett, Louis, Jr. **4**:121
Go Tell It on the Mountain (book) **1**:65–66
Grace, Charles Emmanuel **4**:122
Grace of Monaco, Princess **1**:62
graffiti art **1**:84–85
grandfather clauses **9**:17, 85
Grand Lodge of the Knights of Pythias **1**:104
Grandmaster Flash **3**:114; **4**:123–124
"Grandpop of Bebop" *see* Silver, Horace
Grant, George F. **4**:125
Grant, Ulysses S. **4**:19
Granz, Norman **4**:45; **5**:86
Graves, Earl G. **4**:126
Gray, Wardell **4**:118
Great Awakening **8**:82
Great Compromise (1877) **8**:36, 41
Great Depression **2**:128
Great Migration and urbanization **3**:98; **4**:127–131; **5**:32

Chicago Defender and **1**:7; **4**:129
Migration of the Negro paintings **6**:107
Spencer R. Crew and **3**:45
Greaves, William **4**:132
Green, Al **3**:35
Green, Frances H. **4**:9
Green, Jerome **3**:92
Greene, Claude **1**:23
Greene, Joe **4**:133
Greener, Richard Theodore **6**:104
Greenfield, Elizabeth Taylor **5**:4
Greenwich Village artists **1**:74
Gregory, Dick **5**:5
Gregory, Frederick D. **5**:6
Gregory, Roger L. **5**:7
Gregory, Wilton D. **5**:8
Grier, Pam **5**:9
Griffey, Ken, Jr. **5**:10
Griffin, Archie **5**:11
Griffith-Joyner, Florence "Flo-Jo" **5**:12–13; **6**:63
Marion Jones and **6**:50
Griggs, Sutton E. **5**:14
Grimké, Angelina Weld **2**:118; **3**:110
Grimké, Sarah **3**:110
Guinn v. United States (1915) **9**:84, 85
Guitar Slim **2**:110
Gullah **9**:46
G-Unit **4**:42
Gunn, Moses **5**:15
Guy, Buddy **10**:54
Gwynn, Tony **5**:16

H
Haden, Charlie **3**:22
Hagler, Marvin **5**:17
Halevy, Joseph **4**:51
Haley, Alex **5**:18–19
Hall, Lloyd **5**:20
Hall, Prince **5**:21
Hamer, Fannie Lou **1**:129; **3**:132, 133; **5**:22–23; **6**:69
Hamilton, Lisa Gay **5**:24
Hammer, M. C. *see* M. C. Hammer
Hammond, John **5**:86
Hammon, Jupiter **5**:25; **10**:67
Hampton, Henry **5**:26
Hampton, Lionel **6**:52
Hampton Institute **5**:44
Hancock, Herbie **3**:69; **5**:27
Handy, W. C. **3**:19; **5**:28–29; **7**:113; **8**:8
Hanh, Thich Nhat **5**:92
Hansberry, Carl A. **3**:88
Hansberry, Lorraine **1**:66; **5**:30–31
Hansberry and Others v. Lee (1940) **3**:88
see also civil rights
hard bop **7**:114
see bebop
Hardin, Lilian *see* Armstrong, Lil
Harlem Commonwealth Council (HCC) **5**:118
Harlem Globetrotters **2**:106; **3**:25
Harlem Renaissance **1**:81, 82; **3**:118; **5**:32–33; **9**:40
Alain Locke and **6**:128
Arna Bontemps and **2**:10
Countee Cullen and **3**:52
Dorothy West and **10**:62
Gwendolyn Bennett and **1**:106
Jacob Lawrence and **6**:107
Joel Augustus Rogers and **8**:115

Langston Hughes and **5**:106
Marita Bonner and **2**:9
Nella Larsen and **6**:99
Rose McClendon and **7**:38
Rudolph Fisher and **4**:44
Wallace Thurman and **9**:112
Benjamin Brawley's views on **2**:26
Opportunity magazine **6**:17
Harlem Writers' Guild **1**:36
Harlem Youth Opportunities
    Unlimited **2**:132
Harper, Ben **5**:34
Harper, Frances **5**:35
Harper's Ferry assault **1**:102; **2**:102;
    3:75, 109; **5**:107; **6**:97; **8**:30,
    36; **9**:121
Harrell, Andre **3**:30; **5**:36
Harrington, Oliver **5**:37
Harris, Barbara **5**:38
Harris, Bernard, Jr. **5**:39
Harris, Franco **5**:40
Harris, Patricia Roberts **5**:41–42
Harris, Rebert **3**:35
Harrison, Hubert Henry **5**:43
Hart, Albert Bushnell **3**:118
Harvey, William R. **5**:44
Hastie, William H. **5**:45; **7**:21
Hatcher, Richard **5**:46
Hathaway, Isaac **5**:47
Hawkins, Coleman **2**:54; **3**:69; **5**:48;
    7:76; **9**:57
Hayden, Robert **5**:49; **10**:29
Hayes, Elvin **5**:50
Hayes, Isaac **5**:51
Hayes, Roland **5**:52
Hayes, Rutherford B. **4**:19
Haynes, Marques **3**:25
Hays, Rutherford **3**:97–98
HBCUs see Historically Black
    Colleges and Universities
Healy, Eliza **5**:53
Healy, James **5**:54
Healy, Michael **5**:55
Healy, Michael Morris **5**:53, 54, 55,
    56, 57
Healy, Patrick **5**:56–57
Hearns, Thomas **5**:17, 58
Heart of Atlanta Motel v. United
    States (1964) **9**:18, 84, 85
Heavy D. **3**:29
Height, Dorothy **5**:59–60
    see National Organizations
Hemings, Sally *see* Hemmings,
    Sally
Hemmings, Sally **1**:72; **5**:61; **10**:10
Hemphill, Essex **5**:62
Henderson, Fletcher **1**:42; **5**:48, 63;
    8:8, 65; **10**:130
Henderson, Rickey **5**:64
Hendricks, Barbara **5**:65
Hendrix, Jimi **3**:9; **5**:66–67
Henson, Matthew **5**:68
Herc, Kool DJ **4**:123, 124
Herman, Alexis **5**:69
Herndon, Angelo **3**:62; **5**:70
Hero Ain't Nothin' but a Sandwich,
    A (book and play) **2**:118
Herriman, George **5**:71
Higginbotham, A. Leon, Jr. **5**:72
Higgins, Billy **3**:22
High Court of Swing **10**:46
Highlander Folk School, Georgia
    2:133
Hill, Anita **5**:73–74; **9**:102

Hill, Henry A. **5**:75
Hill, Lauryn **5**:76; **6**:9
Hilliard, Amy **5**:77
Hilliard, Asa G. III **5**:78
Himes, Chester **5**:79
Hines, Gregory **5**:80
Hinton, William **5**:81–82
hip-hop **4**:36, 123; **5**:76; **6**:102;
    7:115; **9**:31
Hirt, Al **7**:18
Historically Black Colleges and
    Universities (HBCUs) **3**:16;
    5:83–84
    see also Tuskegee Institute
History of the Negro Race in
    America (book) **10**:95
Hodges, Johnny **4**:12; **5**:85
Holiday, Billie **5**:86–87; **7**:114;
    9:54
Holland–Dozier–Holland
    Berry Gordy and **4**:120
    Brian and Eddie Holland and
        Eddie **3**:112; **4**:120
    Lamont Dozier and **3**:112
Holly, Buddy **3**:92; **5**:67
Holmes, Larry **5**:88; **9**:65
Holyfield, Evander **4**:54; **5**:88, 89;
    6:83; **7**:82; **10**:5
Holy Ghost Boys **7**:50
Homestead Subsistence Division
    program **3**:67
Homicide: Life on the Streets
    (TV series) **2**:24
Hooker, John Lee **5**:90
Hooks, Alvin **2**:33
hooks, bell **5**:91–92
Hooks, Benjamin L. **5**:93–94
Hootie & the Blowfish **8**:121
Hoover, Herbert **1**:114
Hoover, J. Edgar **2**:46; **4**:97; **9**:15
Hoover, Lou Henry **3**:84
Hope, John **5**:95
Hord, Fred **5**:96
Horizon **10**:46
Hormel, James **5**:42
Horne, Lena **5**:97
Horton, Lester **1**:15
Hotel Rwanda (film) **2**:111
Hot Five **1**:42
Hot Mikado, The **2**:28
House, Son **6**:32
House Un-American Activities
    Committee **8**:101; **10**:129
Houston, Charles H. **5**:98–99; **7**:20,
    21
Houston, Whitney **2**:41; **5**:100
Howard University **7**:20
How Stella Got Her Groove Back
    (book and film) **7**:54
Hubbard, William **5**:101
Huckleberry Finn (film) **7**:111
Hudson, Hosea **5**:102
Hudson-Weems, Clenora **5**:103
Hue and Cry (book) **7**:57
Huff, Leon **4**:90; **5**:104
Hughes, Carrie Langston **5**:107
Hughes, Cathy **5**:105
Hughes, Langston **1**:52; **3**:67, 118;
    4:39; **5**:33, 106–107; **10**:29
    and Bessie Smith **9**:54
    and Rose McClendon **7**:39
    and Zora Neale Hurston **5**:113
    Benjamin Brawley's views on **2**:26
Hughes, Louis **5**:108

Hughley, D. L. **5**:109
Hughleys, The (TV show) **5**:109
Humphreys, Richard **5**:83
Hunter, Alberta **5**:110
Hunter-Gault, Charlayne **5**:111
Hurricane, The (film) **2**:98
Hurricane Katrina **3**:99; **10**:63
Hurston, Lucy **5**:113
Hurston, Zora Neale **3**:118; **5**:33,
    112–113
    Alice Walker and **10**:22
Hutchings, Phil **2**:86
Hutton, Bobby **3**:6
Hyman, "Flo" **5**:114

I

Ice Cube (O'Shea Jackson) **3**:113,
    131; **5**:115; **9**:38
Ice T (Tracy Marrow) **5**:116
"If We Must Die" (poem) **7**:52
I Know Why the Caged Bird Sings
    (book) **1**:37
Imes, Samuel **5**:117; **6**:99
Imperium in Imperior (book) **5**:14
Incidents in the Life of a Slave Girl
    (book) **5**:134
In the Heat of the Night (film)
    8:32–33
Innis, Roy **5**:*118*
International African Service
    Bureau **4**:94
International Colored Unity League
    5:43
Invisible Man (book) **4**:14, 15
Iraq, war on (2003) **2**:92; **8**:50
Islam **8**:83
Island in the Sun (film) **1**:99; **3**:54

J

Jack Benny Show, The **1**:31
Jackie Brown (film) **5**:9
Jackson, Bo **5**:119
Jackson, Curtis, III *see* 50 Cent
Jackson 5 **5**:120, 129
Jackson, Janet **5**:121
Jackson, Jesse **5**:122–123; **6**:53;
    9:27
Jackson, Jesse, Jr. **5**:124; **8**:39
Jackson, John **5**:125
Jackson, John A. **10**:78
Jackson, Mahalia **4**:66; **5**:126–127
Jackson, Maynard H., Jr. **5**:128
Jackson, Michael **3**:35; **5**:121,
    129–130
    and the Jackson 5 **5**:120
    and Quincy Jones **6**:53
Jackson, Nell C. **3**:10
Jackson, O'Shea *see* Ice Cube
Jackson, Reggie **5**:131
Jackson, Samuel L. **5**:132;
    8:*117*
Jackson, Shirley Ann **5**:133
Jacobs, Andrew, Jr. **2**:92
Jacobs, Harriet **5**:134
Jakes, T. D. **6**:4
Jamal, Ahmad **3**:69
James, Daniel "Chappie", Jr. **6**:5
James, Henry **1**:66
James, Larry **4**:26
James, LeBron **6**:6
James, William **3**:118
Jamison, Judith **6**:*7*
Jay-Z (Shawn Carey Carter) **3**:55,
    56; **6**:8; **7**:116

jazz **7**:114
    avante-garde **1**:55
    cool **3**:69; **7**:114
    free **1**:55; **3**:22
    hard bop **1**:131; **9**:30
    soul **1**:12
    see also bebop
Jazz at Lincoln Center (JALC) **7**:18
Jazz Hounds **9**:*57*
Jazz Messengers **1**:131; **7**:85;
    9:30; **10**:46
Jean, Wyclef **5**:76; **6**:9
Jefferson, Thomas **1**:72; **5**:61; **10**:127
Jeffries, Jim **6**:23
Jeffries, Leonard **6**:10
Jelly Roll Morton *see* Morton,
    Jelly Roll
Jemison, Mae C. **6**:11–12
Jenkins, Clarence "Fats" **3**:25
Jennings, Thomas **2**:17; **6**:13
Jet (magazine) **6**:25, 26
Jeter, Derek **6**:14
Jews, black **4**:51; **8**:83
Jim Crow laws **2**:127; **3**:95, 97, 98,
    99; **4**:19; **9**:17, 83
Johns, Barbara **6**:15
Johns, Vernon **1**:10, 11; **6**:15
Johnson, Andrew **4**:19
Johnson, Ben **6**:118
Johnson, Charles (writer) **6**:16
Johnson, Charles S. (educator) **5**:33
Johnson, Earvin "Magic" **4**:126;
    6:18–19
Johnson, George E. **6**:20–21
Johnson, Georgia Douglas **6**:22
Johnson, Gertrude **6**:26
Johnson, Hazel W. **7**:65
Johnson, Jack **3**:24; **6**:23
Johnson, James P. **1**:82, 83
Johnson, James Weldon **2**:66;
    3:118; **5**:32; **6**:24
Johnson, John H. **6**:25–26
Johnson, John Rosamund **6**:24
Johnson, Judy **6**:27
Johnson, Katherine G. **6**:28
Johnson, Lyndon B. **1**:13; **2**:130;
    3:98–99, 106; **8**:44
    and Robert Clifton Weaver **10**:53
    and Thurgood Marshall **7**:21
Johnson, Michael **6**:29
Johnson, Rafer **6**:30
Johnson, Robert (musician) **5**:67;
    6:31–32
Johnson, Robert L. (entrepreneur)
    6:33–34, *35*
Johnson, Sheila Crump **6**:33, 35
Johnson, William H. **6**:36
Johnson-Brown, Hazel **6**:37–38
Johnson Products **6**:20
Jones, Absalom **6**:39
Jones, Deacon **6**:40
Jones, Edith Irby **4**:8
Jones, Edward P. **6**:41
Jones, Elaine R. **6**:42–43
Jones, Eugene Kinckle **6**:44
Jones, (Everett) LeRoi *see*
    Baraka, Amiri
Jones, Frederick M. **6**:45
Jones, Grace **6**:46
Jones, James Earl **6**:47
Jones, Lois Mailou **6**:48
Jones, Marion **6**:49–50
Jones, Norah **2**:110
Jones, Paul R. **6**:51

Set Index

Jones, Quincy **5**:129; **6**:52–53; **10**:14, 40
Jones, Roy, Jr. **6**:54
Jones, Ruth *see* Washington, Dinah
Jones, Madame Sissieretta **1**:73; **6**:55
Joplin, Scott **6**:56–57; **7**:114
Jordan, Barbara **2**:121; **6**:58; **8**:42
Jordan, June **5**:23; **6**:59
Jordan, Louis **2**:110; **4**:45, 46
Jordan, Michael **6**:60–61; **8**:114
Jordan, Tom **10**:27
Jordan, Vernon E. **6**:62
Journal of Black Studies **1**:45
Journey of Reconciliation **7**:53; **8**:126
Joyner, Marjorie Stewart **6**:63
Joyner-Kersee, Jackie **6**:64
Julian, Percy **6**:65
Jump Start (comic strip) **1**:44
Just, Ernest Everett **6**:66–67; **10**:131

K

Kappa Alpha Psi fraternity **1**:17
Karenga, Maulana **1**:75; **3**:118; **6**:68–69
Kasdan, Laurence **9**:39
Kawaida **6**:68
Keith, Damon J. **6**:70
Kelley, Robin **6**:71
Kelly, Leontine **6**:72
Kelly, Shirley Pratt **6**:73
Kennard, William E. **6**:74
Kennedy, Annie Brown **6**:75
Kennedy, Harold Lillard, Jr. **6**:75
Kennedy, John F. **3**:98–99; **7**:10; **10**:53
Kennedy, Robert F. **6**:30; **7**:53
Keyes, Alan L. **6**:76
Keys, Alicia **6**:77; **8**:56
Kincaid, Jamaica **6**:78
King, B. B. **4**:12; **5**:67; **6**:79
King, Coretta Scott **6**:80; **9**:50
    Martin Luther King, Jr., and **6**:84
King, Dexter **6**:81
King, Don **6**:82–83; **9**:27
King, Martin Luther, Jr. **2**:129, 130; **3**:118; **6**:84–85; **8**:44
    and Harry Belafonte **1**:99
    and Mahalia Jackson **5**:126, 127
    and the Montgomery bus boycott **2**:129; **8**:15
    and Ralph Abernathy **1**:10, 11
    and Ralph Bunche **2**:66
    and Vernon Johns **1**:11
    assassination **6**:85, 94
    Bayard Rustin and **8**:126
    Benjamin Mays and **7**:31
    favorite song **3**:106
    "I Have a Dream" speech **2**:130; **3**:98; **6**:84, 85; **7**:120
"King of the Blues" *see* King, B. B.
"King of Ragtime" *see* Joplin, Scott
Kings of Rhythm *see* Turner, Ike; Turner, Tina
King Oliver *see* King, Joe "King"
Kingsley, Anna **6**:86–87
Kingsley, Zephaniah **6**:86–87
Kitt, Eartha **6**:88
Knight, Gladys **6**:89
Knight, Suge **6**:90–91; **9**:62
Knights of White Camellia **3**:97
Knowles, Beyoncé *see* Beyoncé
Korbel, Josef **8**:89
Kountz, Samuel **6**:92–93
Kravitz, Lenny **5**:67
Krazy Kat (cartoon strip) **5**:71

Ku Klux Klan **3**:97; **4**:19
Kwanzaa **6**:68–69
Kyles, Samuel "Billy" **6**:94

L

LaBelle, Patti **6**:95
Lady Sings the Blues (book) **5**:87
Lady Sings the Blues (film) **8**:58, 119
Lancet (newspaper) **2**:19
Langston, Charles Henry **6**:96–97
Langston, John Mercer **6**:98
Langston, Mary Leary **5**:107
"Larcenous Lou" *see* Brock, Lou
La Revue Négre **1**:61
Larsen, Nella **5**:117; **6**:99
La Salle, Eriq **6**:100
Last Poets **6**:101–102; **9**:13
Latimer, George and Rebecca **6**:104
Latimer, Lewis H. **6**:103–104
Law, Oliver **6**:105
Lawrence, Jacob **1**:93; **6**:106–107; **9**:4
Lawrence, Martin **6**:108
Lee, Barbara **2**:121
Lee, Canada **8**:33
Lee, Debra L. **6**:34
Lee, Malcolm D. **6**:109
Lee, Sheila Jackson **2**:121
Lee, Spike **5**:109, 132; **6**:109, 110–111; **10**:42
Leidesdorff, William **6**:112
LeNoire, Rosetta **9**:134
Leonard, Buck **6**:113
Leonard, Sugar Ray **5**:58; **6**:83, 114–115; **8**:111
Lewis, Bill **6**:116
Lewis, Carl **6**:117–118; **8**:51
Lewis, David Levering **6**:119
Lewis, Edmonia Mary **6**:120
Lewis, Lennox **5**:89; **10**:5
Lewis, Reginald F. **6**:121
Lewis and Clark expedition **10**:127
liberation theology **3**:31
Liberator (newspaper) **3**:109
Liberia **1**:134; **2**:116, 126–127; **8**:36; **9**:48, 129
    Alexander Crummell and **3**:49–50
    Augustus Washington and **10**:34
    John Russwurm and **8**:124
    Marcus Garvey and **4**:97
    Martin Robinson Delaney and **3**:81
    Daniel Coker's visit to **3**:15
Life (magazine) **8**:13–14
Liles, Kevin **6**:123
Lil John **6**:122
Lillie, Frank **6**:67
Lincoln, Abraham **2**:126–127; **3**:96; **4**:16, 17, 19; **8**:36
    and Frederick Douglass **3**:109
Liston, Sonny **1**:21; **6**:124; **8**:19; **10**:5
Literacy Volunteers of America **1**:30
Little, Cleavon **5**:15
"Little Jazz" *see* Eldridge, Roy
Little Richard **6**:125–126
Little Rock High School crisis **1**:88; **2**:128; **3**:98; **7**:97; **8**:38; **9**:18
Little Stevie Wonder *see* Wonder, Stevie
little-theater groups **7**:39, 111
Llewellyn, Bruce **6**:127
Locke, Alain **2**:134; **5**:33, 113; **6**:128–129
    and William H. Johnson **6**:36
Loguen, Jermain **6**:130
Long, Nia **6**:131

Lopez, Jennifer **3**:30
Lorde, Audre **6**:132
Los Angeles, mayors
    see Bradley, Thomas
Louis, Joe **3**:26; **6**:133; **10**:20
Loury, Glenn C. **6**:134
Love, Nat **7**:4
Love Unlimited **10**:71
Loving v. Virginia (1967) **9**:84
Luckett, Bill **4**:79
Lyle, Ron **4**:54
Lynch, John **3**:97; **4**:18; **7**:5
lynching
    antilynching bills **3**:100; **10**:75
    Ida B. Wells-Barnett and **10**:57
    Walter F. White and **10**:79

M

Ma Rainey *see* Rainey, Ma
Mac, Bernie **7**:6
Madhubuti, Haki **2**:39; **7**:7
Mahoney, Mary Eliza **7**:8
Malcolm X **3**:31; **4**:35; **5**:19; **7**:9–10, 126; **9**:15, 23
    Denzel Washington and **10**:39
    Elijah Poole and **7**:9, 10, 102
    Spike Lee and **6**:111
Malcolm X (film) **6**:111
Malone, Annie T. **7**:11–12
Malone, Karl **7**:13–14
Malone, Moses **7**:15
Mandela, Nelson **2**:31; **8**:33
Manhattan Project **10**:85
Marable, Manning **7**:16
March on Washington (1963) **1**:11; **3**:98; **7**:120; **8**:38, 69
Marciano, Rocky **7**:79
Marcuse, Herbert **3**:60, 61
Marley, Bob **7**:29
Marrow, Tracy *see* Ice T
Marsalis, Ellis, Jr. **7**:18
Marsalis, Wynton **3**:48, 69; **5**:27; **7**:17–18
Marshall, Kaiser **8**:65
Marshall, Paule **7**:19
Marshall, Thurgood **2**:129; **5**:84, 99; **7**:20–21, 119; **9**:17, 18, 85
Mason, Biddy **7**:22
masons **5**:21
Massie, Samuel **7**:23
Master P (Percy Miller) **7**:24
Mathis, Johnnie **7**:25
Matrix, The (film), sequels to **8**:26
Matthews, James Newton **3**:120
Matthews, Victoria Earle **7**:26
Matzeliger, Jan **7**:27
Mayfield, Curtis **5**:67; **7**:28–29
Maynard, Robert **7**:30
Mays, Benjamin **1**:107; **6**:85; **7**:31
Mays, Willie ("Say Hey Kid") **7**:32–33
Mazama, Ama **7**:34
McAdoo, Bob **7**:35
McBay, Henry **7**:36
McCall, H. Carl **7**:37
McCall, Oliver **5**:88
McClendon, Rose **7**:38–39
McCovey, Willie **7**:40
McCoy, Elijah **7**:41
McDaniel, Hattie **7**:42–43; **10**:79
McDemmond, Marie **7**:44
McDonald, Gabrielle Kirk **7**:45
McFerrin, Robert **1**:34; **7**:46
McGirt, James E. **7**:47

McGruder, Aaron **7**:48
McGruder, Robert **7**:49
M. C. Hammer **7**:50–51
McKay, Claude **5**:33; **7**:52
McKinney's Cotton Pickers **2**:93
McKissick, Floyd **4**:131; **7**:53
McLaurin v. Oklahoma State Regents (1950) **9**:84
McMillan, Terry **1**:59; **3**:90; **7**:54
McNabb, Donovan **7**:55
McNair, Ronald E. **7**:56
McNeeley, Peter **6**:83
McPherson, James **7**:57
McQueen, Butterfly **7**:58
McSon Trio **2**:109
meat-curing **5**:20
melanomas **3**:12
Memories of Childhood's Slavery Days (book) **2**:73
"Memphis Blues" **5**:28, 29
Menard, John W. **3**:97; **8**:40, 41, 42
Men of Honor (film) **2**:22, 23
Meredith, James **7**:59
Merrick, John **7**:60
Messenger (magazine) **8**:69
Method Man **7**:61
Mfume, Kweisi **7**:62; **9**:27
Micheaux, Oscar **7**:63
Middle Passage (book) **6**:16
military and African Americans **7**:64–65
Miller, Cheryl **7**:66
Miller, Connery and Henrietta **7**:68
Miller, Dorie **7**:67–68
Miller, Kelly **7**:69
Miller, Marcus **3**:69
Miller, Percy *see* Master P
Million Man March **8**:39
Millions More Movement **8**:39
Mills, Florence **7**:70; **8**:102
Mingus, Charles **3**:69; **7**:71; **8**:98
Minton's Playhouse **7**:76; **8**:11
Mississippi, University of **7**:59
Mississippi Freedom Democratic Party (MFDP) **1**:129; **5**:22
Mississippi Freedom Summer **8**:38
Missouri Compromise (1820) **9**:8
Missouri ex rel. Gaines v. Canada, Registrar of the University of Missouri, et al (1938) **9**:84
Mitchell, Arthur **7**:73; **8**:43
Mitchell, Roscoe **7**:74
Modern Negro Art (book) **8**:47
Mohammed, Warith Deen **4**:36
Molineaux, Tom **7**:75
Monk, Thelonious **3**:28, 69; **4**:12; **7**:76–77; **10**:91
Montgomery bus boycott **1**:10; **6**:84–85; **7**:128; **8**:15, 37
    and civil rights **2**:126–131
Montgomery Improvement Association (MIA) **6**:84–85
Moon, Warren **7**:78
Moore, Archie **7**:79
Moore, Audley **7**:80
Moore, Cecil B. **7**:81
Moore, Harry and Harriette **9**:18
Moorer, Michael **7**:82
Moorish Science Temple of America **1**:23
Morgan, Garrett **7**:83
Morgan, Joe **7**:84
Morgan Lee **7**:85

Morial, Marc H. **7**:86
Morrill Act (1862) **5**:83
Morrill Act (1890) **5**:84
Morrison, Toni **7**:87–88
Morton, Jelly Roll **7**:89
Mos Def **7**:90
Moseley-Braun, Carol **3**:99
Moses, Edwin **7**:91–92
Moses, Robert Parris **7**:93
Mosley, Tim "Timbaland" **1**:4
Mosley, Walter **7**:94
Mossell, Sadie Tanner *see*
    Alexander, Sadie Tanner
    Mossell
Moten, Etta **1**:79; **7**:95
"Mother of the Blues" *see* Rainey, Ma
Motley, Archibald **7**:96
Motley, Constance Baker **7**:97
Motley, Marion **3**:25; **7**:98
Moton, Robert **7**:99
Motown **1**:115; **8**:87; **9**:32
Muddy Waters *see* Waters, Muddy
Muhammad, Benjamin Franklin
    7:100
Muhammad, Elijah (Elijah Poole)
    1:22; **3**:31; **4**:33; **7**:101–102
    and Louis Farrakhan **4**:35
    Malcolm X and **7**:9, 10, 102
Muhammad, Wali Fard *see* Fard,
    Wallace D.
Muhammad, Wallace Fard *see* Fard,
    Wallace D.
Murphy, Al **5**:102
Murphy, Calvin **7**:103
Murphy, Eddie **7**:104–105
Murphy, Isaac **3**:24; **7**:*106*
Murray, Daniel A. P. **7**:107
Murray, Eddie **7**:108–109
Murray, Pauli **7**:110
Muse, Clarence **7**:111
music and African Americans
    7:112–115
muslim *see* black muslims; Black
    Panther Party
Muste, A. J. **8**:125–126
Myrdal, Gunnar **2**:66

N

NAACP *see* National Association for
    the Advancement of Colored
    People
NAACP v. Alabama (1958) **2**:97
*Narrative of the Life and Adventures
    of Henry Bibb, An American
    Slave* (book) **1**:117
Nas (Nastradamus; God's Son) **7**:11
National Association for the
    Advancement of Colored
    People (NAACP) **1**:60, 115; **2**:5,
    127, 128; **3**:38, 98; **7**:117–118;
    8:37; **9**:83–85
    anthem **6**:24
    antilynching campaigns **3**:100
    Benjamin L. Hooks and **5**:94
    campaigns **7**:119
    Cecil B. Moore and **7**:81
    Myrlie Evers-Williams and **4**:31
    Roy Wilkins and **10**:87
    Septima P. Clark and **2**:133
    Thurgood Marshall and **7**:20
    Walter F. White and **10**:79
    W. E. B. DuBois and **3**:117
    William Montague Cobb and
        3:13

Legal Defense and Educational
    Fund (LDF) **2**:128, 129;
    6:42–43
National Association of Black
    Journalists (NABJ) **7**:120; **9**:78
National Association of Colored
    Women (NACW) **2**:48; **3**:20;
    7:26; **10**:57
    Mary Eliza Church Terrell and
        9:97, 98
National Association of Negro
    Musicians **3**:86
National Bar Association (NBA)
    1:20; **7**:120
National Center for Neighborhood
    Enterprise (NCNE) **10**:121
National Coalition of Blacks for
    Reparation in America **7**:120
National Council of Negro Women
    (NCNW) **1**:115; **2**:96; **7**:118–119
    Dorothy Height **5**:59–60
    Edith Spulock Sampson and **8**:128
National Era (newspaper) **2**:102
National Medical Association (NMA)
    1:112; **10**:93
National Negro Congress (NNC) **3**:67
National Negro Opera Company
    (NNOC) **4**:28
national organizations **7**:117–*120*
National Public Welfare League **5**:14
National Rainbow/PUSH Coalition
    5:123, 124, 125
National Ummah Group **2**:47
National Underground Railroad
    Freedom Center **3**:45
National Urban League (NUL) **2**:55,
    128; **3**:98; **7**:118
    Eugene Kinckle Jones and **6**:44
    Marc H. Morial and **7**:86
National Women's Suffrage
    Association (NWSA) **2**:102
Nation of Islam (NOI) **1**:22; **8**:37, 83
    Elijah Muhammad and **7**:101,
        102; **8**:37–38
    Louis Farrakhan and **4**:35–36
    Malcolm X and **7**:9, 10; **8**:38
    Wallace D. Fard and **4**:33
Native Son (book) **4**:15; **10**:29,
    124–125
Nat Turner's revolt **9**:47, 128–129
Naylor, Gloria **7**:121
"Negro" Abraham **7**:122
Negro Convention Movement **3**:75
Negro Digest **6**:25–26
Negro Folk Symphony **3**:74
Negro History Week **10**:120
Negro National League (NNL)
    1:100; **4**:61, 62
Negro People's Theater (NPT) **7**:39
Negro World (newsletter) **4**:84, 95, 96
Nell, William C. **7**:123
Nelson, Prince Rogers *see* Prince
Neville, Aaron **7**:124
New Edition **2**:41
Newman, Fred **4**:81
New Negro Movement
    Messenger magazine **8**:69
    see Harlem Renaissance
New Negro, The (book) **2**:134; **5**:33;
    6:129; **10**:74
Newsome, Ozzie **7**:125
Newton, Huey **2**:131; **7**:126–127; **9**:14
New York Renaissance (the Rens)
    3:25

Nguzo Saba **6**:68
Niagara movement **3**:98, 117, 118;
    7:117; **8**:37, 72; **9**:117; **10**:36,
    122
    conferences (1905) **10**:57
Niggaz With Attitude (NWA) **3**:113,
    131; **5**:115, 116
Nineteenth Amendment **2**:127; **8**:42
Nixon, E. D. **7**:128; **8**:15
Nixon, Richard M. **2**:131; **3**:33
Niza, Fray Marcos de **4**:24
Non-Violent Action Group (NAG) **2**:85
Norman, Jessye **1**:34; **7**:129–130
Norris v. State of Alabama (1935) **9**:84
Northside Testing and Consultation
    Center **2**:132
North Star, The (newspaper) **3**:109;
    8:35
Norton, Eleanor **7**:131
Norwood, Brandy Rayanda *see* Brandy
Notes of a Native Son (book) **1**:66
Notorious B.I.G (Biggie Smalls)
    3:29; **6**:91; **7**:132; **9**:24
Nuriddin, Jalal Mansur **6**:101
NWA *see* Niggaz With Attitude

O

Obama, Barack **3**:99; **7**:133
Oberlin College, Ohio **9**:98
Oberlin-Wellington Rescue **6**:96–97
Occustat system **4**:5
Ocean's Eleven (film) **2**:111; **3**:71;
    7:6
Ocean's Twelve (film) **2**:111; **7**:6
Oliver, Joe "King" **1**:42–43; **7**:114,
    134
Olympic Games (1936) **3**:26; **8**:7
Olympic Games (1956) **8**:122
Olympic Games (1960) **8**:122
Olympic Games (1968) **4**:26; **8**:38;
    9:59; **10**:6
    George Foreman and **4**:53–54
Olympic Games (1976) **7**:91
Olympic Games (1980) **3**:79
Olympic Games (1984) **6**:117–118;
    7:92
Olympic Games (1988) **5**:12, 13;
    6:118; **7**:92; **8**:86
Olympic Games (1992) **6**:118; **8**:51,
    103
Olympic Project for Human Rights
    (OPHR) **4**:26; **9**:59
Onassis, Jacqueline Kennedy **9**:131
O'Neal, Shaquille **8**:4
O'Neal, Stanley **8**:5
O'Neill, Eugene **8**:100
Operation Breadbasket **5**:124; **6**:53;
    9:26
Operation PUSH *see* People United
    to Save Humanity
Opportunity (magazine) **6**:17, 44
Organization of African American
    Union **7**:10
Ornette Coleman Quartet **2**:114
Oscar Stuart v. Ned (1858) **6**:13
Oubré, Alondra Y. **8**:6
Our Nig (book) **10**:108
Our World (magazine) **3**:67; **9**:50
OutKast **1**:105; **8**:56
Overton, Anthony **6**:21
Owen, Chandler **8**:68–69
Owens, Dana *see* Queen Latifah
Owens, Jesse **3**:26; **8**:7

P

P. Diddy *see* Combs, Sean
Pace, Harry Herbert **5**:29;
    6:25; **8**:8
pacemakers **2**:16
Page, Alan **8**:9
Paige, Satchel **8**:10
Palmer, Alice Freeman **2**:42
Pan-Africanism **1**:134; **4**:96–97;
    8:36
Parker, Charlie "Bird" **3**:69; **7**:114;
    8:11–12, 98; **10**:68; 91
Parks, Gordon **8**:13–14
Parks, Rosa **1**:10; **2**:92, 129; **3**:98;
    6:84; **8**:15, 37
    Condoleezza Rice and **8**:89
    TV movie about **3**:58
Parks, Sarah Ross **8**:13, 14
Parks, Suzan-Lori **8**:16
Parsons, Richard **8**:17
patents **4**:115; **6**:13, 64, 103
    heating **4**:5
    laws concerning **2**:17
Patterson, Audrey **3**:11
Patterson, C. R. **8**:18
Patterson, Floyd **6**:124; **8**:19
Patterson, Frederick D. **1**:79
Patton, Antwan "Big Boi" **8**:20, 56
Paul, Clarence **10**:115
Paul, Mahalia "Duke" **5**:127
Pauling, Linus **2**:21; **6**:12
Payton, Walter **8**:21
Pearl Harbor
    Dorie Miller and **7**:67–68
Peary, Robert E. **5**:68
Peete, Calvin **8**:22
Peliklakaha *see* "Negro" Abraham
Penniman, Richard Wayne *see*
    Little Richard
Pennsylvania Society **8**:34–35
People United to Save Humanity
    (PUSH) **5**:123, 124; **6**:53
Perpetual Mission for Saving Souls
    of All Nations **10**:19
Persian Gulf War **7**:65
Petry, Ann **8**:*23*
P-Funk **3**:113
Phat Farm **9**:32
Philadelphia Human Rights
    Commission **1**:20
Philadelphia Plan **1**:13; **4**:47
Phillips, Andre **7**:92
Philly Soul Sound **4**:90; **5**:104
Picasso, Pablo **6**:129
Pickens, William L. **1**:79
Pickett, Bill **8**:24
Piece of Mine, A (book) **3**:37
Pinchback, P. B. S. **8**:25, 42
Pinkett-Smith, Jada **8**:26
Pippen, Scottie **8**:27
Pippin, Horace **8**:28
Pitman, William Sidney **8**:29
Pittsburgh Courier (newspaper) **1**:79
Planned Parenthood Federation of
    America (PPFA) **10**:47–48
Pleasant, Mary Ellen **8**:30
Plessy v. Ferguson (1896) **3**:98;
    5:84; **7**:20–21; **8**:36; **9**:17,
    83, 84
Plumpp, Sterling **8**:*31*
Poitier, Evelyn **8**:32, 33
Poitier, Sidney **1**:98; **2**:89; **3**:54, 99;
    8:*32*–33, 101; **10**:39

political movements **8**:34–39
    see national organizations
political representation **8**:40–45
    see civil rights; voting rights
Pollard, Fritz **3**:25; **8**:46
Poole, Elijah *see* Muhammad, Elijah
Poor People's Campaign **3**:133
    see March on Washington
Porgy and Bess (film) **1**:57, 58;
    2:89; **3**:72; **7**:46
Porgy and Bess (musical) **1**:36, 79
Poro Colleges **7**:12
Porter, James Amos **2**:104; **8**:47
Potter's House, Dallas **6**:4
Powell, Adam Clayton, Jr. **3**:118;
    8:48, 72, 126; **9**:26, 78
Powell, Bud **8**:98; **10**:91
Powell, Colin **7**:64, 65; **8**:49–50
Powell, Mike **8**:51
Pratt, Elmer Geronimo **3**:14
Preminger, Otto **3**:54
Price, John **6**:96, 97
Price, Leontyne **5**:65; **8**:52–53
Price, Wesley **3**:18
Primettes *see* Supremes, the
Primus, Pearl **8**:54
Prince (Prince Rogers Nelson) **5**:67;
    8:55–56
Proposition 54 **3**:32
Prosser, Gabriel *see* Gabriel
protein structure **2**:21
Provident Hospital **10**:93, 94
Provincial Free Man (newspaper)
    2:101–102
Pryor, Richard **7**:105; **8**:57–58; **9**:7
Public Enemy **4**:36
Puckett, Kirby **8**:59
Puff Daddy *see* Combs, Sean
Pullins, Al "Run" **3**:25
Purple Rain (album and film) **8**:55
Puryear, Martin **8**:60
PUSH *see* People United to Save
    Humanity; Rainbow/PUSH
    Coalition

Q

Quakers **8**:34; **9**:47
"Queen of the Blues" *see* Smith,
    Mamie; Washington, Dinah
"Queen of Happiness" *see* Mills,
    Florence
Queen Latifah (Dana Owens)
    1:125; **8**:61
"Queen Mother" *see* Moore, Audley
"Queen of Soul" *see* Franklin, Aretha

R

Rabb, Maurice F. **8**:62
race riots **4**:129, 130
racism **3**:95
radio, Cathy Hughes and **5**:105
Ragtime (film) **8**:117
ragtime ("rag") **7**:114
    Scott Joplin and **6**:56–57
Rainbow/PUSH Coalition **5**:123,
    124, 125; **8**:39
Raines, Franklin D. **8**:63
Rainey, Joseph H. **3**:97; **8**:64
Rainey, Ma **8**:65–66; **9**:53
Raisin in the Sun, A (film and
    play) **4**:121; **5**:30–31; **7**:43;
    8:33, 92
Randall, Dudley **8**:67
Randall, Harrison M. **5**:117

Randolph, A. Philip **5**:32; **8**:68–69
    and Bayard Rustin **8**:125, 126
Randolph, Virginia **8**:70
Rangel, Charles **8**:44, 71
Ransier, Alonzo J. **3**:97
Ransom, Reverdy C. **8**:72
rap **4**:36, 123, 124
    crunk **6**:122
    East Coast-West Coast
        feud **6**:91
    gangsta **6**:91; **9**:13, *122*
    Gospel **7**:51
"Rat Pack" **3**:71, 72
Ray (film) **4**:63
Ray Charles *see* Charles, Ray
Ray, Charles Bennett **8**:73, 74
Ray, Charlotte **8**:73
Ray, James Earl **6**:81, 94
Raymond, Usher *see* Usher
Readjuster Party **2**:19
Reagan, Ronald **3**:4; **5**:84
Reagon, Bernice Johnson **5**:23
Reason, Charles **8**:74
Reconstruction *see* emancipation
    and reconstruction
Redding, Otis **8**:75–76
Redmond, Charles Lenox **4**:56
Redmond, Eugene B. **3**:119;
    8:77
Redmond, Sarah **4**:57
Reed, Emma **3**:10
Reed, Ishmael **8**:78
Reed, Willis **8**:79
Reeves, Dianne **8**:80
*Regents of the University of
    California v. Bakke* (1978) **9**:84
religion and African Americans
    8:81–83
    black theology movement **3**:31
Remember the Titans (film) **2**:11
Rens, the (New York Renaissance)
    3:25
Republican Party **2**:35; **4**:18
Reuben, Gloria **8**:84
Revels, Hiram R. **3**:97; **4**:18; **8**:42, 85
Revolutionary People's
    Communication Network **3**:6
Revue Nègre, La **1**:61
Reynolds, Butch **8**:86
Rhodes, Ted **3**:26
Rhone, Sylvia **8**:87
rhythm and blues **7**:115
Rice, Condoleezza **8**:88–89, 90
Rice, Constance **8**:90
Rice, Jerry **8**:91
Richard, Little *see* Little Richard
Richards, Keith **6**:32
Richards, Lloyd **8**:92
Richie, Lionel **5**:130; **8**:93–94
Richmond, Bill **7**:75
Rickey, Branch **8**:107
Rillieux, Norbert **8**:95
Ringgold, Faith **8**:96
Riperton, Minnie **8**:97
Roach, Max **2**:44; **8**:98
Robertson, Oscar **8**:99
Robeson, Paul **3**:25; **5**:97; **8**:33,
    100–101
    influence on Jim Brown **2**:53
    influence on Leontyne Price
        8:52, 53
Robinson, Bill "Bojangles" **2**:28;
    3:71; **8**:102
Robinson, David **8**:103

Robinson, Eddie **8**:104
Robinson, Frank **8**:105
Robinson, Jackie **1**:6, 101; **2**:128;
    3:26; **4**:105; **7**:33; **8**:106–107
    influence on Eddie Murray **7**:109
Robinson, Jo Ann **2**:129
Robinson, Mallie McGriff **8**:107
Robinson, Rachel **8**:107
Robinson, Randal **8**:108
Robinson, Smokey **3**:35; **4**:119,
    120; **8**:109
    Stevie Wonder and **10**:114
Robinson, Sugar Ray **3**:69; **4**:105;
    8:110–111
Roc-A-Fella Records **3**:55, 56; **6**:8
Rock, Chris **8**:112
Rock, John S. **8**:113
Rodman, Dennis **8**:103, 114
Rogers, Joel Augustus **8**:115
Rolle, Esther **8**:116
Rollins, Howard E., Jr. **8**:117
Rollins, Sonny **8**:12
Roosevelt, Eleanor **8**:127
    and Marian Anderson **1**:34
    and Mary McLeod Bethune **1**:115
Roosevelt, Franklin D. **1**:114–115;
    2:128; **3**:29, 98; **8**:43; **9**:22, 85
Roots (book) **5**:18, 19
Roots (TV series) **2**:74; **5**:15, 19
Rorty, Richard **10**:61
Ross, Diana **4**:120; **8**:93, 118–119
Rotary Connection **8**:97
"Round Mound of Rebound" *see*
    Barkley, Charles
Rowan, Carl **8**:120
Roye, Edward James **3**:50
Rucker, Darius **8**:121
Rudolph, Wilma **8**:122
Ruggles, David **1**:52
"rumble in the jungle" **4**:54; **6**:82
Rush, Benjamin **3**:127
Russell, Bill **2**:106; **8**:123
Russwurm, John **8**:124; **9**:48
Rustin, Bayard **1**:10; **8**:125–126

S

Salem, Peter **7**:64
Sampson, Edith Spurlock
    8:127–128
Sanchez, Sonia **8**:129
Sanders, Barry **8**:130
Sanders, Deion **8**:*131–132*
Sanford, Adelaide **8**:133
Saperstein, Abe **3**:25
Sarandon, Susan **9**:27
Satcher, David **8**:134
"Satchmo" *see* Armstrong, Louis
Sauanaffe Tustunaage *see* "Negro"
    Abraham
Savage, Augusta **6**:107; **9**:4
Savoy Ballroom **7**:114
Sayers, Gale **9**:5
"Say Hey Kid" *see* Mays, Willie
"scat" singing **1**:42–43
    Ella Fitzgerald and **4**:45, 46
SCEF *see* Southern Conference
    Educational Fund
Schmeling, Max **3**:26
Schomburg, Arturo Alfonso **9**:6
Schultz, Michael **9**:7
Schuyler, George **1**:60
SCLC *see* Southern Christian
    Leadership Conference
Scott, Dred **9**:8–9, 83

Scott, Harriet **9**:8, 9
Scott, Jill **9**:10
Scott, Wendell **9**:11
Scott-Heron, Gil **2**:79; **9**:12–13
Scottsboro Boys **5**:70
Scott v. Sandford (1856) **8**:36; **9**:46,
    83, 84
Scowcroft, Brent **8**:89
Seacole, Mary **2**:87
Seale, Bobby **2**:131; **7**:127; **9**:14–15
Second Amendment **5**:118
segregation **2**:127–130; **3**:95;
    9:16–19, 85
    Charles H. Houston's battle to
        end segregation **5**:98–99
    desegregation in the military **7**:65
    segregation in education **2**:132;
        7:20–21; **9**:17
    segregation and integration
        9:16–19
    see also color bar and professional
        sports; discrimination; Jim Crow
        laws; Little Rock High School
        crisis; Montgomery bus boycott;
        political movements
Seifert, Charles **9**:20
Selby, Myra C. **9**:20
Selma to Montgomery march
    (1965) **3**:67
Senate Committee on Unamerican
    Activities **5**:107
Sengstacke, John **1**:7; **9**:21–22
"separate but equal" policy **3**:98;
    5:99; **8**:36
separatism **8**:34–35
servants, indentured **3**:97; **9**:45
Seven Cities of Cibola **4**:24
Seventeen Messengers **1**:131
Seward, William **9**:121
Shabazz, Betty **7**:9; **9**:23
Shadd, Abraham **2**:102
Shaft films **5**:15, 51; **8**:14; **9**:39
Shakur, Assata **2**:86
Shakur, Tupac (2Pac) **3**:29–30;
    5:121; **6**:91; **7**:132; **9**:24,
    62, 122
Shange, Ntozake **5**:31; **9**:25
Shankar, Ravi **3**:28
sharecroppers **3**:97
Sharpton, Al **2**:50; **9**:26–27
Shaw v. Reno (1993) **9**:84
Shays's Rebellion **5**:21
Sheffield Resolves **4**:76
Shelley v. Kraemer (1948) **7**:43; **9**:84
Shepard, Mary L. **4**:57
She's Gotta Have It (film) **6**:110–111
Shorter, Wayne **3**:69
Show Boat (film and musical) **8**:100
Shuffle Along (musical) **1**:130; **7**:70;
    9:40
Shuttlesworth, Fred **1**:10; **9**:28
Sibelius, Jean **1**:33
Sierra Leone Colony **3**:51
Sifford, Charlie **3**:26; **9**:29
Silver, Horace **1**:131; **9**:*30*
Simmons, Russell **4**:36; **9**:31–32
Simmons, Ruth **9**:33
Simone, Nina **5**:31; **9**:34
Simpson, O. J. **3**:89; **9**:35–36
    Johnnie Cochran and **3**:14
Sinatra, Frank **3**:71; **5**:87
Singleton, Ben **9**:37
Singleton, John **4**:43; **5**:115;
    9:38–39

"Sir Charles" see Barkley, Charles
Sissle, Noble 1:130; 9:40
sit-ins 2:85; 8:38
Sizemore, Barbara 9:41
Sklarek, Norma Merrick 9:42
Skyloft Players 5:107
Slater, Rodney 9:43
slavery 3:95–96; 9:44–49
  and suffrage 8:40
  Anna Kingsley and 6:86, 87
  Annie L. Burton's description of
    2:73
  Cinqué and the Amistad case
    2:124–125
  civil rights and 2:126–127
  Dred Scott and 9:8–9
  Gabriel's rebellion against 4:86
  literacy and 5:83
  music and 7:112; 9:46
  religion and 8:81–83
  Nat Turner's revolt 9:47, 128–129
  slave culture 9:46
  see also emancipation
  and reconstruction; political
  movements; Supreme Court;
  Underground Railroad
Sleet, Moneta J., Jr. 9:50
Smalls, Biggie see Notorious B.I.G.
Smalls, Robert 9:51
Smiley, Tavis 9:52
Smith, Ada Beatrice Queen Victoria
    Louise Virginia see Bricktop
Smith, Bessie 5:110; 8:8; 9:53–54
Smith, Emmitt 9:55
Smith, Jonathan see Lil John
Smith, Kemba 6:43
Smith, Lee 9:56
Smith, Mamie 5:48; 9:57
Smith, Otis 8:43
Smith, Ozzie 9:58
Smith, Tommie 8:38; 9:59
Smith, Trevor, Jr. see Busta Rhymes
Smith, Will 8:26; 9:60
Smith Act Trial 3:46
Smithsonian National Museum of
    American History (NMAH) 3:45
Smith v. Allwright (1944) 7:20;
    8:42–43; 9:84
SNCC see Student Nonviolent
    Coordinating Committe
Snipes, Wesley 9:61
Snoop Dogg (Calvin Broadus)
    3:113; 9:62
Snow, Valaida 9:63
Snyder, Gary 5:92
Social Gospel movement 9:98
Social History of the American
    Negro, A (book) 2:26
Soldier's Play, A (play and film)
    4:82
Soledad Brothers trial 3:61
Song of Solomon (book) 7:87, 88
Sonny Boy Williamson I see
    Williamson, John Lee
    "Sonny Boy"
Souls of Black Folk, The (book)
    3:118; 7:16; 8:37
Soul Stirrers 3:34, 35
Southern Christian Leadership
    Conference (SCLC) 2:40, 129;
    3:98; 7:119; 8:38
  Andrew Jackson Young and
    10:128
  Fred Shuttlesworth and 9:28

Jesse Jackson and 5:124
  Martin Luther King, Jr., and 6:85
  Maya Angelou and 1:37
  Ralph Abernathy and 1:10–11
  Wyatt Tee Walker and 10:30
Southern Conference Educational
    Fund (SCEF) 1:60
Southern Poverty Law Center
    (SPLC) 2:5
Southern Road (book) 2:56
South Park (TV series) 5:51
Sowell, Thomas 9:64
space race 2:108
spectroscopy, infrared 5:117
Spelman College 3:16, 132
Spiller, Bill 3:26
Spinks, Leon 1:22; 9:65
Spiral 1:94
spirituals 7:113; 8:82
sports, color bar and professional
    3:24–26
Sprewell, Latrell 9:66
"Stagecoach Mary" see Fields, Mary
Standard, Kenneth G. 9:67
Stanton, Elizabeth Cady 2:102;
    3:109
Stargell, Willie 9:68
Star Trek: Deep Space Nine (film)
    2:37
Starr, Jamie see Prince
State ex rel. Gaines v. Canada
    (1938) 5:99
Staupers, Mabel Keaton 6:38; 9:69
Steele, C. K. 9:70
Steele, Shelby 9:71
Stephen the Moor see Esteban
Stevenson, Bryan 9:72
Steward, Susan McKinney 9:73
Stewart, Maria 9:74
Stewart, Rex 9:75
Stewart, Rod 3:35
Still, William L. 9:76
Sting 5:67
Stockton, John 7:14
Stokes, Carl 8:42, 45; 9:77
Stone, Chuck 9:78
Strayhorn, Billy 4:11, 12; 9:79
Strode, Woody 3:25; 9:80
Strummer, Joe 3:92
"St. Louis Blues" 5:29
Student Nonviolent Coordinating
    Committee (SNCC) 1:11, 60;
    2:5; 3:98; 7:119–120
  H. Rap Brown and 2:46
  James Forman and 4:55
  Stokely Carmichael and 2:85
sugar-refining 8:95
Sullivan, Leon H. 9:81
Sul-Te-Wan, Madame 3:53; 9:82
Summers, Lawrence 10:61
Supreme Court 9:83–85
  and affirmative action 1:13–14
  and the Amistad case 2:125
  see affirmative action; civil
    rights; discrimination;
    political representation
Supremes, the 4:120; 8:118–119
  see Gordy, Berry, Jr.;
    Holland–Dozier–Holland
surgery, open-heart 10:93
Sutton, Percy 9:86
Swann, Lynn 9:87
Swann v. Charlotte-Mecklenburg
    Board of Education (1971) 9:84

Swanson, Howard 9:88
Sweatt v. Painter (1947) 5:72; 9:84
"Sweet Daddy" see Grace, Charles
    Emmanuel
Sweet Honey in the Rock 5:23
Sweet Sweetback's Baadasssss Song
    (film) 1:124; 10:10; 11
"swing" 1:42
syphilis 5:81–82

T
Tamla-Motown 4:119–120
  see Motown
Tandy, Vertner Woodson 9:89
Tanner, Benjamin Tucker 9:90, 91
Tanner, Henry Ossawa 6:36; 9:90, 91
Tanner, Obour 10:67
Tarantino, Quentin 5:9
Tatum, Art 3:19; 4:66; 9:92
Tatum, Reese "Goose" 3:25
Taussig, Helen 10:107, 108
Taylor, Cecil 4:12
Taylor, Lawrence 9:93
Taylor, Major 9:94
Taylor, Paul L. 9:95
Taylor, Robert R. 9:89
Taylor, Susie King 2:87; 9:96
tees, golf 4:125
Temple of Islam 4:33
Terrell, Mary Eliza Church 9:97–98,
    99
Terrell, Robert H. 9:97, 99
Terry, Clark 8:80
Terry, Lucy 9:100
Theater Owners' Booking
    Association (TOBA) 8:66
Their Eyes Were Watching God
    (musical) 4:27
Thelonious Monk see Monk,
    Thelonious
Thirteenth Amendment 2:127; 3:77,
    96; 4:16, 17; 8:36, 40; 9:49
Thirty Years a Slave (book) 5:108
Thomas, Clarence 9:85, 101–102
  and Anita Hill 5:73–74; 9:102
Thomas, Damon 3:114
Thomas, Frank 9:103
Thomas, Franklin 9:104
Thomas, Isaiah 9:105
Thomas, Thurman 9:106
Thomas, Vivien 9:107–108
Thompson, Era Bell 9:109
Thompson, John 4:32; 9:110
Thompson, John W. 9:111
Thompson, Larry D. 9:85
306 Group 1:93
"Three Bs of Education" 2:42
Three-Fifths Comnpromise 8:40
Thriller (album) 5:129
"Thriller in Manila" 6:82
Thurman, Wallace 9:112
Tibbs, Roy Wilfred 4:28
Tilden-Hayes Compromise (1877)
    4:19
Tilden, Samuel 4:19
Till, Emmett 2:39; 3:98; 4:29–30;
    5:103
TLC Beatrice International 6:121
Toler, Ira 6:50
Toomer, Jean 4:39; 9:113
Topdog/Underdog (play) 8:16
Totem Press (magazine) 1:74
Toure, Kwame see Carmichael,
    Stokely

Toussaint, Pierre 9:114–115
Tracy, Christopher see Prince
TransAfrica 8:108
transplants, kidney 6:92–93
Treadwell, George 10:14
Trenton Six case 1:18
Trotter, William Monroe
    9:116–117
Truman, Harry S. 2:128; 7:65
Truth, Sojourner 1:52; 9:118–119
Tubman, Harriet 9:49, 120–121
  film about 5:34
Tucker, C. Delores 9:122
Tucker, Chris 9:123
Turner, Charles Henry 9:124
Turner, Henry McNeal 9:125
Turner, Ike 9:126, 130, 131
Turner, Morrie 9:127
Turner, Nat 3:96; 5:83; 7:113; 8:35,
    82; 9:128–129; 10:18
Turner, Tina 9:126, 130–131
Tuskegee Airmen 3:63; 7:65
"Tuskegee Flash" see Coachman,
    Alice
Tuskegee Institute 3:59, 74
  Booker T. Washington and 10:35
  Henry McBay and 7:36
  Monroe Nathan Work and 10:122
29th Street Saxophone Quartet
    10:46
Twilight, Alexander L. 9:132
"Twist, The" (song) 1:67; 2:123
2Pac see Shakur, Tupac
Twombly, Cy 1:85
Tyson, Cicely 9:133–134
Tyson, Mike 5:88, 89; 10:4–5
  Don King and 6:83
Tyus, Wyomia 10:6

U
Umfundalai 10:58
Uncle Tom's Cabin (book) 9:49
Underground Railroad 2:101; 3:77,
    81, 96; 4:52; 8:35; 9:49
  Frederick Douglass and 3:109
  Harriet Tubman and 9:49,
    120–121
  Jermain Loguen and 6:130
  Oberlin-Wellington Rescue
    6:96–97
  William L. Still and 9:76
United Beauty School Owners and
    Teachers Association 6:64
United House of Prayer 4:122
United Way of America 3:16
Universal Negro Alliance 4:97
Universal Negro Improvement
    Association (UNIA) 2:32; 4:51,
    96, 97; 7:118; 8:37
Upshaw, Gene 10:7
Uptown Records 5:36
urbanization see great migration
    and urbanization
Urban League see National Urban
    League
US 6:68, 69
U.S. Commission on Civil Rights
    (USCCR) 1:113
Usher (Usher Raymond IV) 5:130;
    10:8
U.S. v. Cruikshank (1876) 8:41; 9:84
U.S. v. Reese (1876) 8:41
U.S. v. Sinclair (1971) 6:70

Set Index

V

VanDerZee, James **10**:9
Vandross, Luther **8**:119
Van Lew, Elizabeth **2**:14
Van Morrison **2**:110
Van Peebles, Mario **10**:10
Van Peebles, Melvin **10**:10, 11
Vansant, Iyanla **10**:12
Van Sertima, Ivan **10**:13
Van Vechten, Carl **5**:33
Vaughan, Sarah **10**:14
Vaughn, Mo **10**:15
Vaughn, Stevie Ray **5**:67
Verrett, Shirley **5**:67; **10**:16
Versailles, Treaty of (1919) **9**:117
Vesey, Denmark **3**:96; **5**:83; **8**:82; **9**:129; **10**:17–18
Vietnam War **2**:131; **4**:131; **6**:37; **7**:65
Virgin Islands **1**:17
Voice of the Fugitive, The (newspaper) **1**:117
Voter Education Project **2**:133; **6**:62
voting rights **2**:133; **8**:34, 40–45; **9**:17, 19
    Fanny Lou Hamer and **5**:23–24
Voting Rights Act (1965) **2**:130–131; **8**:38, 43–44; **9**:19
Voting Rights Bill (1965) **3**:99

W

Waddles, Charleszetta "Mother" **10**:19
Waiting to Exhale (book and film) **1**:59; **7**:54; **10**:68
Walcott, Jersey Joe **10**:20
Walcott, Louis Eugene see Farrakhan, Louis
Walker, Alice **5**:113; **10**:21–22
Walker, Madam C. J. (Sarah Breedlove) **6**:20, 64; **7**:12; **9**:89; **10**:23–24
Walker, David **1**:28; **3**:98; **8**:35; **9**:129; **10**:16, 17, 25
Walker, George **10**:88
Walker, Harry **10**:73
Walker, Herschel **10**:26–27
Walker, Maggie L. **10**:28
Walker, Margaret **10**:29
Walker, T-Bone **5**:67
Walker, Wyatt Tee **10**:30
Walker's Appeal **9**:129
Waller, Fats **1**:82, 83; **10**:31
Ward, Clara **4**:66
Ward, Samuel Ringgold **10**:32
Warhol, Andy **1**:84–85
Warwick, Dionne **10**:33
Washington, Augustus **10**:34

Washington, Booker T. **1**:78; **3**:59; **5**:47; **7**:117; **8**:36–37; **10**:24, 35–36
    and Madam C. J. Walker **10**:24
    and Marcus Garvey **4**:96
    and W. E. B. DuBois **3**:118
    Annie T. Malone and **7**:12
    Ida B. Wells-Barnett and **10**:57
    Virginia E. Randolph and **8**:70
    William Trotter and **9**:116–117
    see also national organizations; Niagara movement; political movements
Washington, Buck **10**:37
Washington, Denzel **2**:98; **4**:67; **10**:38–39
Washington, Dinah **10**:40
Washington, Harold **10**:41
Washington, Isaiah **10**:42
Washington, Kenny **3**:25
Washington, MaliVai **1**:48
Washington, Ora **10**:43
Washington, D.C., race riots (1919) **4**:130
Watergate scandal **2**:36
Waters, Ethel **3**:80; **8**:8; **10**:44
Waters, Maxine **2**:121
Waters, Muddy **1**:109; **5**:67; **10**:45, 54
Watson, Bobby **10**:46
Wattleton, Faye **10**:47–48
Wattleton, Ozie **10**:47, 48
Watts, André **10**:49
Watts, J. C. **10**:50
Wayans family **10**:51
W. C. Handy see Handy, W. C.
Weathers, Carl **10**:52
Weaver, Robert Clifton **10**:53
Webb, Alfreda Johnson **6**:75
Welbon, Yvonne **3**:58
Weller, Paul **7**:29
Welles, Orson **3**:69; **9**:39
Wells, Ida B. **3**:98; **4**:109
Wells, Junior **10**:54
Wells, Mary **4**:120
Wells, Ruth **10**:55
Wells-Barnett, Ida B. **10**:56–57
Welsh, Kariamu **10**:58
Wesley, Charles Harris **10**:59
Wesley, Dorothy Porter **10**:59
West, Cornel **3**:118; **5**:92; **10**:60–61
West, Dorothy **10**:62
West, Kanye **10**:63
West African Student's Union **4**:94
Wharton, Clifton R. **10**:65

Wharton, Clifton R., Jr. **9**:33; **10**:64–65
What's Love Got To Do With It? (film) **4**:43; **9**:130, 131
Wheatley, Phillis **10**:66–67
Wheatley, Susanna **10**:66, 67
Whitaker, Forest **10**:68
Whitaker, Mark **10**:69
Whitaker, Pernell **10**:70
White, Barry **10**:71
White, Bill **10**:72–73
White, Charles Wilbert **10**:74
White, George Henry **10**:75
White, Reggie **10**:76
White, Slappy **4**:64
White, Sol **10**:77–78
White, Walter F. **7**:42, 43; **8**:43; **10**:79
White Citizens' Councils (WCCs) **9**:18, 19
Wideman, John Edgar **10**:80
Wiggins, Thomas see Blind Tom
Wiginton, Clarence W. "Cap" **10**:81
Wilder, L. Douglas **5**:7; **8**:42; **10**:82
Wilkens, Lenny **10**:83
Wilkins, Dominique **10**:84
Wilkins, J. Ernest **10**:86
Wilkins, J. Ernest, Jr. **10**:85–86
Wilkins, Roy **8**:68; **10**:87
Williams, Bert **10**:88
Williams, Cathay **10**:89
Williams, Chancellor **10**:90
Williams, Cootie **7**:76–77; **10**:91
Williams, Daniel Hale **10**:92–93
Williams, Fannie Barrier **10**:94
Williams, Geneva **3**:53
Williams, George Washington **10**:95
Williams, Joe **10**:96
Williams, Paul Revere **10**:97
Williams, Peter **10**:98
Williams, Peter, Jr. **10**:98, 99
Williams, Serena **10**:100
Williams, Vanessa **10**:101
Williams, Venus **10**:100, 102
Williamson, John Lee "Sonny Boy" **10**:103
Willis, Bill **3**:25
Wilmington Ten **7**:100
Wilson, August **10**:104–105
Wilson, Cassandra **10**:106
Wilson, "Flip" Clerow **10**:107
Wilson, Harriet E. **10**:108
Wilson, Mary **4**:120; **8**:118
Wilson, Woodrow **9**:117
Winfield, Dave **10**:109
Winfield, Paul **10**:110
Winfrey, Oprah **9**:131; **10**:111–112
Winfrey, Vernon **10**:112

Winkfield, Jimmy **3**:24; **10**:113
Witherspoon, Tim **6**:83
Within Our Gates (film) **6**:129; **7**:63
womanism **3**:31; **10**:22
Woman's Medical College (WMC) **3**:20
Women's Convention (WC) **2**:72
Women's Rights Convention **3**:109
Wonder, Stevie **2**:110; **4**:120; **7**:29; **8**:97; **10**:114–115
Woodard, Alfre **10**:116
Woodruff, Hale **1**:94
Woods, Granville T. **10**:117
Woods, Tiger **1**:26; **10**:118–119
Woodson, Carter G. **2**:66; **10**:120
Woodson, Robert L. **10**:121
Work, Monroe Nathan **10**:122
World War I **1**:7; **7**:64, 65
    Eugene Jacques Bullard and **2**:62
    Horace Pippin and **8**:28
World War II **3**:26; **7**:65
    Benjamin O. Davis, Jr. and **3**:63
    Eugene Jacques Bullard and **2**:62
    Blood for Britain project **3**:116
    segregation in the military **2**:128
Wright, Billy **6**:126
Wright, Dorsey **8**:117
Wright, Eric see Eazy-E
Wright, Erica Abia see Badu, Erykah
Wright, Jeremiah A. **10**:123
Wright, Richard **1**:65; **4**:14, 15; **5**:70; **10**:29, 124–125
Wu-Tang Clan **7**:61
Wyatt, Addie L. **10**:126
Wyclef Jean see Jean, Wyclef

X

X, Malcolm see Malcolm X

Y

York (slave) **10**:127
Young, Andrew Jackson, Jr. **10**:128
Young, Coleman **10**:129
Young, Lester **5**:86, 87; **8**:12; **10**:130
Young, Roger Arliner **10**:131
Young, Whitney M., Jr. **8**:68; **10**:132
Youngblood, Shay **10**:133
Young Negroes Cooperative League **1**:60
Young Women's Christian Association (YWCA) **5**:59
Yugen (magazine) **1**:74

Z

Zaharias, Babe Didrikson **4**:106
Zollar, Doris **10**:134

Picture Credits